AF680628

The Coinage of Chersonesus
IV Century B.C. – XII Century A.D.

V. A. Anokhin

Translated from the Russian by
H. Bartlett Wells

B A R International Series 69
1980

B.A.R.

B.A.R., 122 Banbury Road, Oxford OX2 7BP, England

GENERAL EDITORS

A. R. Hands, B.Sc., M.A., D.Phil.
D. R. Walker, M.A.

B.A.R. Supplementary Series 69, 1979: "Coinage of Chersonesus".

© V. A. Anokhin

The author's moral rights under the 1988 UK Copyright, Designs and Patents Act are hereby expressly asserted.

All rights reserved. No part of this work may be copied, reproduced, stored, sold, distributed, scanned, saved in any form of digital format or transmitted in any form digitally, without the written permission of the Publisher.

ISBN 9780860540748 paperback

ISBN 9781407350134 e-book

DOI https://doi.org/10.30861/9780860540748

A catalogue record for this book is available from the British Library

This book is available at www.barpublishing.com

CONTENTS

Page

INTRODUCTION

Tauric Chersonesus (Χερρόνησος or Χερσόνησος, in the Byzantine period Χερσῶνος or Χερσόνος) occupies a special position in the history of the northern Black Sea littoral. Founded at the end of the Vth century B.C. by emigrants from Heracleia Pontica, Chersonesus soon became one of the sturdiest _poleis_ of that distant frontier of the ancient world, one which played a conspicuous part in the area's political and economic history. At the time when the slave-owning states were breaking up under the pressure of the barbarian tribes Chersonesus contrived to maintain its independence, and it entered the new feudal era as a robust state organism. The history of Chersonesus affords an opportunity to observe in pure form the process of the formation and development of an ancient _polis_, of its decline, and of its transformation, economic and political, into a feudal town.

Chersonesus or Cherson, as it came to be called in the Middle Ages, occupied an important position in the history of the Byzantine Empire. Over the course of many centuries it remained the Empire's faithful ally and subject and performed the function of an outpost in the Crimea and the northern Black Sea littoral. Not infrequently the town found itself in the thick of the political and military events that agitated the Empire, and from the moment the theme was set up it enjoyed certain rights and privileges that put it in an exceptional position.

One of the most important sources for study of the history of Chersonesus is its coins, the issue of which continued with certain interruptions over a period of a millennium and a half. The prime significance of coins as a source is determined by the fact that they concentrate in themselves the characteristics of economic, political, metrological, artistic, epigraphic, technological, and other sorts of records and make it possible to cast light upon the most varied facets of the town's history over many centuries.

But this source has to be painstakingly processed. Despite the fact that the history of the study of ancient and medieval coins of Chersonesus extends over more than a hundred years, the potentials of the numismatic material are only beginning to be unveiled.

Ancient and medieval coins of Chersonesus appear for the first time in the catalogs of various western European collections at the end of the XVIIIth century and the beginning of the XIXth. Museum collections started to receive Chersonesus coins in particular abundance after the Crimea was incorporated into Russia in 1783. One of the most complete publications was the study by the keeper of the Hermitage coin collection, K. Koehler; but this was rather a catalog than an historical investigation.

One may consider B. V. Koehne's inquiry (Koehne, 1848) to have been the first scientific work on the history and numismatics of Chersonesus. He distinguished the main periods in the town's history—Greek, Roman-

Bosporan, Byzantine—and distributed the issues by periods, in the main correctly. Koehne repeated his main conclusions in another work, devoted to the ancient numismatics of the northern Black Sea littoral as a whole (Koehne, 1857). These two inquiries by Koehne are up to the present the only general works on Chersonesus numismatics.

In the second half of the XIXth century we have the fruitful scientific activity of the German numismatist A. von Sallet, who published a number of important articles on Chersonesus numismatics, mainly that of the Roman period (Sallet, 1874; 1877; 1883).

Among the other work of that time one should mention the catalog of the splendid P. O. Burachkov collection (Burachkov), which is a useful guide even to this day. The substantial shortcomings of Burachkov's catalog are the typological method for the description of the coins, borrowed from Koehne, and also the large number of errors, which called for the publication of special "Corrections" (Bertier, 1907a).

An extremely important step in the study of the coins of Chersonesus is associated with the name of A. L. Bertier de la Garde. His protracted study of the ancient and medieval antiquities of the northern Black Sea littoral has placed him among the ranks of the most outstanding Russian specialists in these fields. Bertier de la Garde also devoted great attention to numismatics. He made a substantial contribution towards the classification of Chersonesus currency as a whole by periods and to the chronology of specific issues, and to the metrology of the coins; he determined the starting date for the Chersonesus era; and on frequent occasions he published new types of Chersonesus coins, each such publication being in essence a completed study (Bertier, 1893; 1906; 1912; 1913). One may say without exaggeration that the works of Bertier de la Garde constituted an epoch in the study of Chersonesus numismatics, finally freeing it from the raids of dilettantism.

A. V. Oreshnikov worked hard and fruitfully on the study of Chersonesus coins; he investigated a range of special problems (Oreshnikov, 1918, 1922, 1922a) and published a large number of new types (Oreshnikov, 1884; 1887; 1890; 1913; 1915), although he devoted amost no attention to the questions of the absolute chronology of the coins he published. He did important work in the field of the numismatics of medieval Cherson as a result of which interest in that little-studied department mounted (Oreshnikov, 1905; 1911; 1911a).

During the Soviet period the study of the coins of Chersonesus has in the main evolved along two lines. The first resulted from the publication of excavation materials both of the pre-revolutionary and of the Soviet periods (Oreshnikov, 1890; Belova, 1927; 1931; 1936; 1938; 1941; 1953; 1959; Krushkol; Gilevich, 1959; 1961; 1968; Golenko, 1972). These articles contain exceedingly valuable material on the history of the monetary circulation at Chersonesus—a problem practically unexplored by pre-revolutionary scholarship. Studies on the actual currency of Chersonesus, on its chronology, and on its metrology have been of lesser importance. The works of the most conspicuous Soviet numismatist A. N. Zograph (Zograph, 1922; 1927) are unquestionably the most considerable in these fields. His outline of the currency of ancient Chersonesus raised the study of Chersonesus numismatics to a new level (Zograph, 1951; 1955).

Intensive archaeological investigation of the Chersonesus townsite in the years of Soviet rule has made it possible to accumulate numismatic material, covering a long period, which has afforded occasion for distinguishing new types of ancient and medieval coins of Chersonesus (Belova, 1941a).

In post-war years the study of coins of Chersonesus has been stimulated by finds of hoards from the ancient period (Takhtai; Gilevich, 1959; 1960; 1970) and from the medieval (Gilevich, 1964; 1974; Sokolova, 1971b). An intensive accumulation of finds and a heightening of interest in the numismatic material has had a productive effect upon the study of coins of the Roman period (Anokhin, 1963a) and of the medieval (Sokolova, 1965; 1968; 1971a; Anokhin, 1968).

Despite the progress made in the study of Chersonesus numismatics, the potentials offered by the material accumulated over long years of archaeological investigation are still far from having been exhausted. It seems to us that there is a particularly acute need for a general work on the currency of Chersonesus, bringing together all the main types of coins, affording an idea of the evolution of the mintage as a whole, and touching upon the questions of chronology, systems of numismatic metrology, and the organization of the currency in the various periods. For a number of reasons, the general works which exist at present can no longer satisfy the inquirer who is seeking with the help of the coins to find a solution to the "baffling" problems, as Bertier de la Garde put it, in the history of Chersonesus; and at the same time, publications of coins are strewn among a variety of journals none too easy of access, and they embody a range of inaccuracies.

The study we are offering to the reader's attention represents an endeavor to fill in that <u>lacuna</u> to some extent. For the first time since the studies by Koehne there are set side by side here, and studied, all of the main varieties of the ancient and medieval coins of Chersonesus.

The main tasks we have set ourselves in writing this monograph have been as follows: 1) establishing the relative and absolute chronologies of the coin issues; 2) determining the systems of monetary metrology; 3) studying the problems of the organization of coin production; 4) utilizing numismatic material in order to extend our knowledge of the history of Chersonesus.

The problems listed have been reflected in one way or another in this work. On Plates I-XXXII there are presented the varieties of the coins of Chersonesus that are known to the author and that are in his view the most important. The numbering of the coins illustrated on the Plates corresponds to the order in which the coins are numbered in the catalog.

The catalog also includes coins known from mention in the literature (with reference to the source in question), and also isolated specimens of coins for which (for technical reasons) we failed to secure casts or photographs. Neither class appears in the Plates.

As the work has progressed we have studied the coins from the collections of the State Hermitage, the State Historical Museum (Moscow), the Chersonesus Historical and Archaeological Museum (Sebastopol), the Odessa Archaeological Museum, and a number of other governmental and private collections, and also casts of Chersonesus coins from the Berlin Museum and the British

Museum. The author takes advantage of this opportunity to express his sincere gratitude for many-sided assistance in his work to N. A. Frolova, T. I. Kostromich, and A. M. Gilevich; to his colleagues abroad Dr. H. D. Schultz, Mr. W. Stancomb, Dr. M. J. Price; to the collectors D. P. Vashkov, D. I. Moshnyagin, V. N. Orekhov, V. V. Pereplesnin, and many others who have offered their collections for study.

THE CURRENCY OF CHERSONESUS BY PERIODS

Reducing the coins of Chersonesus to order has been of concern to many students. Koehne in his day already divided the history of the town and its coins into three periods—Greek, Roman-Bosporan, and Byzantine,—yet without offering any justifications for this (Koehne, 1848).

The scientific foundations for assigning the currency of Chersonesus to periods were laid by Bertier de la Garde. He segregated three groups of ancient coins corresponding to the three periods: "nezavisimost" ("independence"); "svoboda" ("Liberty"); and "vol 'nost' " ("privilege"). He dated the period of "independence" from the mid-IVth century to the mid-Ist century B.C.; that of "liberty" from the mid-Ist century B.C. to the end of the IInd century A.D.; and that of "privilege" from the end of the IInd to the mid-IIIrd century A.D. (Bertier, 1906, p. 55-58).

Bertier de la Garde's breakdown by periods contains almost no errors even from the viewpoint of the present way of looking at the evolution of the Chersonesus coinage. Despite the fact that the results he arrived at were based only on numismatic data and bore mainly upon coins, he held it possible to link his system with "changes in the economic position, in governmental organization, and even in the established faith," (Bertier, 1906, p. 57). It seems to be beyond question that his breakdown of the currency by periods may be used as the foundation of a periodical arrangement of Chersonesus history corresponding to the sum total of knowledge which had been accumulated toward the beginning of the XXth century.

For that reason it is not surprising that Bertier de la Garde's views should have determined in many respects the further course of study. Oreshnikov, who some years later turned to a reduction of Chersonesus coins to system, was able to introduce only a few refinements into the chronology of the periods, but he also offered new names for them. Oreshnikov introduced his most substantial alterations into the second period, which he subdivided into two separate ones. As a result the breakdown assumed the following form: Period I—autonomy (IVth-end of IInd century B.C.); Period II—Bosporan influence (end of IInd century B.C.-25/24 B.C.); Period III—the Reign of the Maiden (25/24 B.C.-mid-IInd century A.D.); Period IV—eleutheria (mid-IInd-mid-IIIrd century A.D.) (Oreshnikov, 1913, p. 25-26). Subsequently, after he had separated out the coins of a brief "first eleutheria" (Oreshnikov, 1922a, p. 118), the style "second eleutheria" took hold for Period IV.

In the interests of fairness one must say that the viewpoint from which Oreshnikov set out was inferior to the position taken by the earlier investigator. Where Bertier de la Garde saw in his breakdown by periods a reflection of phases in the economic and historical evolution of the town, Oreshnikov limited himself to matters of coin-grouping alone. This, he held, "should be based upon the data offered by history and by chronology, and upon metrological evidence (Oreshnikov, 1913, p. 23). Indeed, Oreshnikov progressed no farther than this formulation, and the metrology of Chersonesus coins in particular found no reflection in his scheme.

In the ensuing years the breakdown by periods for Chersonesus remained without alterations. A relatively short time ago K. V. Golenko put into circulation a slightly refined designation for Period II—"Pontic-Bosporan influence" (Golenko, 1964). Our examination of the Chersonesus coinage has made it possible to bring to light certain details of the history of the town and of its currency which have had an effect upon the assignment by periods. Least changes of all have affected the first period — that of autonomy. Only its earlier limit has been further defined, at around 390 B.C., justification for which had already been provided by Zograph in his day.

The question concerning the period of Bosporan influence is more complicated. Its opening date —around 110 B.C.— gives no objections. It was precisely as a result of the expedition of Diophantus that Chersonesus was made subject to Mithradates VI Eupator, a matter regarding which we have the altogether definite testimony of Strabo: Chersonesus "earlier enjoyed autonomy, but later, having been devastated by the barbarians, it was forced to accept Mithradates Eupator as its protector ... From those days and until the present the city of Chersonesus has been subject to the rulers of the Bosporus" (Strabo, VII, 4, 3). And further — "now all this country is under the authority of the Bosporan kings, who are appointed by the Romans" (Strabo, VII, 4, 7). But the closing date for the period, and its duration, are open to great question and they depend upon the extent to which one may consider as soundly based the way in which the period of "the reign of the Maiden" is set apart.

In this matter a decisive part was played by the outlook of V. V. Latyshev, who in publishing one of the inscriptions making mention of a "reign of the Maiden" came to the conclusion that "when the govenmental organization of Chersonesus was reformed in Roman times ..... the people of the city determined to regard the Maiden as their eternal queen, not in any merely nominal fashion but with certain functions and attributes of authority" (Latyshev, 1909, p. 321). In his opinion, the monogram signifying the name of the Maiden (Παρθένος) which was so frequently placed upon coins during this period testified that a given coin had been struck in "the reign of the Maiden" (Latyshev, 1909, p. 325).

Developing Latyshev's view, Oreshnikov drew an analogy from the histories of other ancient cities where divinities also appeared in the roles of functionaries. He saw a difference only in the fact that at Byzantium, for example, the divinities were selected as magistrates for a specific period, whereas the people of Chersonesus chose the Maiden as their "eternal queen" (Oreshnikov, 1913, pp. 12-15). He further associated the adoption of the civic era in 25/24 B.C. with the proclamation of the Maiden as "eternal queen" (Oreshnikov, 1913, p. 25).

First of all one must reject categorically any tie between the adoption of the era and the proclamation of the Maiden as "eternal queen" (if indeed such a thing took place at all). Serious objections were advanced against this thesis as early as Latyshev. He considered the weightiest one to be the fact that indication of the year- ΕΤΟΥ[ς]ΡΘ -on a gold stater, and the inscription ΒΑCΙΛΕΥΟΥCΗC are not directly connected and that consequently the legend as a whole cannot be understood as "such-and-such a year of the reign of the Maiden". (Latyshev, 1909, p. 325). Latyshev's view was shared by Zograph (Zograph, 1951, p. 154). In addition to the arguments they advance one should also take note of the fact that the era does not by any means conclude with the end of the "reign of the Maiden" as it apparently ought to. What is more, dating by this era goes on until the eleventh century. It is perfectly plain that during the Christian period there could be no question of any "reign" by a heathen goddess and that with the very victory of Christianity the era would have been forgotten.

The actual thesis as to an "eternal" reign of the Maiden also gives rise to doubts. There are no proofs for this. All the inscriptions which mention a "reign of the Maiden" relate to a later time, and we have no grounds for thinking that this same order of things was observed at the end of the Ist century B.C. and the beginning of the Ist century A.D. True, if the Maiden were to have performed the functions of "queen" on a periodic basis one would expect to find in the inscriptions indications of the number of times she had exercised this magistracy; but this consideration can be of no decisive significance.

But if one speaks of the monogram as one of the signs of a "reign of the Maiden", then a detailed examination of instances of its use bears witness against the thesis of an "eternity" of the reign. This monogram, in its various forms, developed on one of the issues of the beginning of the "second eleutheria" into the goddess's full name —ΠΑΡΘΕΝΟC— is encountered in the form of countermarks on silver and copper coins from the IIIrd century B.C. onward. It is periodically represented in the actual types of coins from the beginning of the Ist century B.C. and to the middle of the IInd century A.D., after which it disappears forever. In the cases where the mongram is placed beside the image of the Maiden it may be considered an explanatory type, but to reduce the significance of the monogram to this function alone would be incorrect. There are two facts which speak against this: in the first place the presence of the monogram beside the hind on the coins of the years 73 and 74 of the Chersonesus era, and in the second place its absence from the large series of tetrassaria of the years 104-120 of the Chersonesus, at a position beside the image of the Maiden. It would seem that the first circumstance testifies in favor of the propostion that the monogram was placed on the coins as an indication of coinage in the period of the "reign of the Maiden"; but the second, backed by a range of instances of the issuance of coins of this time without the monogram, speaks against it.

The question of the ambiguous nature of the coin issues of Chersonesus will be examined below, in our section on the organisation of the currency of the period of "Bosporan influence". For the present we should merely say that with today's knowledge one cannot either substantiate or refute the thesis regarding an "eternal" reign of the Maiden. But it is an indisputable fact that this "eternal" reign had no relationship to the currency. Insofar as it is specifically the currency that is involved, a "reign of the Maiden" as a particular period in its evolution should be ruled out of the breakdown by periods.

How, then, should one style the interval of time corresponding to this period — that is to say, from the adoption of the civic era to the awarding of the "second eleutheria?". From the standpoint of an evalution of the political status of the town the answer is more or less clear. It follows from Strabo's words that the situation of the town in the days of Mithradates VI Eupator and in those of the subsequent Bosporus kings was in no wise different. If in the Ist century A.D. Bosporan influence weakens or even comes to an end, as one may suppose on the basis of the testimony of Pliny regarding the granting of freedom to Chersonesus by the Romans (Plin., NH, IV, 85), still at the beginning of the IInd century it is these same Romans who again subject it to the Bosporus king Cotys II (123-132) (Const. Porph., De them., 2, 12). Accordingly the political influence of the Bosporus was made manifest in one way or another down to the receipt by Chersonesus of the rights of a free city, and for this reason there are grounds for extending to this period also the term "Bosporan influence".

The question of evaluating Bosporan influence in the currency is a little more complicated. If one is to speak of the typology of the coins, then in contradistinction to the Ist century B.C., in the Ist century A.D. and at the beginning of the IInd the influence of Bosporus coin-types is certainly not found. One may acknowledge that in its selection of coin types Chersonesus was not dependent upon the Bosporus, but one cannot say the same thing about the coin mintage in general. Zograph, for example, is convinced that "the gold coinage of Chersonesus has an intimate link with the gold coinage of the Bosporus, it testifies to dependence of Chersonesus upon the Bosporus, and the one is cut off simultaneously with the other". (Zograph, 1951, p. 155).

This assertion is to our mind excessively categorical. The identical regularities which are observed in the gold and copper coinages of Chersonesus and the Bosporus may simply indicate that both were dependent upon Rome. As for dependence of the Chersonesus currency upon that of the Bosporus, this is possible but not beyond dispute; for almost contemporaneously with Chersonesus, Olbia too issues gold coins, but there are no grounds for speaking of its being dependent on the Bosporus.

However these things may stand, dependence of Chersonesus on the Bosporus during the first century and a half of our era is confirmed by literary sources, by evidence of the existence of a symmachy between Chersonesus and the Bosporus, and finally by the striving of Chersonesus to free itself from this dependence by securing the rights of a "free city", and although this dependence finds no patent confirmation in numismatic records, there are sufficient grounds for retaining for this period as well the designation of the "period of Bosporan influence".

The term "Pontic-Bosporan influence" proposed by Golenko for Period II is legitimate. Pontic coinage does actually produce a strong reaction upon the currency of Chersonesus at the beginning of the Ist century B.C. But in order to be fair one should remark that after the downfall of Mithradates VI the coinage of Chersonesus undergoes Roman influence as well, so that it would be more exact to call Period II "the period of Pontic-Bosporan-Roman influence". Yet inasmuch as both the Pontic and the Roman influences were most likely exercised through the Bosporus, and also because it was precisely relations with the Bosporus that determined the domestic and foreign policy of the town and its political status all the way down to the receipt of the "second eleutheria", we still consider it sensible to preserve for Period II the earlier name — that of "Bosporan influence".

ANCIENT CHERSONESUS

CHAPTER I

THE AUTONOMOUS PERIOD
(about 390 B.C.-110 B.C.)

The coinage of Chersonesus during the period of autonomy is represented by a large number of silver and bronze coins varied in types and sizes. The local origin of the coin types, with rare exceptions, prevents one from reliably substantiating an absolute dating for most of the issues, and for that reason the conclusion that such a dating can be deduced only on the basis of painstaking study of the entire currency as a whole is applicable to Chersonesus in greater measure than to any other ancient city of the northern Black Sea littoral.

For this reason the crucial factor for establishing a system covering the whole numismatic material is the production of a sequence of coin issues, or in other words a relative chronology. It has been noted, in particular, that the autonomous coins fall into three categories which are not uniform in the number of issues they contain. The first is made up of coins that bear no inscriptions at all aside from the name of the town in abbreviated form (XEP), the second of coins with supplementary symbols in the form of individual letters or syllables, and the third, the largest, with the full names of moneyer magistrates. Further analysis has shown that the coins without inscriptions are the most ancient. They are supplanted by the coins with abbreviated names or individual letters, and after these there appear the coins with the full names of magistrates. This observation is the foundation of the systematization. The position of this issue or that has been determined through elucidation of the reciprocal relationships between coin types, their degradation or alteration, the analysis of overstrikes and countermarks, etc.

The question of an absolute chronology is more complicated. As will be shown below, about forty series or issues comprising an interval of time lasting about 280 years can be referred to the autonomous period. Making allowance for the contemporaneity of a certain number of issues, one may take it that at Chersonesus an issuance of coins was undertaken about once in every ten years.

A count of the number of magistrates' names produces more or less the same picture. At present about seventy such names, whether complete or abbreviated, are known. Taking into account the need for various adjustments (part of the names have perhaps not come down to us; some of the names apply to more than one period; no names were placed on early coins even though officials of some sort who were responsible for the issuance of coins unquestionably existed; and the like), this number should be increased to some extent. Inasmuch as the office of moneyer magistrate was not individual as had been believed earlier, but collegial (the college consisting of three persons), we can conclude in this case, too, that issuance of coins was undertaken not more frequently than once in ten years. For this reason, in those instances where there is insufficient data for a really precise absolute dating of a given series, the time for each of them has been defined as being the corresponding decade in the order of issuances.

Although we are very well aware of the inadequacy of such a mechanical approach to the determination of the time when coins were issued, we nevertheless see no reasons for avoiding such meticulous datings in favor of broader ones—let us say within the limits of a quarter-century, a half-century, or something like that—once the relative chronology of the issues has been determined. Possibly future inquiries will show how reliable this course may be and to what extent it may approach a definition of the absolute dates of the autonomous coins of Chersonesus.

1. The Opening Date of the Coinage

The earliest Chersonesus coins are the series with the type of a head of the Maiden, left, on the obverse and of a fish and a club on the reverse (Plate I, 2-7). The early date of these coins is attested by the archaic coiffure of the goddess and the fact that the head is turned left, which is unusual for the local coinage. In addition, on one of the variants of the major denomination of the copper (Plate I, 5) there appears a particular abbreviation of the town name (ΧΕΡΣ) which is not encountered again on even a single coin type, something which also bears witness to an inconsistency of typology which is characteristic precisely of the initial phase of a currency (Bertier, 1906a, p. 234).

But the first series does not yield to satisfactory absolute dating, and on that occount in order to clear up the exact date at which the currency of Chersonesus commenced there has ordinarily been taken into account the series of silver coins with a facing bust of the Maiden (Plate I, 23-25). It is true that despite the fact that this series offers a broader opportunity for determining the time of its issuance, the start of the Chersonesus coinage had been defined in differing ways. Thus Bertier de la Garde considered that the first series does not precede by very much the coins with the facing type, which he dated, by analogy with the coins of Heracleia Pontica that have a facing head of Heracles on their obverses, to 350-330 B.C. (Bertier, 1960a, p. 224). Zograph, comparing the Chersonesus coins of the second series with the coins of Larissa, assigned the former to 370 B.C., and the opening series to 390-380 (Zograph, 1951, p. 146). As we can see, the variation in the suggested date of origin of the currency of Chersonesus is considerable.

One must point out that the chronological boundaries for the dissemination of facing types are quite vague. Such types begin to appear sporadically on coins of the cities and dynasts of the ancient world from the end of the Vth century B.C. One may consider as the time of their most widespread distribution the first half of the IVth century, although in some instances they go even beyond the middle of that century. Facing types maintained themselves longest of all in the monetary typology of Rhodes (till the middle of the Ist century B.C.), which is explained by the exceptional popularity of the Rhodian metrological system.

Thus one may recognize as a broad dating for the Chersonesus second series the first half of the IVth century B.C. A considerable period of Chersonesus currency before it assimilated the facing type, such as Bertier de la Garde accepted, seems unwarranted. If, however, one is seeking to establish a narrower date-range for these coins, one should compare them first with the coins of the metropolis of Chersonesus, Heracleia, many-faceted ties with which must have been quite solid during the first decades of the town's existence.

It is true that the Heracleia coins referred to (BMC, Pontus, p. 141) are themselves not altogether firmly dated. Head assigned them to 302-281 B.C. (Head, p. 515), G. Kleiner to 415-364 B.C. (SNG von Aulock No. 536), P. Franke to the time of the reestablishment of a democracy at Heracleia which is to say 288-287 B.C., admitting at the same time a possibility of their having already been struck in the IVth century B.C. (Franke, p. 139, note 40).

To our mind Kleiner's dating is the most likely. The appearance of a facing type in the IIIrd century B.C. seems unlikely. In addition, on the coins issued at Heracleia after the reestablishment of the democratic system the legend ΗΡΑΚΛΕΩΤΑΝ appears, whereas the inscription ΗΡΑΚΛΕΙΑ, appearing on the coins referred to, is characteristic of an early period of coinage. Inasmuch as widespread dissemination of facing types commenced after 388 B.C. (Bertier, 1906a, pp. 222-224), the dating of the Heracleia type can be circumscribed, with allowance for a certain lag, to 380-364 B.C. The Chersonesus coins should likewise be assigned to this period, or if one takes into account the analogy pointed out by Zograph, to the even narrower time lapse of 370-364 B.C.

Bertier de la Garde and Zograph considered that the Chersonesus coins with facing types had been preceded by only one initial series. In our view, there ought also to be placed between them the heavy copper coins with types of the seated Maiden on the obverse and of a butting bull on the reverse (Plate I, 8). The type of the butting bull, which was for some centuries one of the basic subjects for the monetary typology of Chersonesus, represents an almost exact copy of the pose of the bull on coins of Heracleia which may be assigned to 415-364 B.C. (BMC, Pontus, plate XXIX, 11, 13,14; SNG von Aulock, No. 350-352). The engraver of the dies for these coins of Chersonesus was unquestionably working under the influence of the Heracleia type or was even trying to reproduce it as faithfully as possible, whereas the next engraver, to whom the type of the bull on the coins with the facing types belongs, had already somewhat altered this subject.

One may also assign to a rather early period a number of issues of small copper. Among these are the coins with the type of a bull's head on the obverse and of a fish and club on the reverse (Plate I, 9-12); a series of two or more denominations with types of a head of the Maiden on the obverse and of a club in a wreath on the reverse of the larger denomination, and of a fish on the reverse of the smaller (Plate I, 13-18); and two issues with types of a krater and a dolphin on the obverse, and of a club, in a wreath or without it, on the reverses (Plate I, 19-22). The similarity of the subjects, the identity of the diameters of the coins, and the surrounding of the obverse types with borders of dots point toward chronological proximity of all these issues, while the types of the fish and the club bring them close to the first series, and that of the bull to the issue of heavy copper.

Thus if the series with the facing types can be dated to 370-364 B.C., and if the copper coins described above were issued between it and the first series, then the first series and with it the start of the Chersonesus coinage should be assigned to 390-380 B.C. The last date coincides with the dating proposed by Zograph, although our justifications are different.

2. The Chronology of the Coin Issues

Hence the first issue of coins of Chersonesus is a series of several denominations of silver and copper having types in common for all denominations—a head of the Maiden wearing kekryphalos hair-net, left, on the obverse, and a fish and club, facing right, on the reverse (Plate I, 2-7). On the reverses of the coins ones finds the abbreviated name of the town—XEP (or XEPΣ — which became traditional for the entire ancient period. This series may be dated, as we said above, to approximately 390-380 B.C.

One should place immediately after these the heavy copper coins with obverse type of the seated Maiden, testing an arrow, and a hind, and of a butting bull on the reverse (Plate I, 8), these also falling among the most ancient types of the Chersonesus coinage. Zograph's proposed dating of 375-350 B.C. for these coins is too broad and cannot be accepted. The coins were beyond all doubt issued before the series of silver with facing types which are assigned to 370-364 B.C. They may be assigned to 380-370 B.C. This date does not run counter to the most recent dating for the Heracleia coins with the type of the butting bull on the reverse, 415-364 B.C. (SNG von Aulock, No. 350-352).

Matters are more complicated with respect to the problem of the relative and absolute dating of the four issues of small copper coins. The first issue, with obverse type of a bull's head and with a fish and club on the reverse (Plate I, 9-12), belongs to the initial series with respect to its reverse type. The other three issues, with types: head of Maiden-club in wreath (Plate I, 13-15) together with the minor denomination lying close to it (Plate I, 16-18); krater—club in wreath (Plate I, 19-20); and dolphin—club (Plate I, 21-22), also have a certain resemblance to the early coins, although not so obvious a one. We consider it possible to join all four issues together and date them to a single period, the second quarter of the IVth century B.C. One cannot rule out the suggestion that some of them may relate to a later period, yet all subsequent coinage, represented in the main by heavy coins with the names of magistrates, is fairly reliably classified and does not allow one to insert any one of these issues of small copper coins or to attach them as minor denominations.

Next after the series of silver coins with facing types of the head of the Maiden on the obverse (Plate I, 23-25), dated to 370-364 B.C., one may place the relatively rare copper coins, also having the type of the head of the Maiden on the obverse, but a facing lion's muzzle and a club on the reverse (Plate II, 26). Zograph assigns these to the IIIrd century B.C. (Zograph, 1951, plate XXXV, 26). But that dating seems to us impossible for two reasons. In the first place, the Maiden's headdress—with sphendone and kekryphalos—strikes one as rather archaic for the IIIrd century. In the second place, and this is the main point, all copper coins of major denominaitons have in the IIIrd century the names of magistrates, in contradistinction to these. Consequently either we must make an exception for this issue and on that account construct various theories, or else it ought to be placed still within the IVth century. The latter course seems the more plausible. As for absolute dating, these coins might be set side by side with the silver coins of Panticapaeum with the same subject—a facing lion's muzzle—that are dated to the last 15 or 20 years of the IVth century B.C. (Shelov, plate V, 29), except that in these years the names of magistrates are already being placed on coins at Chersonesus. The anepigraphic character of the issue affords the possibility of dating it to the end of the second quarter of the IVth century B.C., placing it after the silver coins with facing types, that is to say approximately to 364-350 B.C.

A lion's head is represented on yet another and exceptionally abundant issue of small copper coins. These are represented by a number of variants differentiated in the turning of the lion's head to right or left, the number of rays to the star on the reverse, the inscriptions, the points, and the arrangement of these between rays (Plate II, 27-32). The similarity of the subject allows one to place them close to the preceding ones, on the one hand, and on the other hand the presence of the letter Π on one of the variants bears witness to the fact that they continued to be issued into the period when the indication of magistrate names was commencing to be introduced into the currency of Chersonesus.

One must not fail to note the connection of the types of this issue and of the immediately preceding ones with the coin types of Panticapaeum, where the lion and star are frequently used as principal or supplementary types in the Vth-IVth centuries B.C. It is curious to add here the comment that among finds of alien coins at Chersonesus the percentage of Panticapaeum coins that may be assigned to the last third of the IVth century B.C. goes up sharply (Gilevich, 1968, p. 11). Both facts bear witness to an intensification of every sort of contact between the two towns. The coin finds reflect first and foremost the commercial and economic aspect of these relationships, and accordingly the increase in the influx of coins should be associated presumably with augmented activity of Panticapaeum merchants and a heightening of the part they played in the internal Chersonesus market.

The issues listed above exhaust the category of Chersonesus coins without supplementary symbols. Transitional between these and coins with full names are issues with abbreviations in the form of a single letter or of several letters. In some instances these abbreviations may be considered the initial letters of the names of magistrates; in others the possibility of such an interpretation appears doubtful or quite out of the question. To the category of the transitional coins one may assign, in addition to the small coins we have mentioned the types lion's head—star, only one issue of silver coins and two series of copper.

One should regard as the earliest of these the silver coins with the type of a head of the Maiden wearing diadem on the obverse and that of a butting bull on a club, right, on the reverse and with the names K or ΖΟΠΥΡΟ (Plate II, 33-34). The curling locks on the head on the Maiden remind one somewhat of the coiffure of Hera on the Heracleia coins dated to the time of Satyros (352-345). But the free handling of the type, the carefree shock of hair with curls projecting here and there, point to a date earlier than the period of the Hera type, which is a little dry in style (BMC Pontus, plate XXIX, 19-20). To our mind these Chersonesus coins should be dated to the 50s of the IVth century. The pose of the bull on the reverse also reminds one of the early Heracleia representations of that animal.

Both the transitional series of copper coins form a compact group having a fairly reliably established relative and absolute chronology. The first of these series is represented by coins of two denominations: the larger one has on its obverse the type of a quadriga right, and on its reverse that of a nude, kneeling warrior with a spear and a shield, left (Plate II, 36-42); III, 43-56); the smaller one has on its obverse the type of a Janus-head and on the reverse a lion clawing down a bull (Plate IV, 57-59).

Coins of the larger denomination are represented by three varieties—without supplementary inscriptions; with the syllables HP, ΛY, and ΣA; and with letters of the Greek alphabet—A, B, Γ, Δ, E, Z, H, I, K, Λ, M, N, Ξ, Π, P, Σ (A to E on the obverse, as are the syllables, and the rest on the reverse). The coins of the smaller denomination constitute a single variety, with the syllables HP, ΛY, and ΣA (on the obverse).

Both the types of the coins of the larger denomination are borrowings (Zograph, 1927). The composition of the obverse is apparently copied from the Sicilian decadrachms and tetradrachms (Bertier de la Garde saw in the figure of the charioteer the Maiden-goddess); the type of the kneeling warrior was considered by Bertier de la Garde to have been affected by the military stratagem used by the Athenian commander Chabrios in the battle at Thebes against the Spartan king Aegislaus, although Zograph was inclined to see in it an agonistic subject. There is a closely similar type on staters of Cyzicus and tetrobols of the satrap Orontes (Zograph, 1927, plate XXVI, H, J). The period of the latter's rule—362 B.C.—provides a reliable lower limit for these coins, the commencement of the issuance of which should consequently be assigned approximately to the middle of the IVth century B.C.

Zograph compared the type of the Janus-head on the obverse of the coins of the smaller denomination with the analogous type on coins of the island of Tenedos (Zograph, 1927, pp. 392-394), inclining toward seeing in it "a head of Dionysus and that of one of the divinities associated with him." Without objecting to this interpretation, one which had already been suggested by Oreshnikov (Oreshnikov, 1887, p. 42) and by Minns (Minns, p. 545), we may draw the reader's attention to the great resemblance of the faces to those representing Zeus and Hera on the silver coins of the city of Cromna (SNG von Aulock No. 183-187). The presence of a wreath on the head of Zeus, the treatment of the beard and head hair, and the profiles of the faces appear very similar. Unfortunately this has little enough to offer us of an absolute dating of the Chersonesus coins, inasmuch as the dating of the Cromna coins is not defined more precisely than within the IVth century B.C.

A great deal of attention has been devoted to the sequence of issues of the coin varieties of the larger denomination. Bertier de la Garde considered that "to begin with they did not engrave any differentiator, next they indicated the issues, and finally they turned to designation of the names of officials" (Bertier, 1912, p. 48). Zograph agreed with Bertier de la Garde save for the single amendment that in his view the coins with syllables preceded the coins with individual letters (Zograph, 1927, pp. 382-382). That sequence of issues seems the most likely to us.

The question of the meaning of the syllables and letters has engaged many investigators. Bertier de la Garde accepted the idea that the letters might have a numerical significance (Bertier, 1912, p. 47). Zograph denied this on the ground that figures of two digits were missing from among them, as were two symbols, the stigma and the qoppa, which were used only in a numerical sense. As for the syllables, he regarded these as the initial letters of magistrate names, yet without denying the possibility that they might be considered the initial syllables of the names of the months of the Chersonesus calendar (Zograph, 1927, pp. 383-384). Gilevich porposed that this question be left open until the whole of the Chersonesus calendar should become known (Gilevich, 1970, p. 5) and until it could be determined whether the coins with the syllables really do precede the coins with the letters; in case the answer there should be in the affirmative, he conceded little likelihood that abbreviation of magistrate names might be seen in the syllables. Gilevich takes as his point of departure the fact that on coins of subsequent issues there are already abbreviated names of magistrates, which are then supplanted by full names of magistrates. As we see, there is no union of minds on this subject.

We have already remarked above that the most probable sequence for the issuance of these coins is: first those without inscriptions, then those with syllables (HP, ΛY, ΣA), and finally those with letters from A to Σ, something which is convincingly demonstrated by the placing of the syllables and of the first five letters on the obverses of the coins. Therefore there is no need to correct this sort of apparently illogical development for the coinage into one which would appear to us more logical, inasmuch as the latter contradicts the factual data. Furthermore, one cannot acknowledge the syllables to be abbreviations of the names of the months, since there are absent from among them abbreviations for three of the five known months of the Chersonesus calendar-Διονύσιος, Εὔ[κλειος], and Λάτοιος. As is apparent from subsequent coin issues, one may regard them only as abbreviations of the names of magistrates. As for the letters, Zograph is entirely right in declining to see numerals in them, yet their signifying the numbers of issues in order seemed to him beyond question. Unfortunately he was silent as to what interval of time corresponded to the single letter, noting only that "the issues succeed one another a good deal more frequently than do those designated by groups of letters" (Zograph, 1927, p. 380). In our view each letter designates an annual issue; any other frequency seems highly improbable and difficult to demonstrate.

Thus we can set down the following: the first coins with the quadriga were issued, in harmony with the usual practice of the early phase of coinage, without any designations, after which a decision was made to place the names of magistrates on the coins. But that order of things was interrupted, and over a period of eighteen years annual issues were identified by letters from A to Σ. With this last the issuance of coins with the quadriga came to an end; so did the practice of designating the annual issues with letters, and the names of magistrates again appear upon coins in their place. The overall duration of the issue of the coins with the quadriga came in this way to about 20 years.

Zograph dated the coins with the quadriga to 350-330 B.C. and it is difficult to object to this. Gilevich has tried to re-date them, holding that the type of the kneeling warrior was associated with military successes of Chersonesus and specifically with the extension of its sway to the southwestern Crimea, something which in his opinion became possible only after the debilitation of the Scythians brought about by the downfall of king Ateius. With this as his starting point he dates the coins with the quadriga to a period not earlier than 339 B.C. (Gilevich, 1970, p. 6).

Yet it is difficult to agree with such a conclusion. If we are to speak of Ateius, we must confess that we have no data on how the defeat of Ateius affected, or that it affected at all, the relationships between the Greek and the non-Greek population in the south-western Crimea. Gilevich shares the viewpoint of A. N. Shcheglov, who considers, along with other inquirers, that Ateius was the ruler of an enormous state, the boundaries of which stretched from the Don to the Danube. At the same time weighty arguments exist which subject this widely held view to doubt (Kallistov). On collating all the reliable facts of the history of Ateius that are known to us we must conclude that after passing the Danube and seizing the Dobrogea Ateius most likely did not maintain ties with the basic motherland of the Scythian world which lay east of the Danube. From the very start of his intrusion into the Dobrogea he disposed of very limited military forces, and the reliable, real kingdom of Ateius to which Philip II aspired and which was intended for Ateius's son was confined to the territory of the Dobrogea (Anokhin, 1973, p. 38-40). Thus it seems unlikely that the defeat and downfall of Ateius could somehow break down military and political equilibrium between Greeks and Scythians in the Crimea. But even if one supposes that the Greeks secured a certain advantage after 339, an actual (still extremely undefined in the chronological sense) territorial acquisition on the part of Chersonesus could scarcely be a justification for changing the dating of the coins. For these reasons we should accept Zograph's dating of the quadriga coins to 350-330 B.C.

There come in to replace them the coins with types of the griffin and the kneeling Maiden with bow and arrow (Plate IV, 60-65, major denomination) and the small coins with a biga on the obverse and a lion with a spear in its jaws on the reverse (Plate IV, 66-67).

Their position can be based upon the following considerations. In the first place, the coins with the biga could appear only after the coins with the quadriga. In the second, the type of the kneeling Maiden is most likely a re-working of the subject on the reverse of the preceding coins. Where in the first case the type of the kneeling warrior was borrowed by the Chersonesus moneyers without any attempt to harmonise it with local cultural and religious tradition, in the second case the place of the warrior came to be occupied by the Maiden-goddess, the protectress and patroness of the town. Bertier de la Garde pointed out that the type of the lion with the spear in its jaws was borrowed from coins of Panticapaeum (Bertier, 1912, p. 54). These latter are dated at present to the period of 375-360 B.C. (Shelov, plate IV, 41), yet it is possible they are set a little too far back. The coins we are describing are dated reliably enough to 330-320 B.C.

On the reverses of the griffin coins, behind the Maiden, we find the initial letters of the names of magistrates—ΠΑ, ΚΡΑ, and ΑΡΙ ; on the reverses of the coins of the smaller denomination, ΠΑ and ΔΑΜΑΡΕ. A special variant of the coins of the larger denomination consists of coins on which the types change places—the Maiden is on the obverse, the griffin on the reverse (Plate IV, 64-65). The shifting to the obverse of the type of the Maiden-goddess is easily explained. Another phenomenon is less comprehensible—the appearance on these coins of abbreviations of what are unquestionably the same magistrate names, ΠΑ , ΚΡΑ, and ΑΡ. We shall speak of this in more detail below.

The next issue of coins, with the types: Maiden—griffin (Plate IV, 68-69; V, 70-74), has to be segregated into a separate chronological group for the following reasons: in the first place, the names of the magistrates are shifted from the obverses of the coins to the reverses, and in the second place it is only the specimens that are evidently the earliest which bear abbreviated indications of names—ΑΙΣ, ΑΙΣΧΙ , and ΘΕΟΠ, —whereas on the remaining coins we already find names in their complete form (with genitive case endings in—o)—ΦΙΛΙΣΤΙΟ ,ΒΑΘΥΛΛΟ, ΧΟΡΕΙΟ , and ΙΣΤΙΕΙΟ . This issue thus opens the mintage of coins with the names of magistrates written out in full. There are attached to it two variants, close in time, of coins with the same types (Plate V, 75-76). Both of these were most likely issued by one and and the same magistrate, Eudromos (ΕΥΔΡΟΜΟ), whose name is placed on the reverse, behind the Maiden's back or beneath the exergue line.

A characteristic feature of all the coins with types of griffin and kneeling Maiden is that they are struck on flans cast by the "Sicilian" technique (Anokhin, 1974). This serves as a supplementary argument in favor of all three of the coin groups being close to one another chronologically. With the cessation of their issue the "Sicilian" casting technique, too, ceases to be used.

New types come in to replace the types described. Among these the main place fell to a type of the Maiden striking a hind with a spear. This composition was copied from a statue-group evidently created in the last decades of the IVth century B.C. The group as sculpture and the coin type that copied it survive into the period of late antiquity—it is just this type which is placed on the reverses of the coins of the concluding issue of ancient Chersonesus.

The type of the Maiden striking the hind appears on copper and on silver coins. In establishing the relatively greater age of the one group or the other one must take into account the following facts. In the first place, among the magistrates who issued copper coins there was an Eudromos (ΕΥΔΡΟΜΟΥ) most likely to be identified with the person who struck the concluding coins of the griffin-Maiden type. The name Eudromos has not been noted on the silver coins. In the second place, part of the silver issue had the rigidly fixed die-orientation (↑↑). This innovation is traced in a number of issues of silver and copper coins of the IIIrd century B.C. But the copper coins with the Maiden striking the hind, like the type which precedes them (griffin-Maiden), have random die-orientation, and accordingly there are no justifications for placing the silver coins in between them. Thus to replace the coins with the griffin-Maiden types there come in the copper coins with the type of the Maiden striking the hind with a spear on the obverse and that of a butting bull above a club, beneath which there were placed the name of the magistrate and a bow in bowcase, on their reverses (Plate V, 77-81). Five magistrate names are known on these— ΕΥΔΡΟΜΟΥ, ΔΙΑΓΟΡΑ, ΚΛΕΜΥΤΑΔΑ, ΣΥΡΙΣΚΟΥ, and ΘΕΟΧΑΡΕ.

One should place after these a series of silver coins consisting of two denominations. The tetradrachms have these types: on the obverse, a head of the Maiden right, behind it a bowcase and bow; on the reverse, a butting bull left, above it a club and the abbreviated name of the town, below the exergue line the name of a magistrate (Plate VI, 82-86). Bertier de la Garde mentions a unique specimen of a didrachm with the same types (see Catalog, No. 87), the present location of which is unknown. Unfortunately he does not indicate the name of the magistrate either. One may suppose, however, that the coin was issued in the name of one of the three magistrates ΑΠΟΛΛΟΝΙΔΟΥ, ΑΔΩΝΟΣ, or ΑΓΑΣΙΚΛΕΩΣ among those who struck tetradrachms, inasmuch as the other three magistrates (ΑΡΤΕΜΙΔΩΡΟΥ, ΙΣΤΡΩΝΟΣ, and ΑΙΣΧΙΝΑ) issued didrachms of another type. These last have on the obverse the same type of the Maiden's head as on the tetradrachms, and on the reverse the Maiden striking down the hind, as on the copper coins (Plate IV, 88-90).

The two issues of coins, the copper and the silver, may be dated respectively to 300-290 and to 290-280 B.C.

Their place is taken by three issues of silver coins having on their obverses the type of a head of Heracles. In each instance the head of Heracles is different. On the obverse of the coins of the first issue a head of the young Heracles facing right is represented, with the Maiden striking down the hind on the reverses (Plate VI, 92). The reverse type indicates that this issue follows upon the ones above. The magistrates' names are ΒΑΘΥΛΛΟΥ and ΗΡΑΚΛΕΙΤΟΥ. The next issue is represented by a unique coin with type of a head of Heracles facing left on the obverse, and the Maiden seated on a throne on the reverse (Plate VI, 93). The name of the magistrate is ΝΑΝΩΝΟΣ. After this one should place some rare coins with type of the head of Heracles facing right on the obverse, and the Maiden seated on a throne on the reverse (Plate VII, 94). On these coins the name of only one magistrate is known— ΖΩΙΛΟΥ. The same name appears among the list of magistrates' names which were placed on the coins of the next issue. The names ΖΩΙΛΟΥ in all likelihood correspond to a single person, something which confirms the chronological proximity of the two issues and the proposed sequence of striking. The three issues described above should be dated approximately to the second quarter of the IIIrd century or, basing ourselves upon the non-coincidence of the names, to 280-270, 270-260, and 260-250 B.C. The silver coin-issues mentioned apparently reflect a period of experimentation in the selection of denominations and weights for coins and of coin typology. They are replaced by a regular issue of silver coins represented by a large number of names on coins and of actual coins themselves, something which testifies to a continuity of mintage.

The new issue is represented by two denominations of silver coins. A head of Heracles right is represented on the obverse of the coins of the larger denomination, on the reverse the Maiden seated on a throne (Plate VII, 95-105); magistrates' names are: ΠΡΩΤΙΠΠΟΥ, ΗΡΑΚΛΕΙΤΟΥ, ΔΙΩΝΟΣ, ΑΠΟΛΛΑ, ΑΠΟΛΛΩΝΙΔΟΥ, ΠΡΥΤΑΝΙΟΣ, ΝΕΥΠΟΛΙΟΣ, ΞΕΝΩΝΟΣ, ΑΓΑΘΟΚΛΕΟΣ, ΑΠΟΛΛΩΝΙΟΥ, ΗΡΑΚΛΕΟΥ, and ΙΣΤΡΩΝΟΣ. The smaller denomination has the same type on its obverse, but on the reverse a butting bull left (Plate VIII, 107-119); magistrates' names are: ΠΡΩΤΙΠΠΟΥ, ΗΡΑΚΛΕΙΤΟΥ, ΔΙΩΝΟΣ, ΑΡΤΕΜΙΔΩΡΟΥ, ΑΠΟΛΛΑ, ΑΠΟΛΛΩΝΙΔΟΥ, ΠΡΥΤΑΝΙΟΣ, ΝΕΥΠΟΛΙΟΣ, ΙΞΥΠΟΡΟΣ, ΞΕΝΩΝΟΣ, ΑΠΟΛΛΩΝΙΟΥ, ΗΡΑΚΛΕΟΥ, ΠΥΡΡΙΝΟΥ, and ΖΩΙΛΟΥ. The total of names is 16. The overall duration of the issue of coins of this series should to our mind be determined as not less than 15-20 years, and they should be dated approximately to 250-230 B.C.

The series described above was the last issue of heavy silver coins at Chersonesus. After them, several series of small silver were struck, sometimes supplemented by one or two denominations of copper. The earliest series among these should probably be considered as being a series of two denominations of silver coins. On the larger there are types of the head of the Maiden, right, in a dotted border on the obverse, and of a butting bull, left, on the reverse; magistrates' names are ΝΑΝΩ, ΜΙΧΑ (the first two letters as a ligature), ΞΑΝΘΟΥ, and ΥΜΝΟΥ (Plate IX, 121-124). On the smaller denomination there is a griffin on the obverse and a bowcase on the reverse; magistrates' names are ΝΑ, ΞΑΝΘΟΥ (Plate IX, 125-126).

Another issue of coins, typologically very close to the silver with the head of Herakles, seems to us somewhat later. These have on the obverse the type of a head of Herakles right, wearing the lion's skin, and on the reverse a butting bull left (Plate IX, 127-129). The names of magistrates are ΗΡΩΙΔ, ΖΩΙΛ, and ΝΕΟΠΟΛΙΟϹ.

The average weight of these is lower. The same types with different weights of coins may be evidence that we are dealing with issues from different periods—if that were not so, denominations might get mixed up. The non-coincidence of certain magistrates' names speaks to the same effect.

We consider it possible to attach to this issue, as a smaller denomination, copper coins with the type of a head of Herakles, right, on the obverse, and of a prow, left, on the reverse (Plate IX, 131-132). The two obverse types exhibit a marked resemblance (cf. Plate IX, 127, 131). Magistrates' names are ΓΕΡΟΝΤΟΣ and ΣΙΔΑΝΟΥ. Many specimens of this type are overstruck on earlier coins. It was most likely coins of the Maiden—bull type that served as raw material for the overstriking. They have in addition a range of countermarks, which in many respects renders the work of elucidating the sequence of operations more difficult. A total of five varieties of the coins may be distinguished, with types: Heracles—prow (1) with monogram  as countermark (e, see drawing); (2) overstrikes on coins already bearing this countermark; (3) with countermark of a "dolphin;" (4) with countermark of a "star;" (5) coins without countermarks.

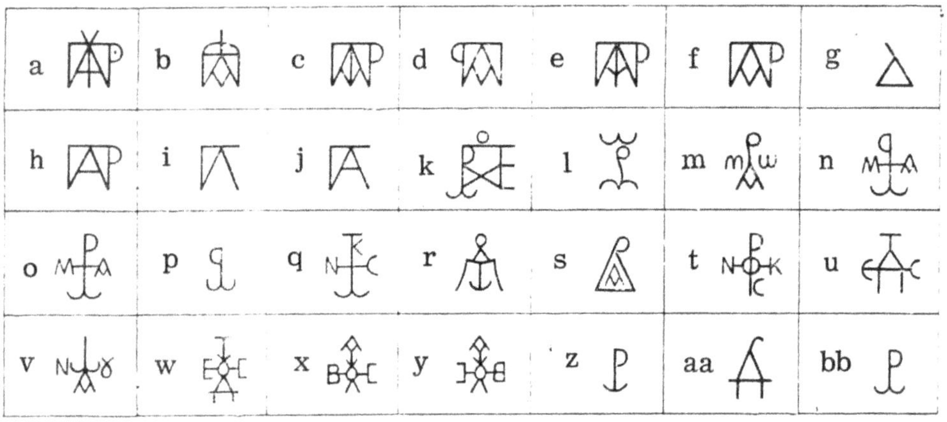

Marks encountered on Chersonesus coins.

Naturally the first two varieties are of the greatest interest. Both of them were published by Bertier de la Garde (Bertier, 1912, plate III, 28, 29, 30), who correctly supposed that "the minting of these coins and their being countermarked took place at the same time or at almost the same time..." (Bertier, 1912, p. 60). This can apparently be explained only as follows: immediately after the commencement of the issuance of the coins a need for countermarking them with a monogram arose. Inasmuch as coins of early issues served as blanks, there might be included for overstriking also a certain number of new coins which had already chanced to receive a countermark. Later these coins received "dolphin" and "star" countermarks. The proposed sequence of operations is conjectural, since it has not proved possible to elucidate this with sufficient assurance from the coins.

The non-coincidence of the names of magistrates on the silver and the copper coins with the head of Heracles obliges one to assign them to different times, yet within the limits of a single decade—220-210 B.C.; the preceding series of silver coins may be dated to 230-220 B.C.

One must place after the issues described a fresh series of coins consisting of two denominations of silver and two denominations of copper. On the obverses of the silver coins there was represented a head of the Maiden, right, with a bow and quiver behind her back. On the reverse of the larger denomination there was the Maiden striking a hind with a spear, and on the smaller denomination a quiver and a bow, string upward (Plate IX, 133-137: X, 138-142). Coins are known having the names of three magistrates—ΥΜΝΟΥ, ΕΥΡΥΔΑΜΟΥ, and ΜΕΝΕΣΤΡ (or ΜΕΝΕϹΤΡΑ).

The larger denomination of the copper coins has on the obverse a similar head of the Maiden, on the reverse a reclining hind (Plate X, 143-144); the names of magistrates are ΞΕΝΟΚΛΕ and ΧΟΡΕΙΟΥ . The smaller denomination has correspondingly a head of the yound Herakles wearing diadem, and a club (Plate X, 145-146); the names of magistrates are the same. There adjoins this series still another, represented only by copper coins, the larger denomination of which has the types: head of Herakles wearing lion's skin—butting bull (Plate X, 147-149). The smaller denomination has the same types as the foregoing one (Plate X, 150-152). The second series was issued by three magistrates—ΑΡΧΙΛΕΙΟ , ΒΟΛΛΙΩΝΟ, and ΜΑΤΡ. The smaller denomination is also known with the name ΔΕΛΦΟΥ (Karyshkovski, plate I, 8); this is likewise incorporated into the series, although it perhaps relates to a slightly later period.

The greater age of the series consisting of silver and copper coins is in our view only slight. Typological and stylistic uniformity enable one to assign the two series practically to a single period, around 210-200 B.C.

Among the copper coins of Chersonesus there is a series of two small groups which as regards their types can still be assigned to the IIIrd century B.C. But it is very difficult to establish their position in the Chersonesus coinage. On coins of the larger denomination there are a head of the Maiden wearing a wreath, left, and the Maiden left, kneeling and shooting a bow; on the coins of the smaller denomination, the protome of a Pegasus left, and a standing warrior with shield and spear (Plate X, 154-155).

As we see, the types of the coins are altogether unusual; they increase the range of types borrowed by the Chersonesus moneyers from the coinages of other towns. It has been possible to find an analogy for the larger denomination among the coins of the Sicilian town of Alaesa ('Αλαίσας). One of the variants of the coins issued in 241-210 B.C. (Head, p. 125-216) has on the obverse the type of a head of Artemis left, as on our coin, and the inscription ΑΛΑΙΣΑΣ ; on the reverse, a kneeling bowman right (Hirsch, plate V, 553). Thus there is every reason to assign this Chersonesus series to the end of the IIIrd century B.C. On the coins of both denominations there appears the name ΑΓΑΣ , which perhaps belongs to the Agasicles who issued the following group of coins. On their obverses there is represented a head of the Maiden wearing a wreath, right, with bow and quiver; on the reverses, a butting bull left (Plate X, 156-157). Magistrates' names are ΑΓΑΣΙΚΛ and ΗΡΩΙΔΑ. A new series of countermarks and overstrikes is associated with this issue in the numismatics of Chersonesus, bearing witness to a crisis of some sort.

The coins described frequently have countermarks in the form of a bird turned right, with its head turning back. Many specimens have two such countermarks each, arranged one against the other on the two sides of the coin. Bertier de la Garde rightly supposed that they were applied by means of hinged dies (Bertier, 1906a, p. 249). True, the dies in the hinged arms were put in place differently (on the coins No. 194 of the State Hermitage and No. 4639 of the Chersonesus State Museum the axes of the paired dies have different orientations). In addition, the following coins have countermarks; silver ones with the types: head of Maiden—Maiden and hind (Plate IX, 137; "star" and "club"), and: head of Maiden wearing mural crown—bow and quiver, with name ΔΕΛΦΟϹ (Plate X, 158; "star" and "club"); copper coins of the type: head of Athena—griffin (Plate XI, 159-160; overstruck on coins already bearing the countermark "dolphin" and of the type: Maiden and hind—bull, and also on coins of the type: head of Maiden—reclining hind; they bear the countermark "star"); copper coins of the type: head of Dioscuros—prow (Plate XI, 165-166; overstruck on coins with the countermark "bird," they bear the countermark "club.").

Although the stamps "star" and "club" are not identical on silver and on copper coins, one can scarcely doubt that they are of the same period. On coins known to us that have both countermarks, they do not overlap each other and for that reason their sequence remains a matter of conjecture. With this qualification, the relative chronology of the copper issues and the countermarks presents itself in the following form:

1. Copper coins of the type: head of Maiden—bull, are issued;
2. The coins are stamped with the countermark "bird";
3. Silver coins with the name ΔΕΛΦΟϹ are issued, and perhaps also copper coins with the type: Herakles wearing diadem—club, bearing the same name;
4. Issuance of coins of the type: head of Athena—griffin, overstruck from coins: a. bearing the countermark "dolphin"; b. of the type: head of Maiden—reclining hind; c. of the type: head of Maiden—butting bull;
5. The countermark "star"; the following are stamped with it: a. head of Heracles—prow; b. head of Maiden—Maiden and hind (silver); c. head of Maiden—bow and quiver, with name ΔΕΛΦΟϹ (silver); d. head of Athena—griffin;
6. Issuance of coins of the type: head of Dioscurus—prow (overstruck from coins with the countermark "bird");
7. The countermark "club"; the abovementioned silver and copper coins with the types: head of Dioscurus—prow, are struck with it.

Unfortunately we have no means of establishing an absolute dating of the issues listed; they can be assigned approximately to the following periods: 1. coins of the type: head of Maiden—butting bull, first decade of the IInd century B.C.; 2. silver coins with the name ΔΕΛΦΟϹ—about 190-180 B.C.; 3. of the type: head of Athena—griffin, around 180-170 B.C.; 4. of the type: head of Dioscurus—prow, around 170-160 B.C.

The silver coins with the name of Delphos, first published by L. N. Belova (Belova, 1941a), have on their reverses the type of a bow, string upward, and quiver. The reverse type points toward their connection with the coins of the preceding series in silver. The type of the obverse—a head of the Maiden wearing mural crown—should perhaps be associated with some sort of military danger threatening from without. We know that in 179 B.C., that is to say at a time close to the date of these coins, Chersonesus concluded a treaty of friendship with Pharnaces I, king of Pontus, according to which the latter undertook to provide aid if "the neighboring barbarians should open a compaign against Chersonesus or against territory subject to Chersonesus" (IosPE, I^2, 402).

Coins of the type: head of Athena—griffin (Plate XI, 159-160; magistrates' names ΑΠΟΛΛΟΔΩΡΟΥ, ΗΡΑΚΛΕΙΟΥ) have as their smaller denomination coins with the same type on the obverse and with Nike on the reverse (Plate XI, 161-163). These latter provide several new names in addition to that of ΑΠΟΛ . Unfortunately the poor preservation of the coins prevents one from reading them with assurance. The type of Nike leads one to suggest military successes on the part of Chersonesus, possibly associated with the conclusion of the treaty mentioned above.

One observes in the monetary typology of Chersonesus a curious tendency to revert to types of the Maiden, or of subjects associated with her, in situations of importance. Thus when coins with types of the head of the Maiden and of a reclining hind were supplanted by coins with the head of Heracles, soon afterwards there appeared a new series of coins on the obverse of which the type of the head of the Maiden was again placed. It is apparently through the same tendency that one should explain the issuance, following upon the series just described, of small coins with a Nike, on the obverses of which there was represented the head of the Maiden-goddess with her attributes, the bow and quiver, behind her (Plate XI, 164). The names of magistrates are no longer placed on these coins.

Coins of the type: head of Dioscurus—prow (Plate XI, 165-166) are dated to the following decade (170-160 B.C.). One such coin (Hermitage, No. 218a) is overstruck upon another upon which there had been the countermark "bird." In its turn it has a countermark "club". The names of magistrates on these coins are ΑΛΚΙΝΟΥ and ΣΙΜΑΙΟΥ . In the same series with them there are conjecturally included as a smaller denomination rare coins with the types of a male head left on the obverse and of a prow on the reverse (Plate XI, 167; cf. Oreshnikov, 1913, p. 35, drawing). These coins also have no names of magistrates. After them there are placed the coins of the type: head of the Maiden—bow and quiver (Plate XI, 168-169), the sole basis for this being the magistrate name ΣΙΜΑΙΟΥ as upon the coins of the preceding series. Their approximate date is 160-150 B.C.

One should remark that establishment of the sequence and make-up of the concluding series of autonomous Chersonesus is made exceedingly difficult through the rarity and poor preservation of the majority of the known coins. The business is complicated to an extreme degree also by the circumstance that at that time many coins with various new types were struck (heads of the Dioscuri, Hermes, Helios, and Apollo for the obverses; Nike , cornucopiae, and tripod for the reverses). these being used as a rule for one or two issues. All of this forces one to regard the dates proposed as being relative and arbitrary in still greater measure than in the cases of the early periods, leaving a possibility for some juggling, although grouping of the issues within the limits of half a century seems fairly well-warranted as a whole. With these qualifications taken into account the chronology of the concluding issues of the autonomous period appears as follows.

To 150-140 B.C. there are assigned coins having on the obverses the head of Heracles right, and on the reverses the beak of a ship, with a club and the name of a magistrate beneath it (Plate XI, 170). The very poor preservation of the coin prevents one even from recognizing it with assurance as being of Chersonesus origin. In this we follow Bertier de la Garde entirely; he had provided a description of them and read the names of the magistrates as ΛΛΚΙΝΟΥ and[ΤΡ]ΥΘΩΝ (Bertier, 1906a, p. 60-61). In his opinion these coins are later than those of the type: head of Athena—griffin. These coins are conjoined with the two issues described above through the reverse type (prow) and the magistrate name ΛΛΚΙΝΟΥ.

One may date approximately to 140-130 B.C. coins of the type: head of Hermes—cornucopiae. They are represented by two varieties, a large one and a small one (Plate XI, 173-174, 175), and are united in a single series. The names of magistrates appear only on the former—ΠΥΘΙΩΝΟ, ΠΡΟΜΑΘΙΩΝΟϹ. Not even the name of the town is placed on the small coins; a small star appears to the right of the cornucopiae. The two sorts of coins look a little disparate in types and fabric, for which reason putting them in a single series appears arbitrary. Some justification for it may be afforded by the circumstance that the two varieties belong to different weight groups and that it does not seem possible to find a pair to either the one or the other of these among coins of other types.

It is apparently to the concluding period that coins fall which have on the obverse the type of a youthful head wearing a wreath, and on the reverse that of a tripod (Plate XI, 176). The type of the tripod and the theophoric name of the single magistrate who issued this coin, ΑΠΟΛΛΩ, enable one to identify the obverse as a head of Apollo. Both types are new for Chersonesus, for which reason the position of the coins among other issues, and also their date of 130-120 B.C., are established provisionally. As an analogy one may name the silver coins of Panticapaeum with the same types, dated to the third quarter of the IInd century B.C. (Shelov, plate VIII, 89). The dating of coins of the type: eagle—goat (Plate XI, 177) and Maiden—goat (Plate XI, 178) is likewise indefinite, and the author has now established that this coins does not pertain to Chersonesus. These small coins are assigned to the third quarter of the IInd century B.C.

One's attention is drawn to the appearance among the coin-types of images of Apollo, Hermes, the tripod, the cornucopiae, all of which bear witness to a certain degree of well-being in the city, accompanied by an upsurge of civilised life, something which is also substantiated by the existence of a large issue of tesserae with a type of Hermes. An impression is created to the effect that in the second half of the IInd century B.C. a considerable economic spurt is experienced. This may possibly explain in some measure the issue, ensuing at the end of the IInd century B.C., of silver coins in greater volume than the town had known in its entire history. Coins of two denominations belong to this last issue of the period of autonomy. On those of the larger denomination a head of the Maiden wearing mural crown, with bow and quiver, is represented with a hind standing right on the reverse; on the smaller one, a beardless head of Heracles wearing diadem, and a club (Plate XII, 179-181, 182-183). The names of magistrates on the heavy coins are ΑΠΟΛΛΩΝΙΔΑ, ΔΙΟΤΙΜΟΥ, and ΜΟΙΡΙΟΣ; on the small ones only the last two are known.

One should also assign to this same series the copper coins the types on which repeat those of the heavy silver save that on the reverse there is represented in front of the hind some object standing vertically, a tree or a trophy (?). The names of magistrates on the copper coins are ΑΠΟΛ, ΣΩΤΗΡΙ, and [Η]ΡΟΞΕ (Plate XII, 184-186). The copper coins were apparently issued somewhat later than the silver ones, but the time difference can scarcely have been great, so that they may practically be considered as being of the same time.

Bertier de la Garde associated these coins with the period of the dependence of Chesonesus on Mithradates VI Eupator, assigning them to the period after 86 B.C., when the stag finally rooted itself in the monetary typology of that king (Bertier, 1912, p. 43). But such a dating is unlikely. The appearance of a hind on Chersonesus coins cannot be regarded as a result of the influence of Mithradates types: it has been encountered on more than one occasion on early coins of the town in combination with the Maiden, so that that animal can be confidently said to be an attribute of the Maiden herself. Moreover, the coinage of Chersonesus in the Mithradatic period, whether in silver or in copper, has an altogether different character, which excludes any possibility of the appearance in it of coins with a vividly autonomous character.

Zograph dated the series described to the period of the wars of Diophantus in the Crimea, considering that in this way the town subsidized the military operations (Zograph, 1951, p. 151). Golenko saw confirmation of this view in the coincidence of the duration of the military operations (three years) with the terms of what he considered to be three annual magistrates (Golenko, 1964, p. 45). Despite the fact that the dating of this series of coins to the period of the wars of Diophantus has never been proved, it may nevertheless be accepted as reliable, at least in general terms—the second half of the IInd century B.C.—although a connection between the wars of Diophantus and the issue is certainly not obligatory. Among the drachmas there is a large quantity of specimens overstruck on coins of early issues of the type: head of the Maiden—Maiden and hind. Bertier de la Garde pointed out instances of overstriking among the hemidrachms as well (Bertier, 1912, p. 38). There are possibly overstrikes among the copper coins as well, some of these standing out through their large flans and weights.

Recently one of the variants of the tetradrachms of Lysimachus type was assigned to the coinage of Chersonesus.(*) On the obverse and the reverse there appear the types usual for these, that is to say a head of Alexander the Great and Athena seated upon a throne with the inscription ΒΑΣΙΛΕΩΣ ΛΥΣΙΜΑΧΟΥ, but beneath the throne are the letters XEP, and before the figure of Athena the monogram ΠΑΡ (e) (Seyrig, 1971, p. 25, figure). As we are aware, many Greek towns issued coins of Lysimachus type distinguished from one another through their varying supplementary inscriptions, symbols, and monograms. The drawing up of a complete list of the poleis that struck such coins has not yet been completed. Among the towns of the northern Black Sea littoral Tyra and the Bosporus issued gold staters of Lysimachus type (Zograph, 1957, p. 26-28; Shelov, plate IX, 104, 107, 108), and the Bosporus issued tetradrachms (Seyrig, 1971, p. 25, note 3). On this account the appearance of Chersonesus in the list in question would in no wise run counter to the general state of affairs. The economic situation of the town at

(*) The author expresses his sincere gratitude to Mr. William Stancomb, who drew his attention to this.

mid-IInd century B.C. (the period to which Seyrig dates the coin) also admits of the possibility of the appearance of a silver coinage. Unfortumately the attribution of the tetradrachm, exceptionally important for the history of the currency of Chersonesus as it is, gives rise to certain doubts. The most substantial one revolves around the considerable stylistic resemblance of the types of this coin, so far as one can judge from the illustration, to those of the gold coin of Paerisades from among Becker's output (cf. Hill, plate V, 73).

True, the tetradrachm comes from a hoard found in Asia Minor (Coin Hoards I, p. 25, No. 80), amid the composition of which two such coins were found. This circumstance significantly increases confidence in their genuineness. We nevertheless consider that definitive resolution of the question depends upon a special study of these coins, something which they certainly deserve.

3. Metrological Standards

The first issue of Chersonesus coins consists of three denominations of silver and two denominations of copper. The weight data for the silver are as follows: large denomination 3.55 g ; medium 2.02; 2.01; 1.97; 1.78 (2); 1.73; 1.65; small 0.55, 0.43; 0.40; 0.38 g.

Bertier de la Garde considered them to be respectively a drachma, a hemidrachm, and an obol of the Phoenician standard (Bertier, 1906a, pp. 233-242). Zograph objected to this identification, terming the standard Rhodian or Chian and pointing to the drachma of that system with norm weight of 3.88 g. (Zograph, 1951, pp. 146-147). One thinks, however, that he too was mistaken.

When we turn to the currency of Chersonesus's metropolis, Heracleia Pontica, we see that at the end of the Vth century B.C. and the beginning of the IVth it is striking silver on the Persian standard. In the first series of coins (with the head of Heracles facing left on the obverse) three denominations are known: a triobol (weight of coins 2.89 and 2.70 g), a diobol (weight range 1.85-1.70 g), and what is evidently a hemiobol (weight 0.41 g); in the second (head of Heracles right) there are a diobol (weights 1.90-1.68 g), an obol (0.92-0.80), and a hemiobol (0.47-0.38 g).

It is not difficult to perceive the complete similarity of the weight characteristics of the Heracleia and Chersonesus coins. The selection of denominations is also close; it is more rational in the Chersonesus series, for in the Heracleia one adjoining denominations are struck, creating a danger of confusing them, whereas at Chersonesus the denominations stand in a 8 : 4 : 1 relationship to one another so that it is practically impossible, even with a considerable variation in weight, to take one for another.

Chronological proximity of the mintages of the two towns is attested, for example, by the fact that both in the one and in the other the same types are used for the different denominations of its coins of a single series. The sole difference between the Heracleia and the Chersonesus series lies in the larger denomination—in the Heracleia one this is a triobol, in the Chersonesus one a tetrobol.

Basing oneself on the drachma weight of 5.40 g presented by Charles Seltman (Seltman, p. 139), the weight norms for the main denominations of the Persian system will be as follows: tetrobol 3.60 g, triobol 2.70 g, diobol 1.80 g, obol 0.90 g, and hemiobol 0.45 g. On comparing with these the average weights of the Chersonesus coins one can see that they are absolutely identical. Thus in our examination of the first Chersonesus silver coins we come to the conclusion that the town commenced to issue them on the Persian metrological standard, taking its direction from Heracleia and other towns of the southern coast of the Black Sea which likewise struck their coins on that standard.

The problem of determining the denominations of the copper coins is considerably more complicated. We are unacquainted with the system of account for copper coins at Chersonesus, and for that reason we shall start from the hypothesis that here, as in Attica, the obol was equal to 8 chalcons, and that there were seven leptons in the chalcon.

The average weight of the smallest coins comes to 0.65 g. They can only be the smallest denomination, the lepton. In that event the weight of the chalcon should come to approximately 4.5 g. Although the average weight of the copper coins of the larger denomination falls considerably below that norm (weight range 3.96-2.03 g), they are nevertheless most likely chalcons, inasmuch as the weight tolerance in ancient copper coins may always be considerable.

The heavy copper coins with types of the seated Maiden testing an arrow and a hind on the obverse, and of a butting bull on the reverse (Plate I, 8) should be accepted as dichalcons—the average weight of the three known specimens in a good state of preservation is 8.96 g.

The small coins with the head of a bull on the obverse (Plate I, 9-12) are in all likelihood two-lepton pieces; their weight reaches 1.5 g.

The question of determining the denominations of coins of the type: head of the Maiden— club in wreath (Plate I, 13-15) is more complicated. On the reverse of one of the coins with the type of the Maiden's head facing right there is a symbol Δ . One can hardly see in this the initial letter of the name of a magistrate—the small coins of the Chersonesus coinage do not as a rule bear such initials. Is it out of the question to suggest that the symbol had a numerical sense, designating the denomination of four leptons? The average weight of the coins comes to 2.30 g, which would correspond to that identification. It is interesting to note that on the reverses of the coins with the head of the Maiden left, three dots appear above the type of the vertically positioned club, something which was perhaps intended to designate another denomination, three leptons. Two coins, one from each of the two variants, would together make up a chalcon.

Whereas all the denominations of the silver of the first series of Chersonesus coins bore the same types, in the next series, with facing head of the Maiden on the obverse (Plate I, 23-25), each denomination is distinguished by a special reverse type. This was unquestionably done in order to differentiate the denominations not only by weight and dimensions, but also by type. The new series is again close in metrological respects to the coins of Heracleia.

Thus Heracleia coins with facing head of Heracles on the obverse are represented by two denominations; coins of the larger weigh 6.70-6.27 g (we are acquainted with four specimens, and the heaviest one is pierced so that its original weight was probably higher); the smaller weighs 0.72 g (a single specimen). The Chersonesus coins are represented by three denominations, the average weights of which are respectively 6.53; 3.37; and 1.54 g. The medium and smallest Chersonesus denominations may be accepted as a tetrobol and a diobol of the same Persian standard, and the largest denomination as an octobol. One's attention is drawn to the fact that the actual weight of the coins, as compared with the preceding series, has gone down so much that only the heaviest specimens just manage to reach the norm. It is difficult to say whether this was the result of a deliberate policy of the Chersonesus moneyers reckoning with a rise in the value of silver in the ancient world, or whether this reflects the influence of Gresham's law or of other causes of some sort. There is no occasion to speculate upon alteration of the metrological standard; to judge by metrological data on the coins, an analogous phenomenon is observed at Heracleia.

Copper coins of the type: head of the Maiden—facing lion's muzzle (Plate II, 26) and: lion's head—star (Plate II, 27-32) are identified respectively as dichalcon and lepton, even though the average weights of the coins relate to each other only as 7:1.

The third issue of Chersonesus silver coins offers a new increase in denomination—the three known specimens of these coins (Plate II, 33-34) weigh 9.91; 9.83; and 9.78 g. The Heracleia coins (of Clearchus) that correspond to them in time have a decidedly broad weight range running from 5.24 to 3.60 g. It seems that the Chersonesus and Heracleia coins may be defined as a didrachm and a drachma of the same Persian standard.

The coins with the quadriga and the Janus-head can only correspond to the dichalcon and chalcon. This relationship of their denominations has already been pointed out by Zograph (Zograph, 1927, p. 386). The same is to be said regarding the series of coins with the types: griffin—Maiden and biga, and: biga—lion. The later issues of coins with the types: griffin—Maiden, and also the coins with the types: Maiden—bull, are unquestionably dichalcons.

After these last, as has already been remarked above, a new series of silver coins was issued. They are represented by two denominations. The average weight of the larger denomination comes to 13.84 g; a unique coin with the same types (see Catalog, No.87) weighs 6.56 g, and the average weight of the smaller denomination, to which this coin too must belong, comes only to 6.73 g.

It is not so easy to determine the metrological standard of the new issue of silver. The half-size denomination of the smaller coins might be identified with the Persian tetrobol, known in early series, but by this time the use of the Persian standard practically comes to an end everywhere in the ancient world. In addition, one would have to define the larger denomination as consisting of 16 obols, which seems utterly improbable.

The currency of Byzantium provides us with an example of the striking of coins close in weight to those of Chersonesus. The city issues tetradrachms and nine-obol coins of the type: Demeter—seated Poseidon. Although the range of weights of the tetradrachms is decidedly broad (14.29-11.67 g as against 14.20-13.70 g for the Chersonesus coins), the two groups are to our mind entirely comparable.

The nine-obol coins have weights within limits of 5.50-4.07 g, the average weight being 4.97 g. Schönert-Geiss defines their metrological standard as Phoenician, and the time of their issuance as being about 250-220 B.C. (Schönert, pp. 56-64).

The weight of the drachma on the Cyrene or Phoenician standard, borrowed in the IIIrd century B.C. by the Ptolemies (something which fostered its widespread popularity in the world of trade), came to 3.40 g. The weight of the Chersonesus drachma (derived from the tetradrachm 3.46 g, from the didrachm 3.34 g) somewhat exceeds the Byzantium weight (from tetradrachms 3.29 g from trihemidrachms 3.32 g), which can be explained through the earlier date of the Chersonesus coins and which offers no obstacle to our defining them as Phoenician or Ptolemaic.

On a majority of Chersonesus coins of this series we find countermarks, imposed in the following order: Monogram ΠΑΡ (a), "dolphin," "thunderbolt". The question of the date of the countermarks and the reasons for their use is one we shall examine below, after we have studied the other issues of silver coins upon which they are likewise found.

After this series of silver, coins with new types were issued with a head of Heracles on the obverse. These are represented by three issues. The three known specimens of the first issue (Plate VI, 92) have weights of 5.23; 5.07; and 4.62 g. (Bertier, 1913, No. 38), and the average weight is 4.97 g, which corresponds to a denomination of nine obols on the Phoenician standard. This denomination was issued at Byzantium, as we have already remarked. Coins on the Phoenician standard were struck at Heracleia as well under Timotheos and Dionysios (345-337) (tridrachms), under Dionysios (337-305) (tridrachms and trihemidrachms), and under Arsinoe (289-281) (tridrachms).

The next issue is represented by a unique coin weighing 10.55 g with type of a head of Heracles facing left on the obverse and the Maiden seated upon a throne on the reverse (Plate VI, 93). On coins of a third issue there are a head of Heracles right, and the Maiden on a throne (Plate VII, 94). Two coins of this type are known; their weights are 6.17 and 4.57 g. The reverse type is of particular interest. Not a matter of chance, in our view, is the fact that on the reverse of the coins of Arsinoe there is also represented the figure of a divinity, Dionysos, seated on a throne, just as on the abovementioned tetradrachms and trihemidrachms of Byzantium there is a figure of Poseidon seated on a throne. The uniformity of the metrological standard and the typology of the coins most likely indicated a definite agreement between these towns in the field of monetary policy. We know that in the IIIrd century B.C. Byzantium and Heracleia formed part of the so-called Northern League, an alliance of the towns of the southern Black Sea coast. The aim of this league was to strive against the Seleucids, who were seeking to expand their holdings at the expense of the independent Greek towns.

Apparently community of interests led them to make their coin issues uniform. Among other towns included in the Northern League were Calchedon, Cius, and Teos. It is still too early to think of Chersonesus having also been a member, inasmuch as it was scarcely threatened by direct military danger from the Seleucids, yet one cannot entirely dismiss such a possibility. In any event, in the field of currency Chersonesus carried on the same policy as other more powerful members of this league, Byzantium and Heracleia.

All three Chersonesus issues are dated to a period around 280-250 B.C. The coins of Byzantium are assigned to a later period—250-220 B.C. (Schönert, p. 58). Of course the dating of the Chersonesus coins is by no means indisputable, but for the sake of fairness the same should also be said of the dating of the coins of Byzantium. We may recall that their early date has been suggested since the days of Svoronos, who identified the names of two officials (out of ten) with ones mentioned in Polybius (Polyb., IV, 47, 4) who represented Byzantium in a dispute with Rhodes over trade tariffs. This identification is doubtful, for example because, as has been noted by a series of scholars, the persons mentioned in Polybius were not eponyms, that is to say they were not identical in function to the persons whose names stood upon coins (Seyrig, 1968, p. 186). Although it is entirely likely that the names of the same persons were indicated in the two cases—Olympiodoros and Hekatodoros—there still was beyond any doubt a difference in time as regards their performance of these separate functions. This difference may have been from a few years to one or two decades. The coins referred to, including those with the names of Olympiodoros and Hekatodoros, were brought to light in a hoard from Büyük-çekmece, which is associated with the Rhodian war of 220/19 B.C. Accordingly the service of the men as eponyms must have taken place earlier than that year. Thus 220/19 B.C. may be taken as a perfectly reliable <u>terminus ante quem</u> for these coins, although it is difficult to say by how much the time of issue stood apart from that date.

The lower date for the coins has been defined in different ways: after Alexander the Great (BMC Thrace, p. 95), 277 B.C. (Macdonald, p. 393), 250 B.C. (Schönert, p. 58), and 235 B.C. (Seyrig, 1968, p. 187). The last date does not leave room for new names or for interruptions in the coinage and for that reason it seems too narrow. Schönert's dating does take that possibility into account, but to our mind not sufficiently. Possibly for the time being one should keep to a general dating between limits of 280-220 B.C. for them.

As has already been pointed out, these three issues reflect a certain period of experimentation in the coinage—optimum weights, types, and denominations are being selected. This is attested by the rarity of the coins, and also by the fact that not one of them bears the countermarks so characteristic of silver coins of this period, and that consequently they were not included among the mass of money in circulation.

To replace these there comes in a mass issue of coins of a new series dating to 250-230 B.C. Its higher denomination has the same types as the preceding one, with insignificant modifications (Plate VIII, 95-105); the lower one, with the head of Heracles on the obverse, has on the reverse the type of a butting bull (Plate VIII, 107-119). These should also be considered tridrachms and trihemidrachms on the Phoenician standard. The average weight of the tridrachms comes to 9.18 g, that of the trihemidrachms to 4.48 g (taking into account even decidedly worn examples). In reality the weight norm for the coins was somewhat higher, coming respectively to 9.40-9.30 g and to 4.70-4.60 g, inasmuch as more than 50% of the coins of both denominations have weights precisely within these limits.

The overwhelming majority of the coins of both denominations are countermarked, first with the image of a dolphin (always on the reverse), then with a thunderbolt (always on the obverse). As we see, they circulated together with coins of type: head of the Maiden—bull; and: head of the Maiden—Maiden and hind. The absence of the monogram ΠΑΡ(a) from among the monograms suggests that the coins are more recent. The reasons for the imposition of countermarks in the ancient world were unquestionably diverse in nature, and they are unfortunately not always comprehensible. Their basic significance nevertheless consisted of extending the circulation of an old coin, perhaps under new conditions. Apparently this is how one should regard the countermarks "dolphin" and "thunderbolt," common to the two series. The countermark "dolphin" is also encountered on many issues of copper coins of the end of the IVth century B.C. to the beginning of the IIIrd century. The time of countermarking may be set at not earlier than the middle of the IIIrd century B.C. Through its use the whole of the town's mass of money—both copper and silver—was probably put upon a uniform footing.

The fact that the money market was in need of being set in order is shown by the great differences in the weight of copper coins of the heavy denomination between those with the types: griffin—Maiden (and ones close to this), and those with: Maiden—bull. The difference between their respective weights was approximately in the proportion 3:2. It is difficult to say whether they preserved their denomination after countermarking, and just what that denomination was. The matter is clearer as regards the silver coins. The two series of silver, 290-280 and 250-230 B.C., consisted of coins the metrological standards of which coincided. But all four denominations were different—tetradrachms and didrachms in the first series, tridrachms and trihemidrachms in the second. Their difference as to types helped in distinguishing the denominations, but their having something in common (which could not always be established on the basis of weight) and their pertaining to the same metrological standard, was certified through the countermark "dolphin." The countermark "thunderbolt," found only on silver coins, apparently reflected some subsequent phase of the coordination process, or else it was associated with a shift in the town's currency to a different metrological standard.

The issues of silver coins examined above enable one to get some idea of the complicated state of the town's finances around the middle of the IIIrd century B.C. They reflected a crisis in the economy, apparently provoked by a reduction in the volume of trade which in the last analysis lowered the influx of precious metal and led to its becoming dearer. Old coin of full weight is taken out of circulation and is converted into treasure. It is precisely from the middle of the second half of the IIIrd century B.C. that we have such important hoards brought to light in the environs of Chersonesus as the Streletski (36 silver and 67 bronze coins) and the Kamyshevski (39 silver and 702 bronze coins) (Takhtai), or the 1966 hoard of bronze coins numbering 643 specimens. In fact the hoards were of greater volume, since a considerable part of the coins of the Kamyshevski hoard and the 1966 hoard were dissipated.

Perhaps one may explain in part through a shortage of silver the issue of small silver coins in two denominations which follows next on this (Plate IX, 121-124, 125-126). The average weight of coins of the larger denomination is 2.29 g, that of the smaller 1.26 g. The weight norms fit easily into the framework of the Phoenician standard, but the denominations in this case turn out to be not entirely ordinary: 4½ obols and 2 obols. As something of an analogy we may take the Heracleia coinage of the period of the rule of Timotheos and Dionysios (345-337), under whom, side by side with coins having an average weight of 9.51 g and most likely constituting tridrachms on the Phoenician standard, there were issued quarters therof, the average weight of which is 2.33 g. It is not without interest to point out that for the currency of the Ptolemies in general an observance of a weight relationship of 2:1 between denominations issued was characteristic. Thus, for example, under Ptolemy III (246-221) there were issued gold coins as decadrachms, pentadrachms, 2½ drachmas, and the half and the quarter of the drachma; and also silver decadrachms, pentadrachms, and pieces of 2½ drachmas (Seltman, pp. 242-243). At Chersonesus this sort of system of denominations did not in practice create inconvenience by reason of its simplicity; the new coins bore the following succession of distinct relationships to the old issues of silver—1 (types: griffin—quiver): 2 (head of Maiden in dotted border—bull): 4 (head of Heracles—bull): 8 (head of Heracles—Maiden on throne).

Another issue of silver coins with the types head of Heracles—bull (Plate IX, 127-129) enables one to divine a shift to another standard of coin weight. The average weight of the new coins comes to 2.04 g. One might have thought of a gradual decline in the weight of coins struck on the same Phoenician standard, but this is improbable. The coins described are most likely hemidrachms on the Attic standard, the norm weight of which ought to come to 2.12 g. Simultaneously with the silver, copper coins were also issued (Plate IX, 131-132), in a dichalcon denomination.

The correctness of the identification of a new metrological standard is confirmed as one examines the next series of silver and copper (Plate IX, 133-137; X, 139-152). The average weights for the denominations of silver are 3.73 and 1.76 g. Bertier de la Garde identified their metrological standard as Phoenician (Bertier, 1913, p. 67), but one cannot agree with this—the weight of the Phoenician drachma comes to 3.40 g. Despite the considerable fall in the average weight of the coins below the norm of the Attic drachmas (4.25 g), this identification is the more probable.

The average weights of the copper coins are 3.50 g and 1.87 g. One's attention is drawn to the closeness of the weight data for the larger denominations, and for the smaller denominations, in the two metals. It is possible that the weight of the Attic drachma was used as a point of departure in the striking of the copper coins, too. The larger denomination of the copper can be identified with the dichalcon, the smaller with its half, the chalcon. Bertier de la Garde saw on the reverse of one of the coins of the smaller denomination the symbol H, the sense of which he did not understand (Bertier, 1906a, p. 253). Such a symbol has not appeared on coins known to us. If he was not mistaken, it would be possible to consider this symbol as an indication of the denomination (ἥμισυς—the adjective "half-") as being equal to one-half that of the heavier copper coin.

It is decidedly difficult to determine the denominations for the series of copper coins of the type: head of the Maiden—kneeling Maiden; and: Pegasus protome—warrior)Plate X, 154-155). The weight of the larger denomination does not even reach two grams (1.78 g), which can only correspond to a chalcon; the smaller denomination, the weight of two coins of which (once in the Bertier de la Garde collection) is unknown, cannot be defined.

The next issue of silver (Plate X, 158) repeats the type of the hemidrachms of the preceding series, which enables one to identify these coins, too, as hemidrachms even though they fall considerably below these in weight (average weight 1.28 g). The quality of the metal of these coins is decidedly low, and individual specimens remind one more of copper. Apparently the state of the town finances at the turn of the IIIrd-IInd centuries B.C. was complicated indeed, something which should perhaps be associated with the appearance of a military threat from the direction of the Scythian kingdom in the Crimea. The Amaga myth (Polyaen., VIII, 56) in all likelihood reflects a true picture of the hostile relations between Chersonesus and the Scythians which drove the town to seek help from the Sarmatians. We know that Gatalus, king of the Sarmatians,was among the allies of king Pharnaces I of Pontus, with whom Chersonesus concluded a treaty of friendship (IosPE, I^2, 402).

The obverse type of the coins we are describing (head of Maiden wearing mural crown) unquestionably served in some measure as the prototype for the silver coins one may assign to the period of the Diophantus expeditions. Prior to these the town was not issuing other silver coins, and on this account hemidrachms long remained the only silver in circulation; and although the town still had available a considerable quantity of that metal, in conformity with Gresham's law ("worse coin drives better coin out of circulation") it was stored away as treasure in the hands of the state and of private persons.

Among the issues of copper coins of the IInd century B.C. one may confidently name dichalcons (types: head of Maiden—bull Plate X, 156-157, average weight 3.23 g ; head of Athena—griffin, Plate XI, 159-160, average weight 3.90 g; head of Dioscurus—prow, Plate XI, 165, 166, average weight 3.25 g; head of Helios—cornucopiae, Plate XI, 173-174, average weight 2.32 g; and: head of Apollo—tripod, Plate XI, 176, weight 1.88 g) and chalcons (types: head of Athena—Nike, Plate XI, 161-163, average weight 2.06 g; head of Maiden—Nike, Plate XI, 164, average weight 1.52 g; head of Maiden—bow and quiver, Plate XI, 168-169, weight 1.70 g). The denomination of a few other issues remains unclear.

The last series is represented by a drachma and a hemidrachm of Attic weight (average weight of the coins repectively 3.81 and 1.62 g), and also by a dichalcon (average weight 2.02 g). One's attention is drawn to the considerable falling off in the weight of copper coins in the IInd century B.C. Apparently it is through the diminution of the weight and diameter of the coins that one should explain the disappearance of the names of officials on the smaller denomination, the chalcon—something which is to some extent of assistance in dating the concluding issues of the period of autonomy and facilitates the distinguishing of their denominations.

4. The Organization of the Currency

The question of the organization of the currency at Chersonesus has not been the subject of special inquiry. One should say that the coins themselves do not afford any information in this regard. With the exception of the names of certain persons which were placed on coins in full or abbreviated form during the entire autonomous period, without indication of their office, almost no symbols are found on the coins which might afford evidence of control over the coinage.

At present we are familiar with about 70 to 80 different names which were placed on coins approximately from the middle of the IVth century to the middle of the Ist century B.C. I. I. Makhov considered that these names were those of members of a college of astynomoi (Makhov, p. 150-183). He reached this conclusion on the basis of a large number of coincidences of names on coins and amphora handles, these names being accompanied in the latter case with an indication of the function.

Oreshnikov subjected this point of view to harsh criticism and rightly pointed out that the mintage of coins could scarcely be in the hands of this second-rank officialdom which for the most part carried out police functions. Oreshnikov considered that the names on the coins belonged to eponymous kings. True, he made this assertion with a good deal of caution and a number of qualifications (Oreshnikov, 1922, p. 113-121). Zograph also considered this deduction to be hypothetical, even though tempting (Zograph, 1951, p.160).

Observations of the coins have shown that some names are repeated on coins known to be of different periods, and that for this reason they should be ascribed to different persons. But an instance is known where coins have established the fact, difficult to explain, of a group repetition of abbreviations of what are apparently one and the same set of names. At issue here are the coins with types of a griffin and a kneeling Maiden. They are represented by two varieties: on the first the griffin is represented on the obverse and the Maiden on the reverse (Plate IV, 60-62); on the second the Maiden is on the obverse and the griffin on the reverse (Plate IV, 64-65). The obverse and the reverse are always distinctly recognizable by reason of peculiarities of the striking technique.

On the coins of the first variety the letters KPA, ΠA, and API appear. They constitute abbreviations of personal names usual for Chersonesus. Exactly the same abbreviations (KPA, ΠA, and AP) also appear on coins of the second variety. The relationship between the issues may be presented as follows. First they commenced to issue the coins with the type of the griffin on the obverse, while the Maiden, one of the main civic divinities, occupied a more or less secondary position—her image was placed on the reverse. After a certain spell of time it was decided that this type-relationship should be altered, and the figure of the Maiden was shifted to the obverse. But the altogether identical selection of magistrates' names runs counter to such a reconstruction of the course of the mintage. It turns out that one and the same set of magistrates takes part in the issuance of coins of the two varieties. Even if one considers that the order in which the magistrates performed their functions might be different in the two cases, the likelihood of such a group coincidence would be decidedly scant. Equally improbable is the proposition that all or some of the abbreviations are to be deciphered into different names; and one should quite dismiss any idea that each magistrate successively or in parallel issued coins of both varieties.

To our mind the only possible explanation of this state of affairs lies in acknowledging that the monetary magistracy of Chersonesus bore a collegate character. The change in the positioning of the types took place while three magistrates were simultaneously performing their function and they left abbreviations of their names on coins of the first and of the second variety. Other facts, too, may be sought out in the currency of Chersonesus which confirm such a conclusion. Thus the didrachms with the type of a head of the Maiden on the obverse and of the Maiden striking down a hind on the reverse were issued under three magistrates - Artemidoros, Istronos, and Aiskhinos (Plate VI, 88-90). All the coins known to date were struck with a single obverse die which, however, was used on two occasions--in its initial state, and after minor touching-up. In both cases it was used by one and the same set of magistrates (although on the coins with the obverse die being used for the second time one reads only the names of Artemidoros and Aiskhinos beyond any question, still the presence of coins of Istronos among the specimens with erased names is entirely admissible). That is to say, one observes the same situation as in the preceding instance, finding a satisfying explanation only on the basis of recognition of the fact that three persons did indeed simultaneously exercise the function. A minor circumstance confirming this deduction is that in many cases the overall number of magistrates issuing coins of a single type or series proves to be three or a multiple of that number.

In itself, collegiality of the monetary magistracy was rather a rule than an exception for the ancient period. It suffices to recall the well-known college of the _tres viri monetales_ of the Roman republic. At Athens four persons were responsible for the issuance of the tetradrachms of the "New Style". At Olbia a "college of seven" and a "college of nine" took part in the issuance of coins. The number of similar examples could easily be augmented.

As we examine the problem of the monetary magistracy at Chersonesus we may seek to identify the college which the magistrates constituted. We should take as our point of departure first of all the proposition that striking of its own coin is one of the most important indices of a town's sovereignty. It is clear that giving effect to the monetary _regalia_ of a _polis_ could not lie in the hands of any second-rate sort of magistracy. What is more, since the well-being of the town and of its citizens depended in many respects upon sensible policy in the field of the currency, the monetary magistracy ought to occupy one of the most important levels in the system of governmental administration. The most suitable for this role was the college of _nomophylakes_. As is apparent from decrees (IosPE, I^2, 343, 347, 351), the college of _nomophylakes_, which was made up of three persons, appears before the organ of supreme authority, the national assembly, together with the dioiketes, that is to say "he who heads the administration," in order to present proposals for laws throughout the whole Hellenistic period. Accordingly it performs one of the most important functions in the system of the democratic state. The very name nomophylax, "the guardian of the law", speaks of its importance. Among the functions of the college of nomophylakes in the field of the striking of coins there was apparently included the determination of any need for the issuance of fresh coins, the selection of the metal in which they should be struck, and also that of one metrological standard or another, that of the coin types, the denominations, and finally determination of the volume of the coinage—perhaps even procurement of the necessary quantity of metal.

The names of members of the college of nomophylakes commenced to be placed on coins of Chersonesus starting with the mid-IVth century B.C. It is difficult to say whether the college of nomophylakes was in charge of the currency in the first decades of the civic coinage or whether there was another order of things, since the early coins do not bear any inscriptions, letters or the like. But during the Hellenistic period all issues were marked with the names of magistrates. The sole exception consists of the coins with the quadriga type on the obverse and the kneeling, helmeted warrior with shield and with spear running transversely on the reverse (Plate II, 36-42; III, 43-56), which demonstrate an entirely different system for designating coin issues.

We have pointed out above that among these coins one distinguishes three successively issued varieties—ones without inscriptions, ones with the syllables ΗΡ, ΛΥ and ΣΑ and finally ones with individual letters of the Greek alphabet from A to Σ The internal arrangement of syllables and letters on the coins (all the syllables, and the letters from A to E, are encountered only on the obverses, the remaining letters on the reverses) bear witness to the fact that in the first place the coins with the syllables preceded the coins with the letters, and that in the second place the letters were set out on the coins in alphabetical order. The coins without any inscriptions were most likely issued earlier than the other two groups.

The coins with the quadriga fall among the very earliest issues of Chersonesus copper (350-330 B.C.). The presence of the three varieties described above within this group enables one to assert that their issuance commenced at the time when the names of magistrates were still not being placed upon coins. After that the mintage continued with the issues distinguished through the names of members of the college of nomophylakes in abbreviated form (three abbreviations are known, which corresponds to the number of the members of that college), subsequent to which this order of things was suddenly changed and the issues came to be marked with letters of the alphabet in order. This practice, however, was not long-lasting. The coins of the type: griffin-Maiden, which came in to replace them, once more came to be designated by the names of nomophylakes, to begin with in abbreviated form, but later in full form. If one takes it that the letters on the coins with the quadriga indicate a count of years, and this is the only possible proposition, then the altered order of designating issues must have been retained at Chersonesus over the course of 18 years.

Such a state of affairs is in our view of considerable interest not only for the history of the Chersonesus currency but also for study of the town's governmental organization, since it offers evidence of a temporary suspension of one of the most important magistrates of the town, the college of nomophylakes, or at least of its complete elimination from control over the issuance of coin.

The practice of designating coin issues with letters of the Greek alphabet existed in many towns, among them Black Sea ones (Istria, Tyra, Olbia). But these facts have not been interpreted in any way. In seeking an analogy we have turned to the currency of Samos, a recently published analysis of which is based upon the community's thoroughly familiar history (Barron).

In the history of the Samos currency two instances of the designation of annual issues by means of letters are on record. The first instance is associated by the author of the monograph, J. Barron, with the Ionian rising of the Greeks against Persian overlordship. The Samos oligarchs, driven out by the Persians, settled at Zankle, where they issued tetradrachms of Attic weight with the letters Α, Β, Δ, Ε and without letters, something which corresponds precisely to the five years of their stay at that town (Barron, pp. 40-43). The second instance relates to the period of the Samos "pentēkontaetía". During this period tetradrachsm of Samos weight were struck: first without any supplementary symbols, later with various symbols (helmet, wheel, astragalus, owl, and others), and finally with letters from Β to Ξ. The author convincingly demonstrates that the change to designation by means of letters is associated with the seizure of power in Samos by the oligarchs in 454-453 B. C. After the Athenian suppression of the uprising on Samos a part of the oligarchs fled to the mainland, where they issued a further two varieties of coins of this type (Barron, pp. 89-93).

Barron's conclusions are built up on a solid foundation of literary and numismatic sources cemented together, and they accordingly strike one as decidedly convincing. The episodes in the history of the Samos currency which are described enable one to draw an important conclusion, having to our mind a general character—namely, that the designation of coin-issues by means of letters in alphabetical order should be associated with the liquidation of democratic institutions and the establishment of an oligarchic form of rule. Apparently a similar situation arose at Chersonesus around 350 B. C. An upheaval occured in the town; oligarchs came into power who did in fact commence to designate coin issues by the years of their rule. The sway of the oligarchs continued through 18 years, after which they were apparently driven out and the earlier democratic system was restored in the town.

Thus the coins with the quadriga have illustrated a transitional period in the history of the Chersonesus currency. Their issue commenced at a time when the names of magistrates were still not being placed on coins, after which it was apparently continued by the newly established college of nomophylakes for a total of one year, before it passed into the hands of the oligarchs. But prior to the coins with the quadriga there had been struck at Chersonesus the group of silver coins with types of the head of the Maiden on the obverse and of a butting bull on the reverse (Plate II, 33-34), on which names appear—ΖΟΠΥΡΟ and Κ (?). These coins are likewise of no little interest.

Inasmuch as they precede the coins with the quadriga, the names on them cannot be regarded as belonging to members of the college of nomophylakes. All the silver and copper coins of earlier issuance are devoid of any sort of inscriptions, and for that reason the coins being examined demonstrate, in our opinion, that there was some other order of mintage. In this connection one's attention is drawn to the difference in the ways of writing the names: one of them is given in full form, the other is abbreviated to a single letter (one cannot assign any other significance to the letter K). One gets the impression that the letter K designated the name of a man well known to the people of Chersonesus. The chronological proximity of the coins to the rule of Clearchus (Klearkhos) at Heracleia enables one to venture a suggestion to the effect that on the Chersonesus coins his name lies latent in the letter K The Chersonesus coins might correspond to the numerous coins of Heracleia itself which bear this same letter.

As we are aware, for a long time the letter K on coins of Heracleia was considered to be the initial letter of the name of that tyrant. Not long ago P. Franke published an article in which he denied the connection of the letters K and Σ encountered upon Heracleia coins, with the names of Clearchus and Satyrus (Franke). He published a number of diobols with the letter K which had been overstruck on coins with the letter Σ. The sequence of the letters, the reverse of the order in which the tyrants ruled, in his opinion allows one to see in them no more than symbols designating issues (Emissionszeichen).

Without denying the weighty significance of Franke's observations for study of the currency of Heracleia, we must at the same time make some comments. In the first place, the fact that of all the letters of the Greek alphabet only two, K and Σ are placed on the coins remains unaltered. In the second place, the dating of the coins in question indisputably coincides with the time of the rule of the two brothers Clearchus and Satyrus, the coins with the letter K unquestionably being earlier in style than the coins with the letter Σ. In the third place, the very circumstance of the overstriking of the coins of the one type into ones of the other testifies to some sort of exceptional event in the course of money matters, perhaps even one running counter to the tenor of the evolution of the currency, and one on that account not actually yielding to decipherment in our day by reason of lack of information on the causes which provoked it. The overstriking constituted an illogical phenomenon as to the meaning of which one may guess, but not as yet be certain. And finally, in the fourth place the two letters cannot by any means be regarded as the same sort of arbitrary supplementary symbols as are the crescent, the bunch of grapes, the ivy leaf, and others encountered on coins of this type, if it were only for the reason that on certain specimens known to us the K is encountered in combination with another supplementary symbol, the one in the form of an ivy leaf (Babelon, plate 55, 7; Franke, plate 1, 1). The latter was in fact the issue symbol in the full sense of the term. Thus the plausibility of seeing in the letters K and Σ the initials of the tyrants Clearchus and Satyrus remains, in our view, as the sole possible or at the least a very considerable one.

Should one not regard the placing of the letter K on the Chersonesus coins as evidence that coins were issued in the name of Clearchus at Chersonesus as well? We know little about the organization of ancient currency in the early periods. In particular, the question of the causes of the appearance of names on the early phases of the coinage of Greek towns has remained almost without study. For the Black Sea littoral examples of this are offered by Olbia (we have in mind the early silver staters with the name EMINAKO) and Callatia, where king Ateius was the initiator of coinage in general and of silver coins in particular (Anokhin, 1973, p. 35). If we are to speak of Heracleia, was the use of the name Clearchus evoked by political motives—acknowledgement of this individual's sovereign powers, —or was it brought on by the tyrant's having provided a certain quantity of silver for the coinage? The latter seems the more probable, inasmuch as in parallel with the coins having the letters K and Σ other coins of the same types are struck, but without letters. The double marking of certain issues—with the letter K and with a supplementary symbol—also speaks in favor of this proposition.

Returning to the Chersonesus issue of silver coins with the letter K , we may conclude that if the name of the Heracleia tyrant Clearchus lies concealed in this letter, then the striking of silver in his name at Chersonesus may be regarded as still another important proof of the existence of close economic and political ties between the town and its metropolis, even of a dependence of Chersonesus on Heracleia. At the same time the issuance of silver in the name of Clearchus (a second such person was the otherwise unknown Zopyros) was perhaps a purely commercial operation, a sui-generis exchange of silver for local merchandise necessary to Heracleia or to the tyrant personally.

Unfortunately the facts which offer any sort of information regarding the organization of the currency at Chersonesus are limited to the instances cited. As we have already remarked, names are regularly placed upon silver and upon copper down to the end of the period of autonomy. It is true that the concluding issues of the smaller denomination of copper, the chalcon, are without names—something most likely to be explainedby a technological cause, the diminution of the diameter of the coin blank. There is a range of issues represented not by three names, but by one or by two. But it would be premature to draw any conclusions from that, inasmuch as the last issue of silver for the autonomous period was carried out by three magistrates.

5. Historical Sketch

With regard to the time and circumstances of the genesis of Chersonesus (cf. Ps. Scyl., 822-827) various opinions have been suggested (Zhebelev, p. 74 ff.). At present a majority of students share the views of A. I. Tyumenev, who assigned the foundation of the town to 422-421 B.C. (Tyumenev, p. 245 ff).

The history of the town during the initial period remains unknown as regards specific facts. Most likely it was a small trading settlement, an emporium (Ps.—Scyl., 68), one of the bases of the Heracleia merchants in the northern Black Sea littoral. The earliest governmental records of Chersonesus are coins, its first series of silver and copper dating around 390-380 B.C. Prior to that Chersonesus either needed no coin of its own, or did not have the right of coinage: the appearance of its own coins should constitute evidence that Chersonesus had become an autonomous governmental organization, a polis.

The formation of the Chersonesus as a state occurred in direct association with the expansion of the Bosporus in the west (Bertier, 1907, p. 196). Despite active support to Theodosia on the part of Heracleia Pontica, the prolonged siege of that town by the Bosporus kings ended with the taking of Theodosia in 387 B.C. The loss of the town, which was presumably Heracleia's main partner in the Crimea, obliged Heracleia to shift the center of its trading operations to Chersonesus, something which fostered its rapid economic growth. For the first half of the IVth century B.C. we note a predominance of Heracleian import ware among Chersonesus finds (Shcheglov, p. 334). The using of coin types in common by Chersonesus and by Heracleia, the observance of a single metrological standard for the striking of coins, and also the suggested issue at Chersonesus in the name of the tyrant Clearchus, bear witness to close economic, political, and cultural ties between the two towns.

Coins also throw light upon the organization of government at Chersonesus in the IVth century B.C. R. A. Novikova arrived at the deduction, while studying the question of the college of nomophylakes, that this was the most important magistracy of Chersonesus (Novikova, p. 106). Numismatic data enable one to fill out this proposition substantially. It has been established that the names on the coins belonged to persons who formed part of a college of three persons, most likely a college of nomophylakes. Thus in addition to their presentation of projected laws to the council and to the national assembly for examination, the nomophylakes carried out the functions of monetary magistrates.

The first instance of the placing of names of nomophylakes (in abbreviated form) upon coins relates approximately to the middle of the IVth century B.C. They are seen upon the initial variants of the coins of the type: quadriga—kneeling warrior (Plate II, 36-38). It is difficult to say whether the formation of the actual college and the entrusting to it of the coin mintage should be associated with this date, or whether it was from this time that their name commenced to be placed on coins. There is an absence of information on this point.

Thereafter the coins with the quadriga are issued annually over the course of 18 years (each issue is signalized by a letter of the Greek alphabet, in order), subsequent to which the names of nomophylakes are again placed on the coins. What we have said affords evidence of the existence at Chersonesus of a form of rule which had eliminated democratic institutions. Comparison with the currency of Samos shows that the practice of designating coin issues with letters of the Greek alphabet is characteristic of an oligarchic form of rule.

The suggested reconstruction of events in the internal political life of Chersonesus in the third quarter of the IVth century B.C., as derived from a basis of numismatic data, may be substantiated by examination of a Chersonesus oath (IosPE, I^2, 401) which was composed at the end of the IVth century B.C. or the beginning of the IIIrd.

First of all, the very fact of the appearance of the oath affords evidence of some sort of exceptional event which occurred at Chersonesus and led to the creation of such an exceptional document. One of the inquirers into the oath, S. A. Zhebelev, has written that: "... the three paragraphs of the oath definitely entitle one to conclude that its composition and promulgation were preceded at Chersonesus by domestic tumults and that these were directed toward the overthrow of the democratic system which had, as one must suppose, been consolidated at Chersonesus since the days of its foundation" (Zhebelev, p. 223). The clause concerning defense of the democratic system was unquestionably intended to avert a repetition of the overthrow. The oath's lines regarding prohibition of hostile action against "non-opting" citizens enable one to suggest the existence of a different category, the "opting" ones, that is to say those who had fled from or had been driven out of Chersonesus after the restoration of the democracy. These same persons were unquestionably set in contrast to that part of the citizens "who had not been declared enemies of the people" (line 40). One should associate with the falling away of some part of the citizen body the mention of territories which the people of Chersonesus had at one time "governed" (line 11).

Zhebelev's suggestion that at Chersonesus only an attempted coup had taken place with the aim of establishing a tyranny, and that the conspiracy had been unmasked and the plotters condemned (Zhebelev, p. 227), has not been confirmed. On the contrary, both the coins and the text of the oath allow one to hold that in reality the conspiracy proved successful. The new authority held on for no less than 18 years, after which the order which had previously prevailed was re-established.

There is indirect information as to what form the new rule took. It may have been a tyranny or an oligarchy. Zhebelev was inclined to favor the former thesis, holding that an oligarchy excludes swearing support to the "liberty" which is mentioned in the oath itself, and supporting his idea through the fact that at that time a tyranny held sway at Heracleia. Despite all the cogency of Zhebelev's deductions, one must nevertheless accord preference to the second thesis. In the first place, the example of Samos affords evidence that an oligarchy might have existed: its coin series issued by oligarchs were also denoted by letters in order. In the second place, oligarchy is unquestionably associated with limitations upon the freedom of the many for the benefit of the few. In the third place, in a later Chersonesus inscription (IosPE, I^2, 355) with which Zhebelev compares the oath, there is constant reference to a certain "tyrant" who had seized power in the town, something the like of which does not appear in the oath. And in the fourth place, one should recall that with Clearchus's coming to power part of the oligarchs at Heracleia were slaughtered and part managed to save themselves throught flight. One of the possible towns where those who had escaped might find refuge was Chersonesus. It is not out of the question that after some time they should have seized power here.

Then what form of rule did the town accept after expulsion of the oligarchs? Novikova considers that the oath signalizes a certain alteration in the direction of greater democratization, yet with preservation of the aristocratic magistracy of the nomophylakes (Novikova, pl 106). One of the most important evidences of democratic transformations lies in the clause of the oath which deals with the obligation to transport grain harvested on the plain only to Chersonesus (lines 48-50). In view of the importance of the matter we shall dwell upon it in more detail.

In the IVth century B.C. extensive territory in the western Crimea became subject to Chersonesus. True, one may speak with confidence only of the coastal strip, the beach-heads on which were Kerkinitis (the modern Eupatoria), Kalos Limen or Fair Haven (the present village of Chernomorskoye) and other less important strongpoints. We do not know the date of the incorporation of this territory into the Chersonesus state. Shcheglov's suggestion that this took place after the Scythian kingdom had become debilitated in connection with the downfall of king Ateius in 339 B.C. is insufficiently backed by arguments.

To designate the territory of the Chersonesus state two terms are used in the oath— χώρα and πεδίον. Zhebelev held that the first name relates primarily to the Chersonesus peninsula as a particular case, but that in general this is the territory directly continguous to the points of settlement—Chersonesus, Kerkinitis, and the rest (Zhebelev, p. 230). By πεδίον he understood the steppe section of the Crimea, adjoining the Chersonesus holdings to the northwest, but not forming part of them. Zhebelev bases this last interpretation upon the definition by Strabo of the Tauric peninsula, except for its mountainous part, as plains (πεδίας). The staking out of the plain (πεδίον) into lots for vineyards (IosPE, I^2, 418) was also referred by this scholar to the territory specified, without his noting any contradiction (how would it be possible to stake out land not belonging to the town?—V. A.). Zhebelev's interpretation seems to us to be in error. In his day little was known about the existence of cleruchies on the Heracleian peninsula (Strzeletski). It now becomes completely obvious that the staked-out plain was cleruchy land, but nothing similar to it has yet been brought to light to the northwest of Chersonesus.

The matter of the plain is not to be shrugged off as merely a terminological dispute. Inasmuch as one of the clauses of the oath obliges citizens to sell or import grain from the plain only at Chersonesus, there arises a question as to what sort of territory this was which was supposed to ensure in adequate measure the supply of the town with grain. Latyshev suggested that this clause had been dictated not so much by concern for the alimentation of the citizens as by a striving of Chersonesus to establish a monopoly on the export of grain (Latyshev, 1909, p. 157).

As has already been pointed out, the people of Chersonesus understood as being "the plain" only the territory of the Heracleian peninsula, that is to say the Chersonesus khōra proper. In that case, the thesis regarding establishment of a monopoly on the export of grain becomes implausible. Most likely the grain cultivated on the Heracleian peninsula should have sufficed for the entire population of the town provided that wealthy landowners should not, in seeking high profits, sell it abroad. Such a possibility was open to them, because on the territory occupied by cleruchy lands there were to the west of Chersonesus three well-provided harbors from which grain might be exported, by-passing Chersonesus. Accordingly this clause of the oath was drawn up in the interests of the poorer sort of town-dwellers, inconveniencing wealthy landowners to some extent. It was most probably adopted under the pressure of the former, inasmuch as it has an alien look among the clauses about safe-guarding the democracy.

The history of the evolution of the two basic coin types—the Maiden-goddess and Heracles—is perhaps a reflection of the struggle between aristocracy and democracy at Chersonesus. From the initiation of the coinage the main position in typology is occupied by the image of the Maiden and of her attributes. The importance of the cult of the Maiden is explained by the fact that in her image there were amalgamated features of the Greek Artemis and of the female divinity of the native population of the Crimea, the Tauri. Settlers always accepted into their pantheon with alacrity the local divinities which protected the territory which they had occupied. The spread of the cult of the Maiden is confirmed by the existence in the town of her temple and of festivals in honor of the Maiden—the Parthenia. The text of the oath places her higher than the Olympian gods and goddesses, and in a number of inscriptions she figures as the protectress who preserves the town from the barbarian. During the course of the entire ancient period the image of the Maiden occupies the central position among the coin types. Considerable popularity was also enjoyed by the cult of Heracles, after whom the metropolis of Chersonesus, Heracleia, had been named. But the Dorian origin of Chersonesus does not of itself totally explain the history of the evolution of images of Heracles in the coin typology. Recollection of the Dorian origin of the town and of Heracleia as metropolis of Chersonesus was preserved at least till the IInd century B.C., but images of Heracles and his attributes already disappear completely from the repertoire of coin types by the end of the IInd century B.C. If Chersonesus was founded as an aristocratic state, then taking into account the information presented above with regard to the significance within the political establishment of Chersonesus of the magistracy of the nomophylakes, characteristic specifically of states with an aristocratic form of rule, one may suppose that the cult of the Maiden enjoyed particular popularity among the aristocracy, whereas the cult of Heracles was disseminated among the democratic strata. The type of Heracles upon coins appears for the first time not earlier than 280 B.C. To judge by the coins, the cult of Heracles became most highly evolved in the IIIrd century B.C. Thereafter, as democratic tendencies within the administration declined, the image of Heracles gradually disappears from Chersonesus coins. The fact that such tendencies were strong in the IIIrd century B.C. is shown by the alternation of coin issues having Maiden and Heracles types. Thus, for example, the head of Heracles is represented on the obverse of silver coins (Plate VI, 92-93; VII; VIII); it is supplanted by the type of the head of the head of the Maiden (Plate IX, 121-124); then the image of Heracles appears again (Plate IX, 127-132); after this, the Maiden (Plate IX, 133-137; X, 138-144), and once more Heracles (Plate X, 147-149).

The appropriation of new territories continued in the IIIrd century B.C. as well, as is attested by the inscription in honor of Agasicles, who staked out plots for vineyards (IosPE, I^2, 418), and also a fragment of an inscription of the end of the IIIrd or beginning of the IInd century B.C. regarding the leasing or sale of land (IosPE, I^2, 403). The expansion of the state through new lands must have had an impact in the form of an upsurge in the prosperity of Chersonesus. In the first half of the IIIrd century B.C. the town issues mass series of silver coins. For comparison's sake we may recall that at that time there is observed in the Bosporus the so-called monetary crisis, which found expression in the complete stoppage of the striking of coins in gold and silver; an analogous phenomenon has been pointed out at Olbia as well. From the same inscription in honor of Agasicles we learn of his constructing defensive walls and setting up a market, which affords evidence of increased material potentialities for Chersonesus. The construction of a theater also falls to the IIIrd century B.C.

Chersonesus maintained cultural ties with Sicily; at the end of the IVth century B.C. the Chersonesus moneyers borrowed a particular technique for the casting of coin blanks which had become widespread in many towns of Sicily and southern Italy (Anokhin, 1974). Nor did links with Sicily break down in later times either. At the end of the IIIrd century B.C. certain types on Chersonesus coins reveal patent influence of the coin types of the Sicilian town of Alaesa (Ἄλαισα). Reciprocal relations between Chersonesus and the island of Delos, one of the largest religious centers of ancient Greece, were intensive. In 276 B.C. the people of Chersonesus offered at the temple of Apollo in Delos three silver flasks weighing 100 drachmas each (Grakov, No. 25-27). Somewhat later, but before 220-221 B.C., they deposited at the same place a considerable sum of money the interest on which, coming to 400 drachmas, went toward organization of festivities in honor of Chersonesus, the Chersonesia (χερσονήσια; Grakov, No. 29-31). A range of evidence regarding ties between Chersonesus and Delphi falls from the first half of the IIIrd century B.C. till the beginning of the IInd (Grakov, No. 12-14).

At the beginning of the IInd century B.C. the situation in the southwestern Crimea changes, and not to Chersonesus's advantage. The economic and military power of the Scythian kingdom in the Crimea gradually mounts, and the kingdom exercises severe pressure upon Chersonesus. At the start Chersonesus contrived more or less successfully to resist the Scythians, something which was doubtless promoted by the conclusion of the treaty with Pharnaces I of Pontus in 179 B.C. (IosPE, I^2, 422). One of the most important provisions of the treaty was the undertaking to furnish aid to the town "if the neighboring barbarians should open a campaign against Chersonesus or against a country subject to the people of Chersonesus, or if they should offend the latter." Gatalus, king of the Sarmatians, was included in the treaty of peace with Pharnaces (Polyb., XXV, 12-14). The legend of the Sarmatian queen Amaga who slew a Scythian king who had carried out raids on Chersonesus (Polaen., VIII, 56) doubtless had some real basis.

Hostile relations between the Sarmatians and the Scythians, possibly occasioned by the treaty ties between the Sarmatians and Chersonesus, ensured the latter a relatively peaceful existence throughout almost the whole IInd century B.C. During that period the town managed to place in order its economy, the strained state of which is seen in the numismatic data from the start of the IInd century B.C. But at the end of that century the Scythians succeeded in neutralizing or even in bringing to their side the Sarmatians. Chersonesus found itself alone facing multitudinous enemies (Scythians, Sarmatians, Tauri); it lost all its holdings in the northwest Crimea and was obliged to turn to Mithradates VI Eupator for help. We are acquainted with the course of events thanks to a Chersonesus decree in honor of Diophantus, a general of Mithradates VI Eupator (IosPE, I^2, 352), and to the information about Chersonesus communicated by Strabo in his "Geography" (VII, 4, 3; VII, 4, 7).

The Scythians evidently came up to the very town itself. Diophantus, as the decree tells us (IosPE, I^2, lines 6-8), "daringly accomplished passage of all his force to the near side, whereupon the Scythian king Palacus suddenly fell upon him with a great horde and he, forced to accept battle, put them to flight." After this he subjected the Tauri of the neighborhood and founded a town. According to the decree this was the sole occasion on which military operations were carried on close to Chersonesus, and on this account there is every reason to compare with this episode the Scythian siege of Ctenus mentioned by Strabo. Most investigators have located Ctenus in the neighborhood of Inkerman. Bertier de la Garde placed it beside Kazachya Bukhta (Bertier, 1907, p. 177ff.). He shared Strabo's opinion regarding the existence in the Kazachya area of an "ancient" Chersonesus, holding that the name Ctenus applied to "the entire northern coast of the Heracleian peninsula, from the Chersonese Beacon to Inkerman" (Bertier, 1907, p. 187, note).

But let us turn to the underlying source. Strabo provides the following information on the locality of Ctenus:1)the Bay of Symbols (the present Balaklava) and Ctenus are the end-points of an isthmus 40 stadia in length, "this being that neck which attaches Chersonesus Minor .... as a part of Chersonesus Major," i.e. the Crimean Peninsula (VII, 4, 2,); 2) "Ctenus is at an equal distance from the town of Chersonesus and from the Bay of Symbols" (VII, 4, 3); 3) "... At a distance of about 15 stadia from the walls of the Chersonesites there is a cape forming a bay of some size pointing toward the town ... This is where Ctenus was" (VII, 4, 7).

Starting from the information cited we can make the following deductions. In the first place, Ctenus was beyond doubt a specific point of settlement, but not a region as Bertier de la Garde believed. In the second place Ctenus, as a point lying the other side from the Bay of Symbols, must have been located somewhere on the northern shore of the Heracleian peninsula, the line between it and the Bay defining an isthmus. In the third place, Ctenus lay at an equal distance from Chersonesus and from the Bay of Symbols, 40 stadia in each case. Inasmuch as this assertion of Strabo's contradicts his own words to the effect that Ctenus was 15 stadia from the walls of the Chersonesites, one may suppose that in the first case he had in mind "old" Chersonesus. Thus Ctenus should be placed in the area of Yuzhnaya Bukhta, an indentation which is equidistant between Cape Chersonese (or Cape Phanar) and Balaklava. The last definition by Strabo fully confirms this deduction—from the walls of the Chersonesites, i.e. from "new" Chersonesus, located on the shore of Karantinnaya Bukhta to the mouth of Yuzhnaya Bukhta is just 15 stadia (about 3 kilometers). Accordingly it is precisely Yuzhnaya Bukhta together with Sarandinakinnaya Balka ravine which runs down to it that make up the neck (ending at Balaklava Bay) which set Strabo's "Chersonesus Minor" apart. The most suitable place for Ctenus is the cape, opposite the present Grafskaya Pristan', which separates Severnaya Bukhta from Yuzhnaya Bukhta.

On the western shore of the cape there is a small cove, and beyond it there is a further small cape, on which Ctenus was evidently located. The heights rising above it had probably been seized by the Scythians. Being deprived of Ctenus threatened the town with decidedly unpleasant consequences. The Scythians would be blockading the exits from Yuzhnaya Bukhta, which apparently served as an important communications channel for the cleruchies lying beside the Sarandinakinnaya Balka ravine, to say nothing of other perils associated with their being in the neighborhood.

The most likely thing is that the operations of Diophantus described in the opening lines of the decree and the description of the defense of Ctenus in Strabo relate to a single event. It would be strange if the decree did not in any way reflect the successful operations of Diophantus, and on this account the description thereof can be harmonized to a certain extent with the course of the defense of Ctenus. Diophantus transferred to "the far side", i.e. across Yuzhnaya Bukhta, but not across Severnaya Bukhta as is usually thought (if the the Scythians had stood at Severnaya Bukhta they could not have threatened the town effectively). Diophantus was in the position of the party undertaking to defend itself—the Scythians attacked first, with Palacus at their head. In Strabo the Greeks were conducting a defense of Ctenus. According to the decree, Diophantus "put the Scythians to flight"; according to Strabo, the Greeks "resisted until they won".

After the withdrawal of the Scythians, who were unaccustomed to conducting prolonged sieges, Diophantus smashed the Tauri of the neighborhood without any apparent difficulty and founded the town of Eupatorium not far away; it should probably be sought on the southern shore of the Heracleian peninsula, in the Balaklava area. After this he set out for the Bosporus, and having accomplished there "in a short time many important feats," returned to Chersonesus. Having brought his force up to strength with a detachment of Chersonites, Diophantus commenced a campaign into Scythia. He overpowered the fortresses of Chabaei and Neapolis (Χαβαίους καί Νέαν Πόλιν), thus subjecting almost all the Scythians. Chersonesus rendered honor to Diophantus "as already saved from the sway of the barbarians." At this point the first year of the war with the Scythians comes to an end; it is ordinarily dated to 110 B.C.

In the following (?) year the Scythians "alienated themselves from the king and altered the state of affairs." Mithradates VI Eupator once more sent Diophantus out with a force. The latter, despite the approach of winter, again advanced with the townsmen against the Scythians, but by reason of foul weather returned to the seacoast, took possession of The Walls and Cercinitis, and set about besieging Kalos Limen. The Scythians brought to their aid the Rheuxinali (Strabo wrote that Palacus was aided by the Roxolani under the command of Tasius, whose force numbered fifty thousand, against six thousand Greeks—Strabo, VII, 3, 17), but they were destroyed. Let us examine this evidence in a little greater detail.

Evidently the coastal strip remained in the hands of the Scythians all this time. The subjection of the Scythians to Mithradates VI put Chersonesus out of danger, but Cercinitis, The Walls, and Kalos Limen remained in Scythian hands. A treaty was concluded between the Scythians and the Greeks. Relying upon it, Diophantus returned to Pontus, but the Scythians "perfidiously" "altered the state of affairs," i.e. they violated some sort of provisions of the treaty. If they had seized Cercinitis and the other points, the decree would have said something about it. A second expedition of Diophantus of 109 B.C., against the Scythians, was not crowned with success. On this account Diophantus directed his forces toward seizure of the coastal holdings of the Scythians. Only in the spring of 108 B.C. did Diophantus organize a third campaign against the Scythian fortress of Chabaei and Neapolis, and this ended successfully. After this he set out for the Bosporus, and in all likelihood he secured from king Paerisades the surrender of authority to Mithradates VI Eupator, whereafter the rising headed by Saumacus broke out. Paerisades was slain, and Diophantus fled on a ship sent from Chersonesus. The rebels took possession of the entire European part of the Bosporus, including Theodosia. Diophantus meanwhile prepared for war. In the spring of 107 B.C. he arrived at Chersonesus with a new land and naval force, and after having inducted a detachment of Chersonesus citizens on three ships he set forth to suppress the rising. It was most likely then that Neoptolemus, admiral of Mithradates VI Eupator, smashed the barbarians in a naval battle in the Straits of Kerch, yet it would seem that earlier, during the winter, they had been defeated in a cavalry battle on the ice (Strabo, II, 1, 16; VII, 3, 18). Evidently it was in 106 B.C., in the month Dionysios (February), that Chersonesus adopted the decree in honor of Diophantus.

Chersonesus emerged from the wars having suffered heavy losses. All its territory in the northwest Crimea had been lost. Under its authority there remained only the Heracleian peninsula, and the city itself lost its independence. It is accepted practice to count from this time the start of a new period in the history of the town, a period of dependence first on the kings of Pontus, and thereafter on those of the Bosporus.

CHAPTER II

BOSPORAN INFLUENCE
(about 110 B.C. — about A.D. 138)

During the period of Chersonesus autonomy the need for a new issue of coins, their denomination, the metrological standard, the types, and the like fall completely within the competence of the college of nomophylakes, who presented corresponding projects of law to the national assembly. After adoption of a decision by the national assembly striking of the coins was carried out, control over this apparently being exercised by this same college of nomophylakes. Such, one must suppose, was the way coinage was issued in each Greek polis which enjoyed sovereignty.

There is no doubt that that process was violated in cases where a town fell into dependence upon one state or another. It might be altogether deprived of the right to issue coin of its own and might evidently therefore, if coinage should become necessary, have to receive appropriate permission from higher authority. In these cases the right of issuing coins, like other rights, depended wholly on the policy of the supreme personality, the king or emperor. It is natural that with change in the superior authority the policy with respect to subject towns might change as well, for the worse or for the better, and for that reason in each such case the town required confirmation of its rights.

As the sources tell us (Strabo, VII, 4, 3), Chersonesus was in this sort of dependent situation under Mithradates VI Eupator. The dependence of Chersonesus —to begin with, upon the King of Pontus, then the kings of the Bosporus, and finally the Roman empire— forces us to approach the task of rendering the Chersonesus coins into system in a different way. Inasmuch as it is now not civic authorities, but Bosporus kings or Roman emperors, who determine monetary policy, altering it to suit circumstances, coin issues must be arranged to the reigns of these. Assignment of issues to the days of one ruler or another is based on analogies with the remaining coinage of that ruler, or else on relative chronology of the actual Chersonesus coins among themselves. From the times of Dynamis Rome intervened a great deal more actively in the internal affairs of the northern Black Sea littoral (for example, the activities of Agrippa), so that it is difficult to say which influence upon the currency of Chersonesus was the determining one — that of the Bosporus, or that of Rome itself. In view of the fact that the typologies of Chersonesus and Bosporus coins of the end of the Ist century B.C. and the first half of the Ist century A.D. are decidedly different, issues may be arranged by periods in harmony with the order of their coinage and without reference to the rule of one king or emperor, or another. The rest of the coins, beginning with A.D. 46, are dated in a majority of cases by years of the Chersonesus era, so that their chronology and reciprocal association do not give rise to any doubts.

1. The Chronology of the Coin Issues

The dependence of Chersonesus upon Mithradates VI Eupator (120-63) unquestionably had to be reflected in coin typology as well as elsewhere. The silver drachmas of the type: head of Maiden wearing mural crown — standing hind (Plate XII, 179-181), can still not be referred to the period of the subjection of Chersonesus to the kingdom of Pontus, as many investigators have thought they could (Zograph, 1951, p. 151), inasmuch as they do not bear any clear signs of the influence of Mithradatic coin types. This view was put forth by Golenko (Golenko, 1964, p. 45), and one cannot fail to agree with it. We have specified above a number of features by reason of which these drachmas cannot be assigned to the period of the Diophantus wars either. The state of affairs in question becomes obvious when one examines the subsequent coin issues, the typology of which finds exact analogies in the currency of the kingdom of Pontus and in that of the Bosporus at the time of Mithradates VI Eupator.

The first issue of Chersonesus that reveals the influence of Pontus types should be regarded not as the silver drachmas with the name of Demetrius, as Golenko proposed, but as the copper coins having on the obverse a head wearing a radiant crown (Helios) facing right, and on the reverse a cornucopiae to either side of which are the caps of the Dioscuri and an inscription Χ - ΕΡ and below this the name of a magistrate —[Η]ΡΑΚΛΕ (Plate XII, 189). With these there are tentatively associated as a smaller denomination the coins with the type of jugate heads of the Dioscuri wearing pointed caps, above each of which there is a star, on the obverse, and of the prow of a ship left, on the reverse (Plate XII, 190). One of these rare coins was in the Bertier de la Garde collection and was published by Oreshnikov (Oreshnikov, 1913, p. 29, illustration). Its location at present is unknown.

For the reverse of the larger denomination there are analogies among the coins of the cities of Amaseia, Amisus, and Sinope in the Mithradatic period (SNG von Aulock, No. 15-16, 69-70, 230-231); for both obverse and reverse, the types on the silver coin of Gorgippia dated by Shelov to 120-100 B.C. (Shelov, Plate IX, 115) offer such analogies. The period of issuance of the Chersonesus coins is defined as the last decade of the IInd century B.C. One may date to the same period a unique coin from the V. N. Orekhov collection (Sebastopol) with a head of the Maiden with bow and quiver on the obverse and with a standing hind on the reverse (Plate XII, 188). In its reverse type it is linked with the last series of silver and copper of the autonomous period, but it does not bear the name of a magistrate — beneath the exergue line there is the usual abbreviation of the town's name.

The next issue, bearing clear traces of the influence of the Mithradatic period, may be considered to be the silver coins having on the obverse a diademed head right, with bow and quiver; and on the reverse, the Maiden striking down a hind with a spear, and the name of a magistrate ΔΗΜΗΤΡΙΟΥ (Plate XII, 191). These coins are the last issue of Chersonesus silver. Golenko finds convincing analogies for them in many issues of the Bosporus cities which have on their obverses a type of Dionysos (didrachms, drachmas, and tetrachalcons). He dates the latter to 90-80 B.C. He also assigns to the same period the Chersonesus coins, but these rather to the beginning than to the end of the period (Golenko, 1964, p. 46). The homogeneity of the Bosporus and the Chersonesus types speaks for itself, although in our view it is preferable to date the Chersonesus coins to 100-90 B.C. when one takes into account the chronology of the suceeding issues. Golenko's thesis to the effect that the absence of the town's name from these coins testifies to attenuation of the town's rights (Golenko, 1964, p. 47) looks less convincing. He adduces as examples the coins of Amisus. Basing ourselves on the mere fact of the subjection of the town to Mithradates we are of course entitled to expect some restriction of rights as well, but this instance can scarcely be regarded as demonstrating anything. In the first place Chersonesus, like Amisus, continues to issue coins with its traditional types, which enable one to determine without fail to whom they belong. In the second place, it is precisely Bosporan towns which issue unified coins with the types of a head of Dionysos on the obverse and of a wreath on the reverse, but mints for which would be impossible to define if it were not that their origin is indicated within the wreath—ΠΑΝΤΙΚΑΠΑΙΤΩΝ ΦΑΝΑΓΟΡΙΤΩΝ, ΓΟΡΓΙΠΠΕΩΝ. The position of Chersonesus, which retained its own types on coins, seems to have been a more priviliged one in the sense of retention of certain rights than that of the Bosporan towns, and for that reason it would still be premature to fall in with Golenko's thesis.

In addition to the abovementioned silver coins Golenko assigns to the period of the subjection of Chersonesus to Mithradates VI Eupator only a single issue of coins (Golenko, 1964, p. 48). He includes in it the following three varieties: 1) bust of the Maiden right, at her back a bow and a quiver (obverse); wreath with a grazing hind in it, beneath this the name of the town (XEP), above it the monogram ΠAP (b) (reverse); 2) head of Maiden right—grazing hind right, beneath exergue line the monogram ΠAP (b) and abbreviated name of town; 3) head of Maiden right—same as on the foregoing but different monogram (d) beneath the fore and hind legs of the hind, beneath the exergue line the name of the town XEP), the letter epsilon in it being of lunate form. Here one should include the variant of the coins which was published in Zograph's book (Zograph, 1951, Plate XXXVI, 20). The location of this coin is not known at present.

To our mind each of the varieties described (Plate XII, 192-195) should be regarded as a separate issue, inasmuch as the monograms have different configurations. At the same time they cannot be separated by any considerable intervals of time on account of the typological similarity of the representations of the head of the Maiden. Golenko considers the coins of the first variety to be the earliest, finding convincing analogies for the obverse on the tetrachalcons of Panticapaeum and Phanagoria which he dates to 100-90 B.C., and on the drachmas of Panticapaeum assigned to 90-80 B.C. (Golenko, 1964, plate I, 15-16). He also dates the Chersonesus coins to 90-80 B.C. But what he considers to be the absence of other types that might be assigned to the period of the reign of Mithradates VI Eupator compels him to date them to a more prolonged period (Golenko, 1964, p. 50). We think there is no need for this, since there are still at least two issues of copper that can be dated to the period of Mithradates VI Eupator.

Thus we assign to the Mithradates period the coins with the type of the facing skull of a hind on the obverse and that of a bow in bowcase on the reverse (Plate XIII, 196). We may recall the fact that Oreshnikov also assigned these coins to the period of Bosporan influence, i.e. to the end of the IInd century B.C. onward to 25-24 B.C. (Oreshnikov, 1913, p. 35-36). Actually in their subject matter they cannot relate to the period of "the reign of the Maiden"; at the same time the absence from these fairly large coins of the name of a magistrate just as categorically obliges one to exclude them from the coinage of the autonomous period. A narrower dating—80-75 B.C., i.e. immediately after the coins of the type: head of Maiden—hind, seems to us possible by reason of the presence upon them of the letter epsilon of lunate form, also noted on the third variety of the coins referred to.

One may also date to the end of the reign of Mithradates VI Eupator (around 75-53 B.C.) copper coins of the type: bust of the Maiden right, bow and quiver at back—eagle on thunderbolt, to right a monogram ΠΑΡ(c) (Plate XIII, 197-198). Zograph assigned these either to the end of the reign of Mithradates VI Eupator or to the beginning of the reign of Pharnaces (63-47), dating them to 70-60 B.C. (Zograph, 1951, p. 152). The author in question started from the proposition that the reverse type had been borrowed from tetrachalcons of Mithradates VI Eupator. These latter are quite reliably dated to the last years of the reign of Mithradates, inasmuch as some of them bear the date ΓΚΣ (223 of the Pontic era or 74-73 B.C., cf. for example Golenko, 1962, plate I, 1). Golenko utterly rejects this date, to our mind so solid, on the grounds that: 1) the Pontic tetrachalcons referred to were still circulating under Asander, who overstruck his own coins upon them; 2) the Panticapaeum coins—obols—with an eagle, which constitute one of the possible prototypes for the Chersonesus type, can scarcely be assigned to the Mithradatic period and should most likely be dated to the time of Pharnaces, even to the end of his reign (Golenko, 1960, p. 36 ff; 1962, p. 50); simultaneously he admits a possibility of these coins having been struck by Chersonesus both under Mithradates VI Eupator and under Pharnaces or Asander; 3) the circumstance, which he has brought to light, of the Chersonesus coin having been overstruck on a coin of Asander enables him to date the Chersonesus coin to a period after Asander assumed the title of King, i.e. to 44-30 B.C. (Golenko, 1962, plate I, 5, p. 51). Despite the seeming persuasiveness of these arguments, they nevertheless cannot be regarded as beyond dispute.

First, as to the overstriking. The doubtful character of the reconstruction proposed by Golenko is obvious enough. Upon comparing the types of the obverse on the Chersonesus and on the Bosporus coins (Golenko, 1962, Plate I, 5b, 6) one may note that the Chersonesus type (to follow Golenko) obliterated a detail on the coin of Asander so prominently raised in relief as was the neck, yet hardly damaged the face or rather left upon it trifling, barely distinguishable outlines. Such a result is possible in a case where at the moment of striking the die is at an angle to the coin, yet in such a case the eagle's head and other details clearly distinguishable on the coin would scarcely have been struck up in full.

If one assumes that it was the Chersonesus coin that was subjected to overstriking, that would correspond to what we see upon the coin—the new type was unable to obliterate completely the old design and it registered most plainly only on the most highly raised details of the old design (the figure of the eagle) but did not reach the less raised ones, particularly the monogram. In this connection the border of the freshly impressed type runs precisely along the outline of the figure of the eagle at the left side. On that basis one can convincingly deduce that it was indeed the Chersonesus coin that served as the blank for the Bosporus coin of Asander of 44-30 B.C. As confirmation of this we may take the fact that it was precisely Pontic coins with the eagle type that were used as raw material for overstrikes in the days of Asander. Probably Chersonesus coins reached the Bosporus together with them. In Golenko's words, "a large part of the Bosporus tetrachalcons of the time of Asander (47-17 B.C.) are overstruck on Pontic tetrachalcons of the type mentioned" (Golenko, 1962, p. 50), that is to say those with the type of the eagle and thunderbolt.

And finally, one cannot at all agree with Golenko admitting a possibility that the Chersonesites used Bosporan obols as a prototype. Unquestionably both the Bosporus and Chersonesus copied at approximately the same time the design of the obols and tetrachalcons of Mithradates VI Eupator. Nor does one, in determining the time of their issuance, have to take into account the fact that the tetrachalcons referred to circulated in the Crimea before the reign of Asander. The Chersonesus coins with the eagle and thunderbolt cannot be separated by any great interval of time from the Pontic ones, and they should be considered practically synchronous. For this reason we regard it as possible that the coins with the eagle and thunderbolt were a concluding issue at Chersonesus under Mithradates VI Eupator, and to date them approximately to 75-63 B.C.

One's attention is drawn to the resemblance between the types of the bust of the Maiden on these coins and on those of the Type: Maiden—hind (Plate XII, 193), but also to the identical configuration of the monograms appearing on them. The two sorts are in fact not greatly separated in time. One should not even exclude a possibility that the coins of the type: Maiden—hind, are synchronous with the coins having the eagle, being a smaller denomination of that series.

We consider it possible to assign a total of only one issue of coins to the period of the reign of Pharnaces (63-47). On their obverses a head right (Pharnaces?) is represented, on the reverses the Maiden at full length, with a bow in her left hand and a dart in the right, and the monogram ΠΑΡ(e) (Plate XIII, 199). One of the coins bears two countermarks in the form of eight-pointed stars, imposed with yoked dies from either side of the coin. The reverse type is the earliest reproduction on coins of a statuary figure of the Maiden in which she is represented as the town's protectress, with a crown upon her head, a bow and arrow in her left hand, and a dart in her raised right hand. This image was also widely used by the Chersonesus moneyers as one of the basic coin types during the first centuries of the Christian era.

Zograph referred these coins to the period of Mithradates VI Eupator; Golenko, to the time of Asander as archon (47-44) or to the year after Asander's assumption of the title of king. Golenko bases his revision of the dating upon the following considerations. He has determined that countermarking with stars was carried out in the Bosporus during the first years (about 40 B.C.) of the kingship of Asander, inasmuch as coins of Asander as archon and also two of the three Bosporan obols assigned to the first years of the rule of Asander as king were subjected to countermarking (Golenko, 1962, p. 53).

In his opinion the Chersonesus coin bearing such countermarks should be assigned to the beginning of the kingship of Asander.

But this deduction is not certain. One can agree with the date of the countermarking, but that gives us no more than a terminus ante quem. Among the coins countermarked at that time there are two obols of Amisus (105-90 B.C.), an anonymous Bosporus obol from the end of the reign of Mithradates VI Eupator, and two Bosporus coins of the time of Pharnaces (Golenko, 1962, p. 53). For this reason it would be at least incautious to believe that the Chersonesus coin turned up in the Bosporus immediately after being issued.

Golenko's attempt to justify the date he proposes for the coins through examination of a Chersonesus inscription (IosPE, I^2, 691) is likewise not entirely successful. We indeed cannot assign these obols to 47-44 B.C., when Chersonesus was enjoying a brief liberty conferred by Caesar, yet there is nothing to prevent our relegating them, with Zograph, to a point in time still in the days of Mithradates VI Eupator. Still, to our mind it would be most preferable to date them to the reign of Pharnaces, if only on account of their unquestionable relative seniority compared with the obols of the "first eleutheria".

We know of two varieties of these obols, The first is represented by coins with the inscription ΕΛΕΥΘΕ[ΧΕΡϹΟΝΗϹ] and a type of a butting bull on the obverse, and with the Maid striking down a hind with a spear, and the monogram ΠΑΡ (h) on the reverse (Plate XIII, 200); the other by coins with the same types exchanging positions: on the obverse is the Maiden with a hind and the inscription ΧΕΡϹ-ΕΛΕΥ, on the reverse the bull and the name ΑΠΟΛΛΩΝΙΔΟΥ (Plate XIII, 201). Oreshnikov linked them with the "first eleutheria" received by Chersonesus from Caesar in 45 B.C., and this should be regarded as the best attribution (Oreshnikov, 1922a).

We place after the coins of the "first eleutheria" a relatively rare issue of copper having on the obverse the head of the Maiden, and on the reverse a caduceus and the monogram ΠΑΡ (f) (Plate XIII, 202). The Maiden's head on these coins and the preceding ones is decidedly similar, and in addition the type is the concluding one in the typological range of the coins of the Mithradates VI Eupator period and that of the first kings of the Bosporus. The next type of the Maiden appears only in the period of the Flavians. On the obverse of the coins new types establish themselves firmly; among these the principal position is occupied by a beardless diademed head, sometimes with a serpent, usually identified with the divinity Chersonas.

Two of the three known coins with the caduceus bear a countermark in the form of a five-pointed star above a crescent—an emblem appearing on Bosporan coins in the period of the rule of queen Dynamis (17-14 B.C.). We have on occasion regarded this countermark as being of Chersonesus, considering it to be evidence of the active intervention of the Bosporus in the operations of the Chersonesus mint (Anokhin, 1963a, p. 16). Unfortunately we were unacquainted with the same sort of countermark on Bosporus coins with the monogram BAE, one of which is mentioned by A. L. Bertier de la Garde (Bertier, 1911, p. 142), and the second published by Golenko (Golenko, 1964, p. 12). The same sort of countermark is also known on a Chersonesus coin of the type: Zeus—thunderbolt (State Hermitage collection). Thus despite Golenko's opinion it is not justifiable to regard the countermark as indisputably Bosporan, any more than Chersonesite. The question of its origin must be left open.

One cannot agree with Golenko and Bertier de la Garde to the effect that these Chersonesus coins were issued at the same time as the Bosporan ones named. The coins with the monogram BAE most likely fall to the time of the sole reign of Dynamis, i.e. 17-14 B.C., which enables one to designate only a terminus ante quem, but not an absolute dating, the justification for which will have be to sought in the rules governing the Chersonesus coinage itself.

The relative chronology of the next issues is also more or less clear. The coins of the type: Zeus—thunderbolt (Plate XIII, 203) which open this series are associated in obverse type with coins of the class: Zeus—Maiden, which in their turn have an extension in a few issues with the same type for the reverse. Less clear is the question of the absolute dating of the issues. What is involved here is the fact that within the time limits for the issuance of the coins of these types there occurred in the history of Chersonesus some important event which led to the adoption of a new calendar, the Chersonesus era. As Bertier de la Garde has established, the event occurred in 25-24 B.C. (Bertier, 1893, p. 60-61), or more exactly in 24 B.C. (Anokhin, 1963). It was usually held that the era was adopted in connection with the proclamation of the Maiden-goddess as "queen" of the town. We too shared that point of view, although we made the final resolution of the problem depend upon full investigation of the coin-series of the end of the IInd century B.C. and of the Ist century (Anokhin, 1963a, p. 14). It was quite natural to seek out numismatic records reflecting the adoption of the era or the event associated with it. Coins of the type: Zeus—Maiden, and the countermark of the monogram ΠΑΡ(f) on coins of the preceding type with: Zeus—thunderbolt, were considered to be such records.

But as we have already said, the adoption of the era and the recognition of the Maiden as "queen" had nothing in common with each other. In reality, in 24 B.C. the Bosporus sought to seize Chersonesus and suffered a setback. The issuance of coins of the type: Zeus—Maiden with monogram ΠΑΡ(f), and the countermark with the same monogram, cannot be regarded as extraordinary phenomena since all issues of the Ist century B.C., with the exception of silver, and copper having the types skull of hind—bow in bowcase, bear this same monogram. Consequently their being connected with this event is possible but not indisputable.

On this account the coins of the type: Maiden—caduceus, and: Zeus—thunderbolt, and also the coins which take their places and have the types: Zeus—Maiden (Plate XIII, 204-205), while close in time to the moment when the era was adopted (all the issues may be dated to the time of Asander as king, i.e. to 44-17 B.C.), nevertheless lack any sufficiently sharply manifested linkage with that event.

The coins of the type: Zeus–Maiden are clearly distinguished from all the subsequent issues; the type of the head of Zeus is treated in the free fashion characteristic of the Mithradatic period. On late coins the type becomes drier and harsher, something which is perhaps a reflection of Roman influence. Among the late coins there is an issue with similar types somewhat differing, it is true, in supplementary details, coin fabric, and weight.

On the obverse there is a diademed head of Zeus right, with a star in front of it; on the reverse the Maiden standing, with monograms ΠΑΡ(f) and ΔΙ (g) (Plate XIII, 206) to the left. On one occasion we divided these monotype yet seemingly not synchronous issues, assigning the latter issue to A.D. 80 (Anokhin, 1963a, p. 29). This was done by reason of the great resemblance of the image of the Maiden on the coins in question to that on the Chersonesus stater of year 104 of the Chersonesus era, and also by reason of a perceptible difference in the style, fabric, and Zeus-head types in the cases of the two classes. But the seemingly weightly arguments in favor of chronological incompatibility of the coins may have another explanation. The resemblance of the Maiden-figures may have been brought about by the presence at Chersonesus of a statue which gave rise to a detailed and many-times-repeated reproduction of it by the engravers of coin dies at differing times. As a second example we may take the statuary group of the Maiden with the hind—representations of it on coins of the beginning of the IIIrd century B.C. and of the middle of the IInd century A.D. are practically indistinguishable. The difference in the styles of the coins can be explained by non-uniform mannerisms in rendering on the part of two engravers. The dating of the coins described should be revised, in the direction of bringing them closer to the prototype and assigning them to the end of the Ist century B.C.

One may date to the same time a unique coin from the collection of V. V. Pereplesnin (Sebastopol) which has the same reverse type as the preceding coins, but on the obverse a bearded head left, similar to the Zeus head but distinguishable by long hair hanging down behind (Plate XIII, 207). The type somewhat reminds one of the traditional image of a Scythian. Before the face there are indecipherable traces of an inscription. It is possible that the finding of a specimen in a better state of preservation would reveal fresh data on this unquestionably interesting issue.

Among the Chersonesus coins at the threshold of our era there is a group the position of which among the other issues has not yielded to reliable classification. On the reverses of the coins there is represented a figure of the Maiden standing and a monogram ΠΑΡ (f), and on the obverse, in place of Zeus, a beardless head wearing a wreath (Plate XIV, 208). At one time, on the basis of the great similarity of the reverse types of these coins and the stater of 158 of the Chersonesus era (Anokhin, 1963a, p. 31), they were dated to the end of the reign of the emperor Hadrian (117-138 A.D.). Now, however, we regard it as possible to join them with the coins of the type: Zeus—Maiden, offering convincing typological analogies, and to date them to the end of the Ist century B.C. or the beginning of the Ist century A.D.

The chronology of following issues has likewise been altered. After the coins of the type: Chersonas—Maiden and monogram ΠΑΡ (h) there are placed coins of the type: Chersonas—Maiden and inscription ΧΕΡ (Plate XIV, 211-212). One's attention is drawn to the disappearance of the monogram, something which will be explained below. The coins are dated to the first quarter of the Ist century B.C. They are supplanted, most probably, by the small coins having on the obverse an analogous type of the head of the divinity Chersonas, and on the reverse a wreath (Plate XIV, 213). These were earlier considered to be a special small denomination, a semis, the existence of which in the system of Chersonesus denominations is no longer upheld. These coins should nevertheless be considered the elder as compared with coins analogous in their types, but considerably heavier (Plate XIV, 214). This sort of sequence can be explained by the fact that types of the divinity Chersonas constitute a stable typological sequence ending with dated gold coins (Plate XIV, 214-216). In the present instance the typology of the coins is of greater importance for determining the relative chronology than are the metrological data for the two groups (the early group is the lighter). Both issues of coins with the wreath are dated within the second quarter of the Ist century A.D.

The concluding period of the coinage of Chersonesus in the days of Bosporan influence is associated with important changes in the field of the currency: the town even issues gold coins, the greater part of these being equipped with dates of the Chersonesus era. This new phase was preceded by events associated with the Roman-Bosporan war of A.D. 45.

As we are aware, the plans of the Bosporus king Mithradates III to achieve independence of Rome were betrayed by his brother Cotys. Forces under the command of the renowned Roman general Aulus Didius Gallus were sent to the Bosporus. The military operations ended with the defeat of Mithradates, who fled, but who after some time was surrendered to the Romans. Cotys was set up on the Bosporus throne.

A flowering of the Chersonesus coinage, the start of which falls to the period of this war, enables one to assert that Chersonesus not only did not stand aside but even played an active part (Anokhin, 1963a, p. 20-21), this probably taking the form of participation of some sort of Chersonesus contingent in the military operations. On this account the victory over Mithradates may be regarded also as a victory for the Chersonesus armed forces. This is attested by the issuance of coins with an image of Nike. In all likelihood Chersonesus hoped to free itself from the Bosporus thanks to this war. The policy of Rome with reference to Chersonesus could not fail to change. It is possible that in addition to the city having helped the Romans in the war with Mithradates, a part was played by their wishing to create in the Crimea a certain counterbalance to the Bosporus—if they confronted each other, they were of lesser danger to Rome. One should point out that rivalry between the two most important states in the Crimea is likewise to be traced in literary sources right down to the IVth century A.D. Commencing with the mid-Ist century A.D. the currency of Chersonesus is under Roman control, and on that account it is well to examine it imperial reign by reign.

The entire coinage of the time of the emperor Claudius (41-54) is represented by dated coins. The earliest of these is probably one dated to the year 70 of the Chersonesus era, i.e. to A.D. 46. Unfortunately a coin with this year appears in the general list of Bertier de la Garde without any indications of its types (Bertier, 1893, p. 66). Such a coin has not been found in the numismatic collections, so that the problem involving it still an open one.

From the year 71 of the Chersonesus era (A.D. 47) we are acquainted with a gold stater with types of a head of the divinity Chersonas wearing a wreath on the obverse, and of the Maiden standing with a hind on the reverse (Plate XIV, 215). To the left of the Maiden there is the monogram ΠΑΡ (h) and the year - AO.

No coins of the year 72 are known. It is difficult to say whether an interruption in the coinage occurs in that year, or whether such coins have merely not yet come to light.

In A.D. 49 (73 of the Chersonesus era) both gold and copper coins were issued. The stater has the same types, but the year numeral is ΟΓ (73) (Plate XIV, 216). On the obverse of the copper coins the head of the divinity Chersonas is represented, with a snake in front of it; on the reverse, a hind standing right, the same monogram, to the right a symbol Δ, beneath this the year ΟΓ, all in a border of dots (Plate XIV, 217).

The volume of the gold coinage was apparently slight: the staters of A.D. 47 and 49 are struck with the same obverse die. In A.D. 50 only copper coins were evidently issued. They have the same types on the obverse and the reverse, with the sole difference that on them there is instead of a Δ, a symbol recalling the stigma (5) and the numerials for the year, ΟΔ (Plate XIV, 218).

In A.D. 51-54 (75-78 of the Chersonesus era) copper coins with other types were issued: on the obverse there are the head of the divinity Chersonas with a serpent, the name of the town (ΧΕΡ) and the year—ΟΕ, OI, * ON, or OH; on the reverse, Nike with wreath and branch left, and to her left the same symbol (5) as on the coins of the preceding year. These types became characteristic over many years for one of the denominations of copper; in the currency of Chersonesus the assignment of special types for each denomination was strictly observed, something which may serve as one among the vivid examples of a conservatism which is not to be traced in the other towns of the northern Black Sea littoral.

The issuance of dated assaria was cut short in A.D. 54, which should be associated with the beginning of the reign of Nero (54-68), who even intended to convert the kingdom of the Bosporus into a Roman province. Limitations in the field of the currency fell to the lot of other Black Sea towns as well: Chersonesus and Olbia cut off their issuance of dated coins. Their striking is resumed at Chersonesus only in the period of the reign of the emperor Titus (79-81). Yet among the undated coins there are two issues of copper which may be attributed to this period with sufficient confidence; one of them is assigned to the reign of Nero.

The undated coins have on the obverse the type of a head of the divinity Chersonas right, with a serpent and a star in front of him; on the reverse, Nike left and the symbol (i) (Plate XIV, 223-225). Both types are very crudely executed, and the ability of the die engravers for some of the concluding variants becomes so degraded that the coins might be called barbarian imitations.

---

* The symbol I is used in place of the Greek sigma.

Naturally there are no grounds for such a view, because all the coins come from the Chersonesus excavations. The following considerations serve as grounds for dating these coins to the reign of Nero. In the first place, they copy dated coins from the end of the reign of Claudius. In the second place, the types of the coins do not allow one to assign them either to the end of the period of Bosporan influence, the coin issues of which are classified reliably enough thanks to the availability of dated coins, and even less to the period of the "second eleutheria", which is characterized by a distinctive coin typology. In the third place, in A.D. 63 Chersonesus underwent an assault by the Scythians and was liberated by the forces of T. Plautius Silvanus, something which affords one the opportunity of supposing a reciprocal connection between the coin issue and this expedition. In the fourth place, the currency of Olbia may serve to a certain extent as an analogy and there we find a range of features similar to the Chersonesus ones. At Olbia the issuance of dated coins is also brought to an end with the beginning of the reign of Nero, and in all likelihood it was resumed only in A.D. 67. Olbia coins are known with the types: Zeus—eagle with letters KA, which are most likely the numerals for a year (21) of the Olbia era, adopted in A.D. 46 (Anokhin, 1971, p. 90).

Dated coins for the period of the reign of Vespasian (A.D. 69-79) are not known either. A number of scholars assign to the time of Vespasian an issue of heavy copper coins which are dated to his reign by a number of indirect indications. These coins have on the obverse the type of a bust of the Maiden with quiver at her shoulder, the monogram ΠΑΡ (h) to the right or to the left, and a circular inscription—ΕΙΡΗΝΗϹ ϹΕΒΑϹΤΗϹ, i.e. "the peace of the Augustus"; on the reverse, the head of a bearded male with the symbol Δ beneath it. On the reverse of a coin of one variant an inscription ΧΕΡϹΟΝΑΣΕΙΤΩΝ has been preserved (Plate XV, 226-227), which was subsequently cleaned off the die and from then on the coins were issued without it. Zograph referred these coins to a time before A.D. 79 (Zograph, 1951, p. 157). He considered it possible to see in the reverse type a portrait of Rhescuporis II (68-92), but that finding is doubtful.

The limitations observed in the currency of Chersonesus under Nero and Vespasian were raised under Titus (79-81). In his time the mintage of Chersonesus assumes the same aspect as it had had in the days of Claudius —gold and copper are struck, and all the coins are dated.

In A.D. 80 (104 of the Chersonesus era) gold and copper coins are issued. On the obverse of the stater there is represented a bust of the divinity Chersonas left, with a crown upon his head that finishes off with three prongs, to the left of it the monogram ΠΑΡ (h) and the date -ΔΡ (104); the whole type is within a border of dots (Plate XV, 228). On the obverse of the copper coins there is a bust of the divinity Chersonas right, a diadem on his head, to his right a lyre, behind a branch, and the inscription ΕΙΡΗΝΗϹ ϹΕΒΑϹΤΗϹ round; on the reverse, the Maiden standing right, with bow and arrow in the left hand and a spear in the right, around this the inscription ΧΕΡΣΟΝΝΕΣΕΙΤ[ΩΝ] ΕΤ[ΟΥΣ] ΡΔ , i.e. "of the Chersonites, year 104"; the types are within dotted borders (Plate XV, 229).

The coins described are to be regarded as the first dated coins after the time of Claudius. Oreshnikov saw on one of the coins the year 103, but on closer examination the second numeral turns out to be a sigma and not a gamma. Attention should also be drawn to the fact that on many early tetrassaria the year numeral signifying 100 (P) is reversed, reminding one more of a qoppa (= 90); but one should reject the possibility of seeing these coins as of the time of Vespasian, because this same way of writing the letter rho is encountered on coins of the year 111 of the Chersonesus era.

The reign of Titus commenced in June of A.D. 79; accordingly Chersonesus required as a minimum about one year in order to retrieve the rights of coinage lost under Nero. Apparently a certain upsurge had already taken place during the days of Vespasian, since copper coins of A.D. 80 in many respects repeat the type of the Vespasian tetrassaria (legend, type of head of the Maiden). Of great interest in this connection are coins struck with obverse dies of coins of Vespasian and of Titus (Plate XV, 230), testifying to a continuity of monetary policy under the two emperors at Chersonesus.

Under Titus, who died on September 13, A.D. 81, only one issue of tetrassaria was struck. They repeat exactly the coins of the preceding year, but they bear another date, PЄ (105) (Plate XV, 231).

No alterations are seen in the currency of Chersonesus during the period of the reign of the emperor Domitian (81-96). The town issues both copper tetrassaria and gold staters periodically but not indeed regularly (this is perhaps to be explained by the fact that some of the dated coins have not come down to us). The tetrassaria of A.D. 82 have the same types and inscriptions, except for the year—P[(106) (Plate XV, 232).

For A.D. 85 we are acquainted with a gold stater and a copper coin. The stater is curious; it offers a new type for the reverse (the obverse has most likely been struck from the same die as the stater of the year 104 of the Chersonesus era)—around the image of the Maiden, beside which there appears the monogram ΠAP (h), a circular inscription BACIΛЄYCHC ЄTOY[C] PΘ has been placed, i.e. "of the reign of the Maiden, year 109" (Plate XV, 233). This sole instance in which the Maiden "regnant" is mentioned on a coin accords very well with the traditional formula of the Chersonesus decrees from the first half of the IInd century A.D. At the same time, as has already been remarked, one must firmly reject the widespread opinion that the year of the "reign" of the Maiden was indicated on the coins.

In A.D. 87 only copper coins were issued—two tetrassaria with the year PIA (111) are known. On the reverse the name of the town—XEP—is added in the legend (Plate XV, 235). For A.D. 96 only tetrassaria are known once more. They preserve the same types and inscriptions, with the exception of the date—PK (120). On a few coins a bucranium has been placed beside the figure of the Maiden (Plate XV, 236-238; XVI, 239-246).

For the striking of tetrassaria an obverse die was prepared which was used, starting with the days of Titus, over a stretch of 16 years. Some of the variants of the tetrassaria of A.D. 96 are also struck with this die. It was used in all the listed years of the coinage, only the reverse die naturally being changed as a new date had to be cut upon it. Of such reverse dies there have been established two for A.D. 80, one for 81, two for 82, and one for 85. As we see, the volume of the mintage was trifling. In A.D. 96 the situation changes sharply. The same obverse die functions with four reverse ones, and in addition 6 new obverses and 11 reverse ones were manufactured, so that a total of 7 obverses and 15 reverses were at work (Anokhin, 1963a, p. 61-63). So sudden an augmentation of the volume of the coinage was most likely evoked by a prohibition by Nerva (96-98) of the issuance of coins, or by the apprehension that such a prohibition was to ensue. For this reason the town issued "illegal" coin; yet, so as not to bring down reproaches on the part of Rome, the coins were marked A.D. 96, that is to say with the last year when coinage was permitted. Some specimens look decidedly degraded in style, which allows one to think of a continuation of their issuance even after the year A.D. 96.

During the period of the reign of the emperor Nerva (96-98) Chersonesus did not issue coins. From the days of Trajan (98-117) there have come down to us a total of two unique coins, a copper and a stater. The copper coin, known from a rubbing made by Oreshnikov (Frolova, p. 105) and from a mention by Zograph (Zograph, 1922, p. 354), has on the obverse the image of a head left, evidently that of the deity Chersonas, somewhat deteriorated through corrosion; on the reverse, an image of the Maiden standing with bow and spear, monogram ΠΑΡ (h), and the year numerals ΡΚ-Η (128), all within a border of dots for both sides (Plate XVI, 247). No information on the weight of the coin has been preserved, but to judge by the diameter (about 22 mm) it was of a denomination smaller than a tetrassarion. The stater has on the obverse the bust of the deity Chersonas left, with a serpent before him and traces of a circular inscription around these; on the reverse, an image of the Maiden standing, as on the copper coin, also the monogram ΠΑΡ (h), and the inscription ЄΤΟΥϹ ΡΛΑ (i.e., "year 131") (Plate XVI, 248). The weight of the stater, preserved in the British Museum, comes to 7.75 g.

The existence of coins of Trajan in both metals affords evidence that during his reign the same policy was enacted with respect to Chersonesus as under the Flavians. But the striking of copper was cut back sharply both as regards coin volume and diminution of the denomination of the copper coins. This should perhaps be seen as a reaction on the part of Rome to the issuance by Chersonesus of tetrassaria for A.D. 96, which, as we have seen, considerably exceeded the usual volume of coinage that had been the practice prior to that year.

Only a single coin falls to the days of Hadrian (117-138)—a stater of the year 134. It has the same types as the stater of the year 107, except that the figure of the Maiden on the reverse is turned the other way and the year is ΡΝΗ (158) (Plate XVI, 249). This stater is the last gold coin of Chersonesus known to us.

We should not be surprised by the absence of copper coins for the period of Hadrian's rule at Chersonesus, inasmuch as the issuance of copper is terminated after A.D. 118 in the Bosporus as well. Cessation of the issuance of copper coins faced the town with the need for meeting the demand for small change in some way or other. On this account there commence to come into circulation old, worn-out coins the lawfulness of which is certified by a countermark representing a small figure of the Maiden standing, with bow and spear, within a border of dots. Such countermarks appear on many tetrassaria of the Flavian period (Plate XVI, 244-245). The countermark is the last numismatic record of Chersonesus for the period of Bosporan influence.

2. The System of Weight and Account

Among the coins of the period under examination we are acquainted with only a single issue of silver. These drachmas, the last in the history of the Chersonesus coinage, bear the name of Demetrius (Plate XII, 191) and are struck on the Attic standard. The average weight of the coins, which are struck in silver of low quality, comes to 3.98 g.

The main class of money entering circulation was made up of copper coins. By this time the weight of the denominations of copper had gone down appreciably—the dichalcon of the end of the IInd century B.C. weighed no more than about 2-3 grams. The opening issues of the period of Bosporan influence to begin with preserve this weight norm, but subsequently the weights of some of the classes of coins were raised. Thus the coins with the large Maiden-bust and the hind (Plate XII, 192) weigh about 6 grams, whereas the weight of the small coins with the same types (Plate XII, 193-195) remains at the preceding level. The denominations of these coins should be defined as respectively a tetrachalcon and a dichalcon. Aside from the tetrachalcons, there are also struck heavier copper coins—obols. The weight of the obol in good state of preservation at the time of Pharnaces (Plate XIII, 199) comes to 17.30 g, suggesting a rather high norm for the tetrachalcon—8-9 grams.

The coins of the "first eleutheria" (Plate XIII, 201) are of definite interest. The average weight of the coins comes to 12.87 g, which points toward an obol, or eight chalcons. But the selection of types: Maiden with hind—bull, which correspond to the denomination of two units, the dichalcon, of the autonomous period, allows one to suppose that these coins, too, were equal to two units of some sort. Zograph regarded them in just that light, suggesting that they corresponded to two assaria (Zograph, 1951, p. 153-154). In doing this he started from the fact that at a still later period, that of the "second eleutheria", these same types were selected for the dupondius—the Maiden with hind, and the butting bull. Golenko holds that so early an orientation toward the Roman system of denominations looks a little unusual and premature for Chersonesus, inasmuch as Bosporus copper of this time retains the same Mithradatic look as before. But Chersonesus may constitute an exception in this regard. One should not lose sight of the circumstances under which the coins were issued: the town, having been under the sway of the Bosporus authorities, finally receives freedom at the hands of the Romans. On this account one can understand the striving of the Chersonsites both to demonstrate their loyalty and gratitude toward Rome, and to set themselves apart from the Bosporus. One surmises that the coins referred to may be identified both as obols and as early dupondii.

The difference in weight from the preceding issue of obols of the time of Pharnaces may also have been a random matter, considering the broad range of weights for the one group and the other, and for that reason it would be premature to base any conclusions on this. Settling the question of the denomination of the coins of the "first eleutheria" would be of appreciable importance for elucidation of the local monetary system of weight and account.

If the coins were simultaneously both obols and dupondii, there would follow from this a correspondence of the local drachma with $\frac{3}{4}$ of a Roman denarius (the drachma is equal to 6 obols, the denarius to 8 dupondii). Accordingly one would have to consider the drachma not Attic, as it is defined from the silver coins with the name of Demetrius, since the Attic drachma was equal to the Roman denarius (Mattingly, p. 95-96), but Rhodian. But if the reduction in the weight of the coins was not a random matter and the coins, being dupondii, corresponded not to an obol but for example to six chalcons, then the Chersonesus drachma pertained to the Attic metrological standard. But the data available do not yet allow one to settle this matter.

The next issues of Chersonesus copper coins are represented only by tetrachalcons. Particular interest is aroused by one of the classes of coins, bearing the type of a head of Zeus on the obverse and that of the standing Maiden, beside whom there are the monograms ΠΑΡ (f) and ΔΙ (g), on the reverse (Plate XIII, 206). The average weight of the coins comes to no more than 4.42 g, whereas the coins of the same sort which preceded them, but which lacked that symbol, weigh on the average 7.22 g. Both the one class and the other may nevertheless be defined with sufficient assurance as tetrachalcons. In that event the symbol (g) may be acknowledged to be the sign of a denomination of four chalcons, * something that would confirm the correctness of our view.

Use of a denomination symbol may have been evoked by a reduction in the weight of the coins. We may recall that an analogous instance is known for the Bosporus: the civic coins of Caesaria (Panticapeaum) and Agrippia (Phanagoria) bear a numerial designation—the symbol H (= 8), pointing toward a denomination of 8 chalcons, or an obol. The exceptionally low weight of civic coins in the Bosporus as compared with regal ones (barely more than one-third as much) was noted also by Zograph (Zograph, 1951, p. 195). A ratio between these coins of Caesareia and Agrippia and those of Chersonesus, amounting to 2:1 is entirely admissible. One should note the chronological propinquity of the coins—the Bosporus ones fall to the reign of Polemon (14-9 B.C.). Despite the relative abundance of the Chersonesus coins, their issuance was not prolonged, since all the specimens known are struck with a single pair of dies.

Over the course of the first half of the Ist century A.D. the weight of the tetrachalcon goes down still further. The average weight of coins of the class: Chersonas—Maiden (Plate XIV, 208-210) comes to 4.53 g; that of those analogous to them, of the class: Chersonas—wreath (Plate XIV, 213) and of ones with the same types as the last (Plate XIV, 214), to 2.71 and 4.04 g respectively.

The very first dated coin for the year 73 of the Chersonesus era (Plate XIV, 217) bears the symbol Δ, which allows one to identify it tentatively as a tetrachalcon. On coins of the next year of the Chersonesus era, 74 (Plate XIV, 218) there is a different symbol (i) in place of the symbol Δ . Inasmuch

---

* In the next chapter we propose a further explanation of this symbol.

as the types and weight norm of the coins remain as before, one may assert that they constitute one and the same denomination. The alteration of the symbol must indicate a shift to another system of account, which can only be the Roman one. But the proposed explanation of the symbol (i) is not sufficiently reliable. If it is to be understood as the numerical symbol for the denomination, a sigma (= 6), then in that event the denomination of the coin would have to be defined as 6 unciae or a semis, that is to say the half of an as. Zograph understood it in just this way (Zograph, 1951, p. 156).

Yet with such a definition as this there arise a range of difficulties. In the first place, if the coins with this symbol are to be recognized as the semis, it turns out that in weight they exceed their Roman equivalent by appromiately twice, whereas the Chersonesus tetrassaria fall to half the Roman sestertius. In the second place, the striking of coins with this symbol and with the same types continued at Chersonesus to the end of the IInd century A.D., whereas in the other Black Sea towns and at Rome itself the semis ceases to be issued after Hadrian. In the third place, a late issue of coins with such a symbol is accompanied by heavier coins identified with the dupondius, the tressis, and the tetrassarion, and for that reason it is more logical to see in the former an assarion rather than a semis. The same finding is also confirmed by the metrological data for the coins, which allow of a 1:2:3:4 ratio with a certain weight tolerance for the copper, but by no means a ratio of 1:4:6:8 (Anokhin, 1963a, p. 48, Plate II). For these reasons definition of the coins under examination as being the semis is unlikely. One should most likely see in them the assarion, and one might tentatively regard the symbol as being that for the assarion.

If we take all the foregoing into account, we would secure a precise date for the shift of local monetary account to the Roman system. Inasmuch as this took place in the first years after the termination of the war of Rome with the Bosporus, in which Chersonesus participated on the side of Rome, a pro-Roman orientation of the town would be even more patent. At this same time Chersonesus also commenced to issue gold coins which have received the name of staters in the literature. In their weights they correspond to the norm for Roman aurei. In addition to these and to two issues of assaria (Plate XIV, 219, 222-225) falling to the concluding years of the reigns of Claudius and Nero, the town issues heavy copper coins defined as tetrassaria; on one of the early varieties there is the symbol Δ (Plate XV, 226). The average weights of the tetrassaria and the assaria do not, however, exhibit strict oorrespondence—the weight of the tetrassaria is palpably low. Under Trajan copper coins of the diameter smaller than that of the tetrassarion for the preceding period (Plate XVI, 247) were issued, but the weight of the unique specimen of the coin remains unknown. Its denomination is conjecturally defined as being the assarion.

3. The Organization of the Currency

We have said that while during the autonomous period the issuance of coins was within the competence of a college of nomophylakes, in the period of Bosporan influence the right to issue coins most likely pertained to the supreme authority, first to Mithradates VI Eupator and the other kings of the Bosporus, and then to the Roman emperors. It was only one or another of the kings or emperors who could sanction the issuance of coins. Consequently all changes on the throne brought in their train a need for confirmation by the new ruler of the rights received earlier. Under such circumstances the organization of the currency at Chersonesus could not fail to change. We do in fact observe a number of new features in the civic coinage. In the first place, these include the rare appearance of the names of individual magistrates on coins and their early disappearance, and in the second place, a gradual incorporation of monograms into the coin type. It is curious to note that although to begin with names and monograms apparently exclude each other, nevertheless despite the disappearance of the names the monograms do not dominate entirely and many of the issues from the middle and end of the period under examination lack them.

Let us examine the question of the names. One can separate out the following issues of coins having the names of sole magistrates: head of Maiden—hind (Plate XII, 187) with the name ΗΡΟΔΟΤ ; head of Helios—cornucopiae (Plate XII, 189) with the name [Η]ΡΑΚΛΕ ; drachmas (Plate XII, 191) with the name ΔΗΜΗΤΡΙΟΥ ; the coin of the "first eleutheria" (Plate XIII, 201), with the name ΑΠΟΛΛΩΝΙΔΟΥ. The coins of these classes are represented by a large number of specimens, so that an appearance of new names among them is improbable as a practical consideration. All the issues involve differing types and different periods of time, so that the fact of the sole exercise by these persons of the office of monetary magistrate is fairly obvious.

Unfortunately, for the time being it is scarcely possible to define the function of the monetary magistrate any more exactly. He may have been the king-eponym, or "the person standing at the head of the administration", i.e. the dioiketes. Inasmuch as in earlier times coins bore the names of members of the college of nomophylakes who together with the dioiketes presented legislative bills to the national assembly, this latter functionary seems to us the most realistic candidate for the office in question.

The imposition of monograms commences with coins of the type: head of Maiden—hind with lowered head (Plate XII, 192). The very first examples of monograms are drawn in differing ways (Plate XII, 192-195; XIII, 199). Later on the stable forms (f) or (h) become rooted. It is not difficult to note that the basis for each of the monograms is one and the same, so that all of them most probably signified the same name Παρθένος. On one of the initial issues of the "second eleutheria" the name of the Maiden is set forth in full in place of a monogram (Bertier, 1906, plate VI, 5, p. 61-62).

Bertier de la Garde made interesting observations regarding the coins of the period of Bosporan influence. He published two coins attributable to the period of the "first eleutheria", one of which bore the name of a functionary and the other a monogram (Bertier, 1906, plate VI, 1, 2, cf. our Plate XIII, 200, 201), and he reached the following important deduction: "Its (the monogram's) being placed upon coins", he wrote, "apparently had some sort of connection with the designation of functionaries: it proves to be the case that the one and the other, the monogram and the name, are incompatible with each other as it were, even on exactly uniform and synchronous coins... It seems to me that this was a consequence of an alteration in the order of the striking of coins. We do not know precisely what it was at Chersonesus, but in general respects one may suppose that all this was within the competence of one or several persons, one among them in fact placing his name upon the coin and being responsible for it, perhaps also being at the same time the eponym: his name, in any event, served to determine the time of issuance of the coin. For some reason or other this order of things was changed and the striking of coins was placed under the direct protectorate of the Maiden, perhaps being set up in conjunction with her temple or being carried out with participation of her priests, in token whereof her monogram was imposed, it being of course incompatible under such circumstances with the name of any functionary whatever" (Bertier, 1906, pp. 62-63).

Bertier de la Garde's suggestion as to a double nature of the coin issues of Chersonesus unfortunately failed to be developed further. In this a decisive part was played by V. V. Latyshev who, in publishing an inscription with mention of "the reign of the Maiden", came to the conclusion that "upon reform of the Chersonesus system of government in the Roman period .... the Chersonesites resolved to regard the Maiden as their eternal queen and indeed .... not merely in name, but with specific functions and attributes of authority". In his conclusion as to the extract from the works of Bertier de la Garde which we have cited above he once more repeated without any qualifications his assertion regarding recognition by the Chersonesites of the Maiden as their "eternal queen"; the monogram, in his opinion, was imposed "to signify that the coin had been struck in 'the reign of the Maiden'" (Latyshev, 1909, pp. 321, 325). Thus he failed to appreciate that incompatibility between the name of an official and the mongram is to be detected precisely upon coins of a single class and time. In his opinion the whole problem revolved solely around recognition of the Maiden as "eternal queen". True, not being a specialist in the field of numismatics, he may not have realized that many issues assigned precisely to the period of her presumed reign fail to bear such a mongram.

We have reached a conclusion above to the effect that the "reign of the Maiden" did not affect the currency. The functions of the king and of the monetary magistrate were separated. In addition to the circumstance noted by Bertier de la Garde that the magistrate's name and the monogram were incompatible, one may list a number of other issues which have no monogram. Moreover, issues with the monogram alternate with others upon which only the name of the town appears. Among such instances we classify: 1) coins of the type: head of Zeus — thunderbolt and inscription ΧΕΡϹΟΝΗϹΟΥ (Plate XIII, 203), which have no monogram — something which presumably thereafter brought about their being countermarked with a monogram; 2) the tetrassarion of the year 104 of the Chersonesus era has the inscription "of the Chersonites", but the stater of the year 109 the inscription "regnant" and a monogram; all the issues of tetrassaria of the years 104-120 lack a monogram; 3) at the very start of the "second eleutheria" the coins of one issue were struck some with a monogram, some without it (Plate XVII, 250, 251).

If one supplements what has been said with further examples of the alternation, in Chersonesus during the period of Bosporan dependence, of coin-issues with a monogram and ones without it, one can deduce that there existed in the town's currency two categories of coinage. One of these is represented by coins bearing the names of civic officials or simply the name of the town ΧΕΡϹΟΝΗϹΟΥ or of the civic community (ΧΕΡΣΟΝΝΗΣΕΙΤΩΝ), most frequently in abbreviated form (XEP); the other, by coins bearing a monogram signifying the name of the Maiden-goddess. These facts afford, as it seems to us, a sufficient basis for defining the first category as a civic coinage, the second as a temple coinage. It follows that Chersonesus issued coins now in the name of the town, now in the name of the Maiden-goddess. In the first instance the coinage was supervised by civic functionaries, in the second evidently by priests of the Maiden's temple.

One can specify two instances of functioning in parallel on the part of temple and of civic issues — in the years 80 and 85 staters and tetrassaria were struck— but they do not afford grounds for holding that the town and the temple possessed discrete rights to strike coins. One might have been able to reach such a conclusion on the basis of Strabo's words regarding the different status in law of the towns and of the priesthood (Strabo, XVII, 3, 24); but at Chersonesus the question was possibly reduced to a matter of who subsidized a coinage in each particular instance — the town or the temple. Even so, the definite autonomy of the priests of the temple of the Maiden (only of her temple?) merits attention.

Thus Bertier de la Garde's view regarding the double nature of the coinage of Chersonesus during the period of Bosporan influence is fully confirmed. It is necessary to add to his deductions only two substantial qualifications. In the first place, he supposed that at the time when coins were issued with the name of an official, and with the monogram (the "first eleutheria"), a shift took place from one system of managing the currency to another. Actually, however, as we have already remarked, such alternation back and forth was of a lasting character. In the second place, Bertier de la Garde considered the existence of a mint attached to the very temple of the Maiden to be possible; this is most unlikely since the coins of the "second eleutheria" which have been mentioned, for example, both those with monogram and those without it, are struck with a common obverse die.

4. Historical Sketch

The political situation of Chersonesus during the period of Bosporan influence has been tellingly outlined by Strabo: "This town formerly enjoyed autonomy, but upon being laid waste by the barbarians it was obliged to place itself under the protection of Mithradates Eupator ... From that time and until this very day the town of Chersonesus has been subject to the masters of the Bosporus" (Strabo, VII, 4, 3). With its loss of independence the town evidently lost interest for historians, and on that account notices regarding it become fragmentary or oblique. One can manage to establish some details on the basis of local sources — for the most part epigraphic ones.

We get information on Chersonesus after the wars of Diophantus from the "Chronicles" of Memnon, describing the history of Heracleia Pontica. During the time when Heracleia was under siege by the Romans in 72-70 B.C., the people of Heracleia twice sent out embassies with a plea for aid. The first mission "to the colonists" was apparently directed only to Chersonesus, the second "to the Chersonesites and the Theodosians in Scythia, and to the dynasts of the Bosporus" (Memn., 47, 49). Both missions were successful. Chersonesus twice rendered aid to Heracleia, selling it provisions (the aims of the second mission are worded less concretely — with a request for an alliance), yet without saving it from utter destruction.

This episode is apparently the last evidence of anti-Roman tendencies in the foreign policy of the Chersonesites. Some years later (65 B.C.) Mithradates VI Eupator's son Machares, who had been left by his father as ruler in the Bosporus, fled to Chersonesus, but ended his life by suicide for fear of being caught by the pursuit (App., Mithr., 102). Yet when Phanagoria raised a revolt against Mithradates VI in 63 B.C. Chersonesus joined in with it. After the downfall of Mithradates VI the northern Black Sea littoral was for practical purposes in the hands of the Romans. Pharnaces, son of Mithradates (63-47), was installed as king of the Bosporus after he had acknowledged subjection to Pompey. Only Phanagoria, which had been the first to rise against Mithradates VI, received liberty and autonomy.

The status in law of the states which had been incorporated to Rome varied. Strabo provides a brief and yet exhaustive characterization of the diverse degrees of subordination: "Among all these lands subject to the Romans part are under the administration of kings, but another part they rule themselves, styling them provinces, and they send in governors and tax collectors. There are also a few free towns (ἐλεύθεραι πόλεις), some of which have associated themselves freely from the start, but others they have themselves set free as a distinction. There are also certain dynasts, philarkhoi, and priests under their authority; these live in accordance with the laws of their fathers" (Strabo, XVII, 3, 24).

Chersonesus, being under the authority of Pharnaces, sought to obtain the status of a free town, which was accomplished under Caesar. After the defeat of Pharnaces the mission of Gaius Julius Satyrus was sent by the Chersonesites to Rome (IosPE, I², 691). The date of the mission is defined as the period between May 46 and January 45 B.C. (Rostovtsev, 1917). The adoption of the decree testifies to the effect that Chersonesus received the rights of a free town. This is also confirmed by the issuance of copper coins of a heavy denomination, obols or dupondii, with the inscription Χερσονήσου ἐλευθερᾶς. But liberty proved shortlived, and after the death of Caesar (44 B.C.) Chersonesus once more found itself in subjection to the Bosporus. The subsequent coinage bears no mention of "liberty".

Starting with April of 24 B.C. Chersonesus initiates a new era (Anokhin, 1963). The decrees dated by this era (already falling, it is true, to the beginning of the IInd century A.D.) also mention "the Maiden regnant" (βασιλευούσης Παρθένου), which has served as a basis for the erroneous thesis that the era was adopted in connection with the proclamation of the Maiden as "regnant".

Other investigators associate the establishment of the era with the receipt by Chersonesus of the rights of a free town at the hands of the emperor Augustus (Belov, pp. 97-98), but this viewpoint, too, fails to stand up to critical analysis. In the first place, there ought to be on the coins a reference to "liberty", as during the period of the "first" and the "second eleutheria"; in the second place, it is for just this period that we have the testimony of Strabo regarding the subordination of Chersonesus to the Bosporus (Strabo, VII, 4, 3). As we are aware, the "first eleutheria" did not evoke the appearance of a special era, and on the other hand the era adopted in 24 B.C. was not changed in connection with the town's receipt of the "second eleutheria" under Antoninus Pius. To put it briefly, the assertion that Augustus granted liberty to Chersonesus in 24 B.C. cannot be justified through facts nor through more or less plausible assumptions.

The event which set a beginning to the new era must have been of enormous importance for the entire future destinies of the town, and it seems to us that we can name it, despite the exiguity of evidence concerning the history of Chersonesus at the end of the Ist century B.C. What is at issue is the incidents related by Constantine Porphyrogenitus in his story about Gicia. This story constitutes, if one will, one of the most curious items in the chapter regarding the history of the town of Cherson which is contained in his manual of precepts "Concerning the Administration of the Empire" (Const. Porph., De adm. imp., 53). After the unflattering evaluation of this chapter by T. Mommsen ("Cherson myths") it remained for a long time outside the field of vision of scholars, who ignored it as a source for the history of the town. R. Garnett subjected the story of Gicia to critical analysis and saw in it a reliable underpinning (Garnett, pp. 100-105). It was he, too, who provided an answer to the question, of interest to us, regarding the causes of the establishment of the era — an answer which stands in need of inconsiderable additions.

Let us recall briefly the contents of the 53rd chapter. It is devoted to the history of the wars of Chersonesus. The first of these, with the Bosporus, was carried on in the days of Diocletian; the second, with the barbarians on the Danube, under Constantine the Great; the third and fourth, with the Bosporus, are not attached to any particular emperor; and the same thing is true of the story of Gicia, but in harmony with the overall exposition of events it has seemed that all three ought to be referred to the second half of the IVth century B.C.

In the story of Gicia an attempt of the Bosporans to seize Chersonesus is described. To that end a son of the Bosporan king Asander married Gicia, a daughter of "the Chersonesus laureate and patrician" Lamachus. A year after the death of Lamachus, Gicia arranged a banquet in honor of her father for all the citizens of Chersonesus, and she promised she would do this annually for the future. Her husband proposed to the Bosporus a plan for seizing the town precisely on the day when Gicia's father would be commemorated. For that purpose warriors, arriving from the Bosporus, were infiltrated secretly into the house the number of whom gradually came to about 200. But on the eve of the festival Gicia's serving-maid accidentally came across the warriors in the cellar and told her mistress about this. The latter exposed the plot to the "patricians", and she was promised in return that after she should die she would be buried within the precincts of the town. While the festival was under way Gicia's residence was burned down along with her husband and all the Bosporans.

Garnett took note of the fact that the general atmosphere of the story of Gicia does not harmonize with the period in which one ought apparently to assign it. In the IVth century Christianity had already become the prevailing religion, but no indications of it are to be found in the tale. On the contrary, festivities with dancing and singing, Gicia's wish to be buried within the town yet not in a church (the place of most honor for the burial of a Christian), attest more strongly a time of paganism. The names of the actors —Lamachus, Asander, and others— also speak of an early time. Garnett noted the coincidence of the name of the Bosporan king in the story with that of a real ruler of the Bosporus, Asander (47-17 B.C.), he attributed the Gicia story to the period of that reign, and he placed the events described in it in direct connection with the adoption of the civic era of Chersonesus which fell, according to Boeckh's determination, to 36 or to 21 B.C. (Garnett, pp. 103-105).

Garnett's deduction seem to us indisputable. After the defeat of Mithradates VI the kings of the Bosporus held under their control probably all of the Greek towns of the Crimea and of the Asiatic side of the Cimmerian Bosporus, including Chersonesus. Only Phanagoria, the first to rise against Mithradates VI Eupator, received autonomy, but as early as Pharnaces (63-47) it was amalgamated with the Bosporus. The dependence of Chersonesus was most likely of a limited nature, and on that account the Bosporus resolved to incorporate it into the body of the Bosporan territory. Like Pharnaces who had seized Phanagoria, Asander sought to overpower Chersonesus, but this was not crowned with success. It is difficult to say whether this took place as described in the Gicia story. In the tale there are unquestionably also legendary details, but the real nature of the basic subject matter —an attempt by the Bosporus to seize Chersonesus— appears to be beyond doubt. Unquestionably the salvation of the town would fully deserve to be signalized by the adoption of a special era.

In the monetary typology of Chersonesus the type of the Maiden with a crown upon her head, with a bow and arrow in one hand, and with a spear raised in the other becomes widely used from about this time onward. The type copies some statue and runs through the entire coinage of Chersonesus. Somewhat later, approximately from the middle of the IInd century A.D., there commenced to be added to it the figure of a hind (possibly the hind formed part of the statuary group). According to the story, the Chersonesites erected two statues of Gicia, one of them supposed to represent her in modest attire as she exposed her husband's plot, but the other "in warlike guise defending the town against the ill-intentioned". The description of the second statue fully corresponds to the early coin type of the Maiden. Of course there is no justification for recognising the image on the coins as being that of a statue of Gicia herself. The version according to which the statue of the divinity is called Gicia beyond all doubt appeared at a later time as a result of an adaptation of remnants of pagan beliefs and "idols" to the new Christian religion. Taken by itself, the fact of the widespread popularity of the type of the protectress-Maiden at the end of the Ist century B.C. and in the first centuries of our era is very notable.

If an attempt by the king of the Bosporus to seize Chersonesus actually took place, the salvation of the town could doubtless be ascribed only to the Maiden, as had occurred on an earlier occasion (cf. IosPE, I^2, 343). One should, it is true, point out that the appearance of the statuary type of the "protectress" Maiden falls to a somewhat earlier date than 24 B.C. — it appears for the first time on a coin dated to the period of Pharnaces.

It is not known how the events of 24 B.C. were reflected in the relationship between Chersonesus and the Bosporus. At a later time fairly intensive links were maintained between them. Thus in one of the inscriptions (IosPE, I^2, 419) the subject is the sending by Chersonesus of an auxiliary detachment to king Polemon (14-9 B.C.) who, as we are aware, conducted extensive military operations in the Bosporus (in particular, he destroyed Tanais) and who was killed in one of the battles. In a second inscription (IosPE, I^2, 354) we are told of an envoy from queen Dynamis (9 B.C. — A.D. 7 being greeted at Chersonesus with great honors); in a third (IosPE, I^2, 573) the name of king Aspurgus is mentioned. Apparently Chersonesus continued to be dependent on the Bosporus and was obliged to assist it with forces.

Zograph considered that the dependence of Chersonesus on the Bosporus was expressed only nominally in a symmachy, but that in actuality the town was in subjection (Zograph, 1951, p. 155). In our view things were otherwise. The town was actually independent of the Bosporus: self-rule existed, signs of the existence of a Bosporan administration are lacking, and coins were issued with local Chersonesus types. In practice the subjection boiled down to the obligation to provide the Bosporan kings with forces in the event of war. The attempt to seize Chersonesus affords evidence of an attempt to alter the existing state of affairs and to include the town within the composition of the kingdom of the Bosporus.

The practical reasons for alteration of the political status of Chersonesus assumed form at the middle of the Ist century A.D. In A.D. 39 the emperor Claudius transferred the kingdom of the Bosporus to Polemon II, a grandson of Polemon I. This action infringed upon the rights of Mithradates VIII, the son of the recently deceased king Aspurgus. Mithradates VIII did not fall in with this decision and proclaimed himself king. The earliest staters of Mithradates VIII are dated to A.D. 39 (Bertier, 1913, No. 108). For reasons that are unknown Rome failed to react in any way to this event. What is more, in A.D. 41 Claudius actually recognised Mithradates VIII as king, handing to Polemon, who had in fact never appeared in the Bosporus, one of the districts of Cilicia. Mithradates VIII cherished plans for freeing himself from Rome, but these became known to the Romans through his brother Cotys.

To eliminate Mithradates VIII from the Bosporus forces were sent under the command of A. Didius Gallus, the governor of Moesia. Mithradates VIII was beaten and fled, hoping to recover the throne with the help of the local tribes. The war took on a lingering character. Even the residents of Byzantium became involved in it. In A.D. 53 they requested from the Roman Senate freedom from imposts. Claudius confirmed the fact that "exhausted by the recent wars with the Thracians and the kingdom of the Bosporus, they stood in need of aid brooking no delay. And he freed them from the payment of imposts for five years" (Tac., Ann., XII, 63). Finally Mithradates VIII was handed over to the Romans, and his brother Cotys was installed as king of the Bosporus, the first coins for him being dated to A.D. 45.

Immediately afterwards considerable alterations likewise take place in the currency of Chersonesus. The town issues gold staters—an altogether unthinkable matter for a town forming part of a dependent kingdom. The earliest stater is dated in the year 71 of the Chersonesus era, i.e. to A.D. 47 but the issuance of dated coins perhaps commenced in 46. A few years later a regular annual coinage of copper coins commences. These last have on their reverses an image of Nike with palm branch and wreath (unquestionable evidence of some form of military success). One can scarcely doubt that these successes were associated with the military operations against Mithradates VIII. In a commemorative inscription in honor of an unknown person (IosPE, I^2, 420) there is mention, among other meritorious deeds, of some sort of activity perhaps of a military character, which took place in the Bosporus. In the same text there is also mention of a mission by this citizen to the ruler of Moesia. The mission has usually been associated with the expedition of T. Plautius Silvanus Aelianus, but it might equally be related to the war against Mithradates VIII.

The exceptional privileges granted to Chersonesus can be explained only by acknowledging that the status of the town had altered. Pliny tells us that Chersonesus was accorded liberty by the Romans (Pliny., NH, IV, 85). Bertier de la Garde, confronting this statement with the issue of coins bearing the image of Nike, suggested that the liberty had in part been won through force of arms (Bertier, 1893, p. 70).

One may also assign to the same time another extremely interesting Chersonesus decree in honor of an unknown figure (IosPe, I^2, 355), one unfortunately preserved only in fragmentary form. The citizen being honoured had been somewhere outside the town, perhaps in connection with the negotiations for liberty (line 14). Upon returning he found the citizens suffering under a tyrant and he contrived to free them without bloodshed. Next there is description of tumults in the town and of the activity of the citizen as an epimēlētes, a repairing of the walls, an overhauling of provisions in connection with an approaching war, assistance to needy citizens in the form of grain. After this there is mention of the Roman emperor, the senate, "the age-old liberty of the Chersonesites." In recreating the text Latyshev admits of the town's receiving liberty (lines 30-31). Further material is to the effect that the partizans of the "tyrant" recognized him once more, but that this time, too, the citizen preserved the town from peril, There follows at the end of the inscription the decision by the council and the people that the person being honored should be rewarded with a gold wreath and a statue.

Chersonesus's receiving new privileges may be ascribed to A.D. 47, or to one of the preceding years (to judge from numismatic data). Hence if in the decree the same event is pinned down, as we believe to be the case, then one may see in the tyrant some local citizen who was a partizan of Mithradates VIII, or even Mithradates VIII himself.

But the thesis which was accepted on the basis of the reconstruction of the lines of the inscription which are of interest to us (IosPE, I^2, 355) runs up against a succession of serious objections. In the first place, as we are aware, the receipt by Chersonesus of liberty under Caesar and Antoninus Pius (the "first" and the "second eleutheria") was accompanied by the issuance of coins with the inscription ΧΕΡϹΟΝΗϹΟΥ ΕΛΕΥΘΕΡΑϹ , yet coins with such an inscription were not issued after A.D. 47. In the second place, one of the indicators of a change in the status of the town is the striking of gold coins. The latest of the staters known to us is dated to A.D. 134, i.e. approximately ten years earlier than the receipt by the town of the eleutheria which the Heracleotes secured for it. It turns out that the town, enjoying some sort of privilege received from the Romans just after 47 B.C., nevertheless still achieves liberty and upon receiving it at once issues coins with the inscription ΕΛΕΥΘΕΡΑϹ . The matter becomes still more complicated through the fact that under Cotys II (123-132), as Phlegon of Tralles informs us (Steph. Byz. s.v. Βόσποροϲ), Chersonesus was once more subject to the Bosporus. The issuance of coins in A.D. 134 after the death of Cotys might be regarded as an evidence of liberation, but then why should the town have been so stubborn about achieving eleutheria?

To us the political status of the town prior to its receiving the "second eleutheria" looks like this. After the Roman-Bosporan war Chersonesus received the rights of autonomy, but not eleutheria. Koehne in his day had already written about the difference between the concepts of αὐτονομία and ἐλευθερία suggesting that the latter is equivalent to the concept of independence, whereas the former signifies government in harmony with the ancient customs of a given town (Koehne, 1848, p. 48-49). The same author adduces a number of examples to the effect that in antiquity these concepts were not always clearly distinguished. On this account Pliny's testimony that Chersonesus was granted liberty by the Romans (always provided he did not have in mind the liberty received from Caesar) should not be understood in the sense that Chersonesus received the rights of a free city (civitas libera). By the time of Pliny these titles had no real significance, so that inexact application of the terms by Romans is easy to explain. The striking of gold by Chersonesus would in our view have been impossible if the town had continued to stand in dependence upon the Bosporus. In evaluating the fact that Chersonesus struck gold coins one should bear in mind that Olbia too (or king Pharzoius) had the same right. One gets the impression that in the period immediately after the war with Mithradates VIII Rome recognized the presence on the northern Black Sea littoral of three more or less important governmental formations: the kingdom of the Bosporus, Chersonesus, and Olbia. Each of these must have been at the very least neutral toward the others; possibly even friendly and allied; and less likely, subject.

Speaking of Chersonesus, this sort of situation continued till the beginning of the reign of Hadrian, or more precisely till A.D. 123. From the communication by Phlegon of Tralles we learn that the emperor subjected certain towns to the Bosporan king Cotys, and Cherson among them. Obviously one should understand by Cotys the IInd of that name (123-132). At that time Chersonesus was not issuing any coins. With the end of Cotys's reign probably the subjection to the Bosporus was cut short as well. Under Rhoemetalces Chersonesus again issues gold coins (the stater of A.D. 134). We are aware that Chersonesus twice sent out to Rhoemetalces successful missions seeking alliance (IosPe, I^2, 423). G. D. Belov holds that this is evidence of a subjection of Chersonesus to the Bosporus (Belov, p. 106). For our part we think that a dependent town would scarcely have sent out a mission of such a nature.

The events preceding the receipt by Chersonesus of the rights of a free city community are associated with the activity of the Chersonesus citizen Ariston son of Attina (IosPE, I^2, 359, 423). In A.D. 130 he occupied the office of secretary to the council. After this he occupied from 131 to 138 a further succession of important offices: he was twice named envoy to king Rhoemetalces, he was elected prodikos and nomophylax, he managed the treasury, he was a priest. At the beginning of the reign of Antoninus Pius (138-161) he was sent as envoy to Rome to negotiate eleutheria. After six years of fruitless activity in Rome Ariston died. From the foregoing it is apparent that Chersonesus did not receive the status of a free city community before A.D. 144 at the earliest.

More successful was the mission of the Herakleotes to the emperor Antoninus Pius (IosPE, I^2, 362, 363), as a result of which Chersonesus received the rights of a free city community.

CHAPTER III

"THE SECOND ELEUTHERIA"

(about A.D. 145-268)

Among the Chersonesus coins of the Roman period one of the most numerous groups consists of coins of various denominations bearing the inscription ΧΕΡϹΟΝΗϹΟΥ ΕΛΕΥΘΕΡΑϹ . All of these, with the exception of the obols of the "first eleutheria", fall to the concluding period of the numismatics of ancient Chersonesus which has received the appellation of the "second eleutheria" in the literature. The term "second eleutheria" may also be regarded as the name for a particular period in the history of Chersonesus when the town, which had for two and a half centuries been under considerable influence from the kingdom of the Bosporus and had even been dependent upon it, enjoys the rights of a free city community (civitas libera).

The coins of the "second eleutheria", decidely varied in style, are exceedingly poor in all possible sorts of supplementary symbols, monograms, and the like. With the exception of the inscription on them that has been mentioned, they bear only from time to time marks of value (Β, Γ , and Δ), and at the very beginning of the period a few issues bear a monogram for the name of the Maiden (but one has her full name—ΠΑΡΘΕΝΟϹ). The absence of dated coins, the quasi-autonomous nature of the coinage, and the barbarized style of the majority of the coins renders their relative and absolute dating difficult .

We have used as the basis of the classification of the coins of the "second eleutheria" the fact, established earlier, of the allocation of a limited selection of types and of their being bound up respectively with the coins of each denomination (Zograph, 1951, p. 152). A total of four denominations were issued—the tetrassarion (types: head of divinity Chersonas on obverse, and Maiden with hind on reverse); the tressis (Asclepius—Hygieia); the dupondius (Maiden with hind—butting bull), and the assarion (two sorts: Chersonas—Maiden, or Chersonas—Nike).

The group most numerous in quantity of variants consists of the tetrassaria, which were struck from the beginning to the end of the period. It is this denomination that became the basis for the classification of the entire Chersonesus currency of the period of the "second eleutheria". The other denominations are distributed more or less satisfactorily in harmony with the style of one or another set of variants of the tetrassaria.

At the start all the coins of the "second eleutheria" were placed in three periods: about A.D. 138-180; about A.D. 180-211; and about A.D. 211-295 (Anokhin, 1963a, p. 33). The boundaries between the periods correspond to the start of the reign of one emperor or another, and the periods themselves embrace the reigns of several emperors. The boundaries between the periods were produced by comparison with the coinage of other towns and they seem reliable enough to our mind. On this occasion they are being justified through certain further observations, so that their reliability is further increased. There has emerged a possibility of arranging all the issues of the "second eleutheria" by reigns of emperors, just as has been done for the coins of the preceding period. In a number of instances the indisputability of assigning a given group of coins to this emperor or that is perfectly evident, but in others it seems problematical. The same is to be said of the dating of issues within particular reigns. One can only hope that in the future fresh observations will make it possible to introduce greater clarity into these important problems.

1. The Chronology of the Coin Issues.

One should assign to the start of the coinage of the "second eleutheria" period coins bearing the divinity Chersonas facing right and with a lyre on the obverse, and of the Maiden standing with a hind, and also the monogram ΠΑΡ (h), on the reverse (Plate XVII, 250). They were perhaps issued even before Chersonesus received liberty, inasmuch as they bear no mention of it. The transitional character of this issue is emphasized by the presence of the monogram so characteristic for the preceding period. One's attention is drawn to a variant of coins close to these in type but having no such monogram (Plate XVII, 251). As we see, the dual character of the coin-issues is also retained at the start of the "eleutheria".

The presence of the monogram provides a sufficiently reliable criterion for segregation of the initial issues of the "second eleutheria". Among these we assign coins of analogous type, i.e. tetrassaria on which for the first time in the whole history of the town's currency the monogram is turned into the goddess's name written out in full—ΠΑΡΘΕΝΟϹ (Plate XVII, 252), and also two issues of the same denomination with monogram or without it (Plate XVII, 253-257). These last offer a curious trait for the characterization of the coinage of this phase: the still not entirely stabilized typology on more than one occasion obliged the engravers to clean away old inscriptions from the dies and to replace them with new ones. The arrangment of the inscriptions ΧΕΡϹΟΝΗϹΟΥ (most frequently in abbreviated form—ΧΕΡ) and ΕΛΕΥΘΕΡΑϹ on obverse and reverse was not constant either, but in the concluding issues of the transitional period the former one became fixed to the obverse and the latter to the reverse.

On the reverses of the tetrassaria the "Maiden-protectress" is represented as on the coins of the period of "Bosporan influence", but the image of a hind is added to this. Apparently this statuary group of the Maiden with the hind, new for Chersonesus), was created (or metamorphosed) between A.D. 96 and 138. This group is reproduced on coins till the end of the coinage, although the hind is sometimes shifted about within the limits of the coin field, appearing now to the right and now to the left of the Maiden, something which is apparently to be explained by different angles for reproduction of the statuary group.

In addition to the tetrassaria, we assign to the opening phase of the coinage in the "second eleutheria" period coins of two further denominations—a dupondius and an assarion. The dupondius repeats the type of the autonomous dichalcons and obols of the "first eleutheria": on the reverse is the Maiden striking down a hind with a spear, plus the inscription ΧΕΡΣΟΝΗΣΟΥ; on the obverse, a butting bull and the inscription ΕΛΕΥΘΕΡΑΣ (Plate XVII, 258-260). Earlier it was thought that the obverse was the side on which the Maiden and the hind were represented (Anokhin, 1963a, p. 66-67), in analogy with early dichalcons; but technological data show us that one should consider the side with the butting bull to be the obverse.

On the obverses of the assaria there is represented a bust of the divinity Chersonas facing left with a branch before him; and on the reverse, the Maiden with spear and bow and the inscription ΧΕΡ—ΣΟ (Plate XVII, 261). The square shape of the letters, the identical abbreviation of the town's name as ΧΕΡ—ΣΟ and its being broken in two by the image, provide the justification for joining together into a single series certain variants of all three denominations (Plate XVII, 254, 260, 261).

The coin classes enumerated make up a relatively compact group with more or less reliably discernable lines of development. Less indicative is a second group of coins to which several issues of tetrassaria, one issue of the tressis (a denomination new for Chersonesus), and of the dupondius belong. One issue of tetrassaria bears the full inscription—ΧΕΡΣΟΝΗΣΟΥ ΕΛΕΥΘΕΡΑΣ (Plate XVIII, 262)—and can be assigned to the transitional coinage; the style of the types does not run counter to this. The other issues of tetrassaria are considerably distinguished from the early ones and should unquestionably be regarded as later (Plate XVIII, 263-265; 267-269). Their types and inscriptions can be regarded to a certain extent as copied.

On the obverse of the tressis Aesculapius is represented standing and facing, with his head turned left and with a serpent-staff; and on the reverse Hygieia holding in her hands a serpent and a patera (Plate XVIII, 266). On the reverse is the sign of the denomination, a Γ. The coins described find a reasonably convincing analogy in one of the issues of tetrassaria and they can be put together with these in a single series (Plate XVIII, 265, 266). One of the variants of the dupondius (Plate XVIII, 270) likewise corresponds with them more or less, but the remaining variants of that denomination are degraded to the point of a complete sketchiness and primitiveness of execution (Plate XVIII, 271, 272). In the other denomination no such thing is encountered, and for that reason the numerous issues of the dupondius may constitute a third and separate chronological group.

Let us examine the absolute chronology of these three groups. Their general dating may be determined as approximately A.D. 138-180. The starting date is given by the commencement of the reign of the emperor Antoninus Pius (138-161), under whom the town received eleutheria; the closing date is delimited by the issuance of a series of coins of four denominations with marks of value at the beginning of the reign of the emperor Commodus (180-192). With this to start from, an early group of coins characterized by a number of transitional features may be dated to the time of the emperor Antoninus Pius and the rest to the reign of the emperor Marcus Aurelius.

The dating of the first group of issues is to our mind convincing enough; with the second, the matter becomes more complicated. The mintages of the other towns of the northern Black Sea littoral show that under Marcus Aurelius Tyra issued no coins at all, the Bosporus cut its coinage back considerably, and the possibility of an issue at Olbia remains to some extent problematical. The currency of Tyra is of particular interest; it has been well studied thanks to the issuance of coins with the titulature of the Roman emperors. There was a time when this circumstance compelled one to suppose the existence of an interruption at Chersonesus too, but at present, if one starts from the logic of the evolution of the Chersonesus coinage itself, such an interruption seems insufficiently demonstrated. In any event, one does not manage to find a more suitable time for the issue of dupondii mentioned above than the end of the reign of Marcus Aurelius. The barbarized style of the coins gives rise to doubt as to their having belonged to the output of the Chersonesus mint. But a suggestion that they did not would be unfounded, inasmuch as such coins are found exclusively in excavations at Chersonesus itself. Is it impossible to associate their appearance with a partial change in the ethnic make-up of Chersonesus during the interval of time indicated, and to regard it as a clandestine or even a lawful output of alien soldiery of the Roman garrison stationed here? What we have said is of course no more than a conjecture, in need of careful reinforcement with additional evidence.

The next chronological period is opened by a series of coins of four denominations—until recently the only complete series (Plate XIX, 273-283). Two denominations in fact bear marks of value—Γ and Δ. The device of designating the various denominations by means of marks of value in the northern Black Sea littoral, if one does not count the Bosporus, commenced to be widely used only at the time of the emperor Commodus (180-192). At Tyra for example, marks of value were placed on all coins starting with the first series of Commodus (Zograph, 1957, plate 2), something which enabled Zograph also to date to this reign one of the series of Olbia coins (Zograph, 1951, p. 143). In our case we too consider it possible to assign to the time of Commodus the Chersonesus series of coins with marks of value that has been mentioned, thus securing a more or less reliable starting date.

The next series of coins consists of two denominations—a tressis and a dupondius (Plate XX, 284-285). The distinguishing feature of these coins is the completeness of the inscriptions, their unique position, and also the occurance of identical errors on each of the denominations—ΧΕΡϹΟΝΗϹϹΟΥ (on the reverse) and ΕΛΕΥΘΕΡΑΑϹ (on the obverse). These peculiarities, and also the free style of the types, afford evidence of a fairly high level of skill on the part of the engraver and allow one to define the coins of both denominations confidently as being the work of a single engraver. We have no data for an absolute dating of the coins of this series, but the relative chronology allows one to assign them with assurance to the reign of Septimius Severus (193-211). What is involved here is the fact that the coins of the next series, issued under the emperor Caracalla, repeat the inscriptions of the series both as to fullness and as to arrangment, and one of the variants even has an analogous error in naming the town—ΧΕΡϹΟΝΗϹϹΟΥ. Accordingly the die engraver for the coins of Caracalla's day borrowed this innovation from the coins of the preceding issue. In saying that the series described should be assigned to the times of Septimius Severus we are nevertheless unable to indicate a more exact date for it than the whole period of the reign of that emperor.

There has usually been assigned to the period of Caracalla a series of three denominations—tetrassarion, tressis, and dupondius—standing out sharply from the general mass of the Chersonesus issues of the "second eleutheria" through the highly artistic types of the coins, and the handsome square shapes of the letters of the inscriptions. One should also associate with these a smaller denomination, the assarion, known from a single specimen in the State Hermitage collection which has unfortunately not been preserved entire (Plate XX, 295).

The whole series is so unusual for Chersonesus that one may almost with conviction speak of it as being the production of a visiting master. The practice of migrating was, as we are aware, widespread in the ancient (and indeed not only the ancient) period. One of the peculiarities of this series is the fact that the image of the divinity Chersonas on the obverse of the tetrassaria has been given the portrait features of certain actual persons considerably differing also in the presence or absence of a wreath on the head, in the coiffure, and in other details. In one of the old descriptions the image of the divinity Chersonas was understood as being a portrait of Caracalla (for example, Trésor, plate XLVII, 10, p. 141). It seemed that the quasi-autonomous nature of the Chersonesus coinage excluded such an interpretation and on that account, even though the series was indeed dated to the time of Caracalla, no further research was undertaken in that direction. A comparison which we have made between types of Chersonesus and Roman coins has led to decidedly interesting and unexpected results.

Thus four types of image differing each from the others have been isolated. The first (Plate XX, 286) is represented by a male bust with a massive beardless head, decorated with a wreath, and having regular but somewhat heavy facial features. This type can unquestionably be identified as a portrait of Caracalla.

The second (Plate XX, 287, 288) beyond doubt conveys a female portrait —there is no wreath on the head, the coiffure is represented in the form of masses of hair carefully parted at the top of the head and brought downward in wavy locks around the head from forehead to occiput. The face has features that are not entirely regular, a long aquiline nose, and sharply delineated nostrils. The similarity of this image with the portrait of Julia Domna does not give rise to any doubts either.

On the third sort of coins (Plate XX, 289) a young beardless male is represented wearing a wreath on his head, with more delicate facial features than in the first series. On the basis of the attributions of the first two portraits, this group might be an image of Caracalla's younger brother Geta, or else of Elagabalus. But the lack of any vividly individual facial features of either person prevents one from making a final choice. The fourth group (Plate XX, 290) also shows a male type of face, but without wreath on the head; no portrait resemblance can be seen, though it reminds one somewhat of the portrait of Caracalla, although the nose and the brow ridges are not so massive.

To what period should these coins be assigned? We know that portraits of Caracalla and Geta are encountered on coins of the reign of their father Septimius Severus. But we cannot date these to that time, since we do not find among the Chersonesus classes a portrait of Septimius Severus himself, he being always represented with a beard. Thus the remaining possibility is that the coins were issued during the years of Caracalla's reign, i.e. in A.D. 211-217. From the practice of the Roman imperial and provincial currency we know that members of the imperial house who bore the title of Caesar were represented without wreath on the head; from this we should conclude that the fourth group conveys a portrait of some person who had that title. But under Caracalla no one bore the title; accordingly this portrait cannot be assigned to his time. But inasmuch as the portrait of a Caesar could not appear on coins without being accompanied by coins of the emperor himself, the last two classes of images should be dated to the reign of Elagabalus (218-222), the third class of portrait being ascribed to the emperor himself, and the fourth to Severus Alexander, adopted by him approximately a year before his death (A.D. 221).

So the tetrassaria of the classes listed should be divided between the reigns of Caracalla and of Elagabalus. The question of the smaller denominations is not clear. It is difficult to say whether they were issued only under Caracalla or only under Elagabalus, or under both Emperors. There is a possibility of dividing them into groups; in particular, on the dupondii the bull is represented facing now left and now right. For the time being it does not seem possible to determine whether this reflects some sort of chronological distinction, or what it may be. The tressis exhibits no substantial variations, to say nothing of the unique specimen of the assarion, and on that account all three smaller denominations are set apart into a group of their own, dated to the periods of the reigns of the two emperors. There are letters ΠΑ on the reverse of the assarion. The question of what these letters mean will be examined below, in the section on the organization of the currency during the period of the "second eleutheria".

Some supplementary remarks may be made on the coins described. Under Caracalla coins of the larger denomination were issued with portraits of Caracalla himself and of his mother, Julia Domna. Inasmuch as it has not been possible to bring to light a portrait of Geta, the striking of this series evidently commenced not earlier than February of A.D. 212—the date of Geta's death. The tetrassaria of the next series were most likely struck with portraits of Elagabalus and of Severus Alexander as Caesar, but it is rather difficult to catch their portrait features in the coin types. This state of affairs should be explained by the fact that the die engraver, living and working at Chersonesus, could avail himself only of a limited quantity of iconographic material, in the main the corresponding imperial coins, and he presumably had not seen a portrait of Severus Alexander even on coins. The coins with the presumed portrait of Elagabalus are dated to the whole of his reign, i.e. A.D. 218-222; those of Severus Alexander to A.D. 221-222.

The next issue of Chersonesus coins (Plate XXI, 296-303) was originally assigned to A.D. 230-250 (Anokhin, 1962, p. 60), but later to A.D. 240-250 (Anokhin, 1963a, p. 44). The considerable gap was explained by the great difference in style and skill of execution discerned between the preceding issue and the one now being described. But that assertion calls for review. First of all, the difference in the execution of the dies (earlier ascribed to the skill of the visiting engraver) cannot afford evidence of a great interruption in time.

The activity of the visiting master continued no longer than ten years, from A.D. 212 to 222, so that the local engraver who took his place could have commenced work in the following year. Furthermore, the preceding issues of coins were struck from reign to reign without any sort of evident interruptions. Consequently it is unlikely that such an interruption would have taken place under Severus Alexander. The issue of coins that we are discussing is represented by a large number of dies (18 obverse and 30 reverse dies, linked with each other) and would suit very well the 13-year duration of the sole rule of that emperor (222-235). There has moreover come to light a possibility for determining more exactly the upper limit for the issue, something we shall have to dwell upon in more detail.

One of the tetrassaria of the issue being described bears a countermark in the form of a letter Γ (Plate XXI, 300). This coin, mentioned by F. Imhoof-Blumer (Imhoof, 1902), is preserved in the Berlin Museum collection. Such countermarks are not found on coins discovered during Chersonesus excavations, so its non-local origin is beyond question. The abundant countermarking of Greek provincial coins belonging to the cities of Asia Minor in the IIIrd century A.D. permits one to assert that this countermark too is of Asia Minor.

The basic mass of Asia Minor countermarks is made up of numerals, marks of value—A, B, Γ, Δ, Є, the stigma, Z, H, I, and IB (West, p. 118-123). The numeral Γ is encountered on the coins of many towns of Pisidia, Caria, Lydia, Ionia, and Bithynia. The greatest interest for us may be offered by the countermarks on coins of Heracleia Pontica and Tium, ties with which are traditional for Chersonesus and are confirmed both by coin finds (Gilevich, 1968, p. 21) and by epigraphic data (Solomonik, 1964, No. 13).

The countermarks on the coins of Heracleia and Tium have a uniform triangular shape of punch corresponding to the outline of the letter Γ (SNG von Aulock, No. 389, 415, 956). This allows one to think that they were imposed in a single town, most likely Heracleia. This is confirmed by the greater quantity and later date of the Heracleia coins; the coins of Tium are dated to the time of Septimius Severus (193-211), those of Heracleia to the time of Caracalla (211-217), Balbinus (238), and Gordian III (238-244).

The coins of the emperors named will hardly have been conntermarked in succession. It is most probable that this operation was carried out during some brief interval of time on all the coins that made up the composition of the monetary circulation. When did the countermarking occur? The last coins of Heracleia, with countermark H, are assigned to the time of Philip the Arab (244-249). According to data from the von Aulock collection (SNG von Aulock, Heft 2 and Heft 15) the city did not issue coins between the reigns of Philip and Gallienus (253-268), and the coins of this last emperor no longer have countermarks. Accordingly the most likely time for imposition of the countermarks was 249-253 A.D. It is to just that period, in particular, that the last countermarked coins of Nicomedia fall (Trebonianus Gallus, 251-253 A.D.). One must point out that mass countermarking of coins in all likelihood took place twice in Asia Minor—at the middle of the IIIrd century and evidently under Aurelian (270-275), but inasmuch as earlier coins of each of the cities were included in the countermarkings, the picture as a whole becomes a little blurred.

However that may be, there is every reason to suppose that the Chersonesus coin was countermarked at Heracleia in the middle of the IIIrd century. But some time must have elapsed before it arrived at Heracleia, and for that reason the upper date for it should be considerably lowered, limiting the issue as a whole to the time of Severus Alexander.

The tetrassaria of the next issue repeat the class of the preceding coins, being distinguished only through the presence of the letter B cut on the dies of some variants of the reverse (Plate XXI, 304). Earlier we considered it possible to associate the appearance of the letter B , which can only be a mark of value indicating a reduction of the coin's worth to one-half, with the reform of Aurelian and with the monetary policy of the emperors of the subsequent period, when one observes an analogous phenomenon in the coinages of a number of towns, and to date it to 275-285 A.D. (Anokhin, 1963a, p. 44-46).

The dating of the preceding issue to the days of Severus Alexander forces one to re-date these coins as well. As has already been said, in the middle of the IIIrd century A.D. a mass countermarking of coins with marks of value was carried out. Without finally deciding upon the question of the causes of such an operation, we do consider it possible to put forward a suggestion to the effect that it was associated with a need to regularise the currency. The majority of the towns issued coins without marks of value and the diversity of coin types, and likewise considerable fluctuations in sizes and weights, created problems in monetary accounting and circulation. The countermarks were intended to contribute to the introduction of order into the monetary economy. It is not out of the question that the countermarking should have been carried out with the observation of certain standards of weight and size for one denomination or another, and that for that reason a coin of a large denomination which failed to correspond to the norms might be countermarked with the mark of a lesser denomination. The average weight of the Chersonesus denominations fell considerably below the norms for the corresponding denominations of the coins of Asia Minor. For example, the average weight of coins of the issue being described comes to 4.93 g. For comparison's sake we may cite the average weights of countermarked coins of Heracleia Pontica from the von Aulock collection: H (8)—12.62 g; Z (6)—9.79 g; Δ (4)—6.91 g; Γ (3)—6.10 g. (SNG von Aulock, Heft 2; Heft 15). The Heracleia countermark of the symbol on the Chersonssus coin testifies that at Heracleia this tetrassarion was valued at no more than a tressis. We think that the appearance of the symbol B on tetrassaria of this issue ought to be regarded as an occurrence of the same sort. Apparently the reform carried out in the middle of the IIIrd century affected Chersonesus too. Inasmuch as the weight of Chersonesus tetrassaria lagged considerably behind the norm for the denomination in question, the coin was made equivalent to a dupondius, and on that account the corresponding symbol was cut into the punches prepared. The countermarking in Asia Minor took place in the middle of the IIIrd century; the Chersonesus issue, for its part, should be assigned to a slightly later time, tentatively to the first years of the reign of Gallienus.

The next and last issue of coins of ancient Chersonesus was the most massive of all: to strike it no less than 7 obverse and 44 reverse dies were used. A majority of the variants are linked with one another through dies in common, so the issue was fairly compact in time. The coins retain the type peculiar to tetrassaria (Plate XXI, 306-308), but the image of the divinity Chersonas on some of them bears more resemblance to a portrait of the emperor Valerian (253-260) on coins of the town of Tium (Plate XXI, 308; SNG von Aulock, Heft 3, No. 1036-1037). This provides us with some supplementary arguments in favor of dating the issue tc the time of Gallienus. Chersonesus evidently shared the fate of the majority of other Greek towns, which ended their mintage under that emperor.

2. The Organization of the Currency

During the period of Bosporan influence the issuance of coins at Chersonesus was carried out interchangeably either in the name of the town or in the name of the Maiden goddess (Temple issues). The issuance of civic coins fell within the competence of some sort of individual magistrate, most likely a dioiketes. From the middle of the Ist century B.C. they stopped putting names on these coins and it is difficult to say what the system was in the subsequent years. Data on this matter are missing from the coins, but one may assume that matters having to do with minting continued to be handled by one of the highest offices of the town's government.

Evidently the currency was organized in the same way at the beginning of the "second eleutheria": coins are issued both with a monogram of the Maiden's name (in one case the full name) and without it. But soon this order of things was broken down and all the way down to the end of the period coins are issued only in the name of the town. We have spoken above about the double nature of the coinage during the period of Bosporan influence as having depended on who was financing a coin issue in each particular instance—the civic authorities or the Maiden's temple. One must suppose that given the fact of the "second eleutheria" the town had sufficient opportunities for the issuance of coins; it is quite likely that the coinage was subsidized entirely or in part by the Roman authorities. One is likewise impelled toward this deduction by the circumstance that the coins lacked any sort of supplementary symbols or inscriptions indicating a civic magistracy responsible for the issue.

The finding of the unique assarion now preserved at the State Hermitage (No. 311 b; Plate XX, 215) enables one to present the organization of the currency of Chersonesus for the period of the "second eleutheria" in another light. On the reverse of this coin, to the left of the figure of Nike, there are two letters—ΠΑ. No traces of any other letters are visible (true, a part of the coin flan has failed to be preserved). Evidently the reverse legend was limited to these letters.

The preceding issues offer a possibility for two different explanations of these letters. In the first place, they may be understood as the first syllable of the Maiden's name—ΠΑΡΘΕΝΟϹ. One might argue that we are urged toward such an explanation by the name of the goddess written out in full on one of the coins of the start of the period—the sole word present on the coins outside the slogan ΧΕΡϹΟΝΗϹΟΥ ΕΛΕΥΘΕΡΑϹ. But such a reading strikes one as unlikely. It is difficult to concede that the name of the goddess should have appeared after a prolonged interruption of 70-80 years, and in such an unusual abbreviation at that. In addition, the inscription ΠΑΡΘΕΝΟC had been placed beside the image of the Maiden herself, whereas here we have a figure of Nike. For this reason greater attention is merited by the symbols placed upon coins with the Nike type.

A total of three issues of such coins are known: the first is of A.D. 51-54; and the form of the symbol is (i); the second is of the time of Nero, and the form of the symbol is the same; the third is of the time of Commodus, and the form of the symbol is (j). Should one not consider both varieties as ways of writing the letters ΠA in a monogram? In itself the evolution seems convincing enough, and the odd initial form of the symbol can be explained by a striving to avoid its being confused with the monogram for the Maiden's name.

In that event we are in a position to suppose that on all coins with the Nike type on the reverse, that is to say the smallest denomination, the assarion (?), the office of the first archon was indicated—the πρῶτος ἄρχων. There is nothing surprising in this. As we are aware, the mintage of Olbia was in the hands of first archons. Their names, together with indication of the office in the form of a monogram made up of the letters ΠA, are regularly placed upon Olbia coins of the Ist-IInd centuries A.D. (Zograph, 1951, p. 141, 145). Apparently at Chersonesus the first archon could issue coins in his own name only rarely, and then only the smallest denomination. Probably considerations of an economic character exercised decisive influence.

The sole weighty argument against the thesis of the identity of the symbols (i) and (j) with the letters ΠA, and against the correspondence of both sets with an abbreviated designation of the office of first archon, is the fact that on the small coins with the hind types (see Catalog of Coins, No. 217 and 218) the first symbol comes to take the place of the delta which had earlier been understood as being the mark for the denomination of four units, the tetrachalcon. But if one takes it that both symbols relate to indications of the same type (and the decipherment of the first as an abbreviated designation of the office of first archon does strike us as convincing or at least as possible), then this in its turn leads to another and still more curious argument to the effect that the symbol Δ signifies the office of the dioiketes (ὁ ἐπὶ τᾶς διοικήσεος).

There is nothing unexpected about this proposition either. We have said earlier that at the beginning of the period of Bosporan influence the coinage passes into the hands of a single individual who may most likely have been precisely the dioiketes. According to epigraphic records this office exists at Chersonesus before the middle of the Ist century B.C. An exception is the inscription in honor of Ariston son of Attina (IosPE, I^2, 423), which is dated to the middle of the IInd century A.D. and in which his having filled this office, associated with elucidating the state of the town's finances, is mentioned. On coins the office of the dioiketes may have been indicated even at the end of the Ist century B.C. (see Catalog of Coins, No. 206, monogram g). The first archon figures regularly as being among the principal officials only from the IInd century A.D., but the earliest inscription with mention of this office relates to the beginning of the Ist century A.D. The transition of the main functions of administration from the dioiketes to the first archon during the course of the Ist century A.D. seems evident enough in accordance with the epigraphic data. In decrees of the first third of the IInd century A.D. the dioiketes is no longer mentioned. The inscription in honor of Ariston allows one to suppose that that office was established only when need dictated, and most likely with limited tasks and powers. In conclusion we should remark that what has been said about the system for the organization of the currency at Chersonesus in the first centuries of our era has been built up on the basis of the few data offered by the coins available to us, and that it is to be regarded as merely conjectural. In order to clear up the question definitively one must have at hand fresh supplementary materials.

3. Historical Sketch

At the beginning of the IInd century A.D. the internal situation in the Crimea became more complicated, something which was apparently brought about by some peril from without. During the time of Hadrian (117-138) the town twice sent out missions to the Bosporan king Rhoemetalces; the aim of one of the missions was to conclude an alliance.

The receipt by Chersonesus of the status of a free city community was accompanied by the introduction of Roman forces for its defense, so that the danger of war fell away for some time. One may suppose that the granting of liberty was not an act of "graciously granted benefactions" as the decree put it, but that it was one of the most important measures to strenghten Roman positions in the Crimea. Chersonesus becomes a base for Roman forces. There were stationed in the city detachments of the Ist Italian, XIth Claudian, and Vth Macedonian legions, and also auxiliary forces. There was also located here the military tribune, who commanded all the land and naval forces of the Romans in the Crimea (a squadron of the Flavian fleet of Moesia was stationed at Chersonesus).

Within Chersonesus itself there was a detachment headed by a centurion (IosPE, I^2, 404). In one of the inscription fragments (IosPE, I^2, 405) there is discussion of the marking off of limits within which, perhaps, the Roman legionaries were to dwell. One of the duties of the centurion was to collect various taxes, which were entered in the treasury and were earmarked for maintenance of the force. For the end of the IInd century A.D. we have correspondence of Chersonesus with the legate of the province of Moesia, under whose command the Roman forces in the Crimea were, regarding τέλος πορνικὸν tax on prostitution collected at Chersonesus (IosPE, I^2, 404). Rostovtsev holds that this impost was levied probably from the beginning of the "second eleutheria". During the joint rule of Marcus Aurelius and Lucius Verus (161-169) or that of Marcus Aurelius and Commodus (177-180) it was revised. In Rostovtsev's opinion the revision consisted in reduction of the sum that went for maintenance of the Roman soldiers, and corresponding augmentation of the share that became available to the town. An attempt on the part of the soldiers of the garrison to restore the tax to the earlier amount in fact led to a lawsuit in which the legate stood on the side of the Chersonesites (Rostovtsev, 1916, p. 66-67). The inscription falls to A.D. 185-186.

In another inscription, also falling to the period of the emperor Commodus, the subject matter is apportionment of funds from the Chersonesus treasury for the maintenance of the Roman garrison (Solomonik, 1964, No. 14).

At the end of the IInd century and in the first half of the IIIrd century A.D. intensive construction work went on in the town. Part of it was unquestionably linked with reinforcement of the town's defenses—walls and towers are built or repaired (IosPE, I^2, 438, 439; Solomonik, 1964, No. 25, 26); other parts, with civilian construction-terms, a building for the agoranomy, and temples are erected (IosPE, I^2, 440-444; Solomonik, 1964, No. 26, 1973, No. 133).

At Chersonesus, as at other towns, a cult of the emperors was established, and likewise an office of archpriest (Solomonik, 1964, No. 13). Roman influence places its mark upon many features of Chersonesus life, commencing with the use of a Roman monetary unit, the denarius (IosPE, I^2, 440-444, 446) and extending to the adoption of Roman names. The name Aurelius won particularly widespread acceptance, and one should presumably associate this with Caracalla's edict of 212 A.D. granting all residents of the empire the rights of citizenship.

During the period of the "second eleutheria" coins are issued with the inscription ΧΕΡϹΟΝΗϹΟΥ ЄΛЄΥΘЄΡΑϹ , i.e. "of free Chersonesus". The types of the coins are inveterately local ones—The Maiden with hind, the divinity Chersonas, Nike, the bull. Roman influence makes itself felt in the appearance upon the coins of images of Aesculapius and Hygieia, who enjoyed particular regard among the Roman legionaries. Under Caracalla and Elagabalus images of the divinity Chersonas were given portrait features of the emperors and of members of their families. It is possible that the same picture held for subsequent years, but the low level of engraving skill preveneted their conveying a portrait likeness. The uniformity of the coin types unfortunately deprives one of any opportunity to trace particulars of the historical evolution of Chersonesus in the second half of the IInd century A.D. and in the IIIrd.

One must point out that from the IIIrd century we have only fragmentary data containing almost no facts concerning the town's history. Some light is thrown upon events at the end of the IIIrd century A.D. by coins, but their issue most likely comes to an end under Gallienus (253-268). For the subsequent period one notes a lacuna in epigraphic and literary notices concerning Chersonesus right down to the time of Diocletian (284-305). One may suggest that in those intervening fifteen years there were no Roman forces at Chersonesus. We are aware that Roman settlers and forces in neighbouring Dacia were withdrawn under Aurelian (270-275). It is just for that period that we have extremely strong pressure of barbarians upon the empire, ending with their defeat. But is it only cessation of the currency and absence of Roman forces that characterize the situation of Chersonesus during that period?

From the information on the history of the town at the end of the IIIrd century and in the IVth that is gathered together in Constantine Porphyrogenitus we know that under Diocletian Chersonesus conducted a successful struggle in the Bosporus, helping Rome to repel the pressure of the barbarians. As a reward for this Diocletian granted the town liberty and atelia, i.e. freedom from imposts. But "liberty", as we know, had been received by Chersonesus under Antoninus Pius and the town still enjoyed it under Gallienus. In all likelihood the withdrawal of Roman forces and the cessation of coinage had

had been accompanied by Chersonesus's loss of the status of a free town; or better put, that status was not confirmed by some one of the intervening emperors—Claudius II (268-270) or Aurelian. This can to some extent be explained by the strain the empire underwent in striving against the barbarians.

The course of events suggested is reinforced by the information contained in Const ntine Porphyrogenitus regarding the outcome of the second war on the Danube (the first war, with the Bosporus, took place between A.D. 284-292; Garnett, p. 102), in which Chersonesus took part.

The war was waged between A.D. 323 and 337. In gratitude for its assistance, Constantine the Great confirmed the liberty and exemption from taxation which had been granted the town, issuing an appropriate edict, and he also conferred a number of other honors. The greatest interest lies in the installation at Chersonesus of a detachment of ballistarii numbering one thousand rations of grain. The Chersonesites designated the families which were to receive this ration and which were to provide soldiers for the detachment.

Some years after the events described Chersonesus waged two wars with the Bosporus. In the first war the Bosporus suffered a defeat at Kafa (Theodosia). The boundary between Cherson and the Bosporus was in fact set at that place. In the second war the Bosporus would seem to have suffered an even more crushing defeat; its force fell prisoner, but was released "out of compassion", with the exception of a few, who were kept "for agricultural work". A new boundary was established at Kybernike (Cimmerica?) forty miles from the Bosporus. "From that time", Constantine Porphyrogenitus writes, "the kingdom of the Sarmatians in the Bosporus was overthrown".

It is unquestionable that the information preserved by Constantine Porphyrogenitus had a basis in reality. Numismatic data may afford a measure of confirmation: as we are aware, the coinage of the Bosporus came to an end in A.D. 332.

The presence at Chersonesus of a detachment of ballistarii is pinned down by a number of epigraphic sources (IosPE, I^2, 449; Latyshev, 1896, No. 7). According to Constantine Porphyrogenitus this detachment was made up of Chersonesus residents. In the text of his history there is no mention of the presence at Chersonesus of any forces other than the civic levy. Ballistarii had already taken part in the war with the Bosporus under Diocletian. But in "The Lives of the Bishops of Chersonesus" there is mention of the arrival in Chersonesus in A.D. 325, accompanying the bishop Capitonus, of a detachment of 500 soldiers which thereafter remained at Chersonesus (Latyshev, 1906, p. 41, 62). A. L. Yakobson is inclined to put faith in this last source (Yakobson, 1959, p. 18). To our mind the data of Constantine Porphyrogenitus are the more plausible. The Chersonesus ballistarii were typical representatives of frontier forces, milites limitani et riparienses. "Associated with the calling of the soldier in these forces was the use of lands, and in this connection there was in operation here as early as the IIIrd century the principle of the hereditary nature of military service which in the IVth century was instituted as a general principle in the empire, being extended also to other fields of activity" (Kulakovski, p. XXIX). Apparently only the superior command staff could be appointed from Constantinople, persons like the comes Diogenes who is mentioned in an inscription in honor of the emperor Zeno.

One should p int out that strengthening of the defense capability of Chersonesus by the central authority received a great deal of attention. A certain range of epigraphic records consists of inscriptions concerning the erection of defensive walls. The persons carrying out construction operations not infrequently belonged to the corps of officials of high station. Concern for the strenghtening of Chersonesus comes through particularly during the period of the Hunnish invasion, after which only Chersonesus remained inviolate throughout thewhole northern Black Sea littoral. This is attested, for example, by an inscription of the time of the emperors Valentinian, Valens, and Gratian, falling to A.D. 370-375 (IosPE, I^2, 449); and also one of the emperors Theodosius and Arcadius (A.D. 383-395; IosPE, I^2, 450).

Chersonesus enjoys certain economic privileges. Of great interest is an inscription, unfortunately poorly preserved, which affords evidence that the town had the right of trading with the surrounding peoples (Shangin, No. 11). It is curious to note that the inscription fragment which was found is part of a decree of the emperor Honorius (A.D. 395-423) confirming these rights which had already been received by Chersonesus under his father, the emperor Theodosius (379-395).

Over the course of many years Chersonesus serves as a regular place of exile for persons dangerous to the empire: the fidelity of the town ensured reliable safekeeping. In A.D. 363-364 a future claimant to the throne, Procopius, who was a relative of the emperor Julian, sought to hide here; but "he observed that the town's residents merited no trust, and fearing to be handed over to persons who had come to seek him" he fled (Zos., IV, 5, 2). After having experienced failure in his plot against the emperors Valens and Valentinian in A.D. 366, Procopius was exiled with his partisans to this very same Chersonesus. Under Leo I (457-474) Timotheus Ælurus, patriarch of Alexandria, was exiled to Chersonesus; later on many other personalities were exiled hither as well. In the literature of the day there assumed form a concept of Chersonesus as a wild place set apart from all the world, where exiles dragged out a weary existence, their situation actually not being distinguished from that of the local residents. This is the way the town is presented to us in the letters of Pope Martin (middle of the VIIth century). Of course the exiles had to undergo various physical and still more powerful emotional sufferings, but may this not have affected the objectivity of their evaluation? One supposes that it would not be right to take in any absolute sense the opinions of such persons as these regarding Chersonesus. In the IVth and Vth centuries Chersonesus was an ordinary provincial town, small in area and in the number of its residents and yielding place to the capital in many other respects. Life there was presumably hard as a result of the constant military dangers, But during the period of the barbarian invasions this was more the rule for the majority of frontier towns than the exception. In comparison with the other ancient towns of the northern Black Sea littoral Chersonesus was viable enough not only to survive but even to emerge from this tempestuous time without substantial damage to its political and economic status.

MEDIEVAL CHERSON

CHAPTER I

THE POLIS PERIOD
(A.D. 474-834)

Chersonesus terminated the issuance of its own coin under the emperor Gallienus (A.D. 253-268). The requirements of the town's monetary circulation were satisfied through the use of provincial coin, the underlying mass of which was made up of the product of the mints of Nicomedia and Constantinople (Gilevich, 1968, p. 57).

Resumption of the activity of a mint at Chersonesus, or Cherson as it came to be called in the Middle Ages, falls to the time of the emperor Zeno (474-481). The granting of the right of coinage to Cherson was probably one among a number of measures the enactment of which contributed to a strengthening of the town, which performs an important function as one of the strongpoints at the approaches to the frontiers of the empire. Under the emperor Zeno the town's defensive walls were restored, as is attested by a well-known inscription of A.D. 488 in honor of the emperor (Bertier, 1893). Perhaps one should also assign to the same time the initiation of the town coinage, by virtue of which the construction work was to be financed.

The currency of the "polis" period is characterized by the following features: the town issues coins irregularly, the types of the coins corresponding in the main to empire-wide models; the usual method for manufacturing coins was striking, and it was probably only at the very end of the period that a shift was made to casting. The greater part of the coins bears the names of Byzantine emperors, thanks to which almost no particular problems with their attribution arise.

1. The Chronology of the Coin Issues

Coins of the emperor Zeno struck at Cherson were segregated out by L. N. Belova (Belova, 1941a, No. 2). They have on the obverse the bust of the emperor and an inscription DN ZENO PF AVG, on the reverse a figure of the emperor standing, with a spear and with a prisoner at his feet, and the legend CONCODIAR (the engraver left out the letter R and put it at the end of the legend; Plate XXII, 309). Finding of these coins exclusively on the territory of Cherson and their absence in other Byzantine towns make this attribution convincing enough.

No Cherson coins are yet known for Zeno's successor the emperor Anastasius (491-518), although one cannot entirely rule out the possibility of assigning a few types of coins of that emperor to local production. The same may be said regarding coins of Justin (518-527). But I. V. Sokolova's attempt to distinguish coins of Justin I cannot be regarded as successful. Let us dwell upon this in a little more detail.

In a note published not long ago Sokolova examines copper coins with the type of an emperor's bust on the obverse and a standing figure of the emperor on the reverse (Sokolova, 1971a, pp. 66-68). These coins had been assigned by Belova among those of Cherson and dated to the period of Justinian I (Belova, 1941a, No. 3). Sokolova describes in detail the coin classes, represented by a type of the emperor on the reverse with a cross in his right hand and an orb in the left, and distinguishes three groups. Let us introduce in brief form her characterization of each of the groups: "1. On the obverse a head of the emperor painstakingly engraved, with good rendering of the face and eyes; the diadem ends in a bow in front, and the inscription is complete and readily legible ..."; "2. The engraver's cutting is harsher in the image of the emperor on the obverse, there is no uniformity in the rendering of the diadem, and the inscription is less correct ... " "3. This image of the emperor on the obverse is the coarsest; the nose, brows, and eyes are rendered at times with a single flourish ..." (Sokolova, 1971a, p. 67). A number of variants of the inscription correspond to each class, from the correct DN IVSTINIANVS to distortions of the most various sorts, particularly in the third group. It is precisely among these last that Sokolova picks out coins of Justin.

To our mind this investigator's description and legend samples convincingly show that we are confronted by nothing more than varying stages of degradation and distortion of the inscriptions of the underlying class, for which reason the endeavor to decipher in some of them the name of Justin I looks unconvincing, and the assertions that "the differences in the legends ... cannot be a matter of chance," and that "one cannot explain them as errors or as carelessness on the part of the die engravers" simply unwarranted and contradictory to the facts. In addition, there should unquestionably have been placed at the beginning of the whole group the coin with the inscription DN IVSTINIANVS on the obverse and VICTORIA AVGGGE on the reverse (Plate XXII, 310), this having served as the prototype for all the other varieties within this class. The reverse sequence, i.e. from coins with degraded types and legends pertaining purportedly to Justin I and leading to the specimen described, strikes one as simply unthinkable. The existence of mutilated inscriptions obliges the investigator to be extremely cautious, the more so when he is dealing with the distinguishing of an issue by a new ruler. Of course the search for new classes must be continued, but it should be based upon solid factual data admitting of no ambiguous interpretation. For this reason we should at present retain Belova's attribution of the coins in question (to the time of Justinian I).

Two classes of coins fall to the time of Justinian I: those with a figure of a warrior, and those with a monogram incorporating the name of the town. The coins with the warrior type should be considered the earlier; like the issues of the time of Zeno which precede them, they lack the features of specifically civic coins. They are represented by three varieties distinguished as to reverse type: 1) the emperor standing, in military dress, holding a long cross in his right hand and in the left an orb; on one of the variants the inscription is VICTORIA AVGGGE, but on the majority of the variants of this variety it is as on the coins of the remaining varieties—VICTOR (Plate XXII, 310, 311); 2) the same, but he rests his left hand upon his shield (Plate XXII, 312); 3) the same, the head turned right; he holds a standard (labarum) in his right hand, the left rests on the shield (Plate XXII, 313). Sokolova describes a variant of the coins of the third variety, on the reverse of which the emperor holds an orb in his left hand, but we have not succeeded in finding such a coin either in museum collections or in private ones. On the obverse of all three varieties a bust of the emperor is represented facing right, with a diadem on his head and the inscription in the fullest unmutilated form—DN IVSTINIANVS PF AVG.

As for the chronological sequence of the varieties, only the first can be the earliest; the remaining ones are distinguished by smaller coin size and for that reason they are most likely later. The general dating of each of the varieties is obscure, as is that of the issue as a whole; it may be set conjecturally in the first half of the reign.

The second issue of Justinian is represented by coins having a bust of the emperor on the obverse as on the preceding coins, and the inscription DN IVSTINIANVS PP AVG (sometimes also in more abbreviated form); on the reverse the monogram (k), incorporating the name of the town—ΧΕΡϹΩΝΟϹ or ΠΟΛΙϹ ΧΕΡϹΩΝΟϹ (Plate XXII, 314). All the coins are splendidly executed and exhibit no features of degradation of the types, although errors are indeed encountered in the inscriptions. Dating them to the second half of Justinian's reign is also conjectural.

Wroth called the coinage of Cherson in Justinian's time (having in view only the coins with the monogram) "rare and inconsiderable," conceding that they might be supplemented with other coins (of the class: Wroth, I, p. XVIII; plate X, 14-61). Such coins have been found during excavations at the town, but not very frequently, and for this reason the question of their belonging to Cherson remains open.

The next coins of Cherson in point of time are represented by three different series. The first is made up of coins having on the obverse a type of two standing figures and the inscription ΧΕΡϹΩΝΟϹ, on the reverse a single figure and a mark of value—M (40 nummia) on the follis and K (20 nummia) on the half-follis (Plate XXII, 315, 316).

The coins of the second series have the same types, but the name of the town is written with an omicron (ΧΕΡϹΟΝΟϹ), and the marks for the denomination are respectively H (8) and Δ (4), i.e. 8 and 4 pentanummia (Plate XXII, 317-319). On coins of the third series the same types and denomination marks appear as on the second series, but the inscriptions are different—DN MAVRIC PP AVG (Plate XXII, 320, 321).

Sabatier also described a coin with the denomination mark M and the inscription DN MAV PP AV (Sabatier, I, plate XXVI, 21), but I. I. Tolstoi doubted its existence (Tolstoi, issue No. V, p. 577). Such coins are not represented in the collections of the Chersonesus and other museums, so that the question remains open for the present.

Investigators have unanimously assigned all three series to the reign of the emperor Mauricius Tiberius (582-602) on the basis of the legend on the coins of the third series. The images of the two figures on the obverse and the single one on the reverse have been regarded as those of the emperor, his wife Constantina, and their son Theodosius, who was born in A.D. 584 and who received the title of Augustus in 589. Oreshnikov was unacquainted with the finding of coins with the numeral K at Cherson, and of coins with the titulature of the emperor, for which reason he did not recognize them as having been struck at Cherson (Oreshnikov, 1905, p. 4). Tolstoi numbers the coins of all the series among the issues of Mauricius Tiberius (Tolstoi, issue No. V, plate 40; 41).

What is the sequence as among these series? One should unquestionably regard as the first the series with the numerals M and K, as on empire-wide coins. The next is most likely the series with the numerals H and Δ and the name of the town, indicating successorship of the type; the concluding one would be the series with the emperor's titulature. Coins of Heraclius also retain the titulature of the emperor. This sort of sequence appears the most logical from the standpoint of the evolution of the coin type. Can one date all three series to the time of Mauricius Tiberius without qualification? We think one must answer this question in the negative.

Two circumstances constitute obstacles to dating the three series to the time of Mauricius Tiberius. In the first place, if the striking of the coins commenced from the moment when Theodosius was named Augustus, i.e. in 590, all three series with differing types would have had to be issued within limits between 590-602, which is unlikely. The smaller denomination of the second series is known in such a large number of variants, sharply distinguished one from another in style, that to wedge their issuance into a few years does not appear possible. In the second place, if we assign the coins described to Mauricius we expose their failure to correspond with empire-wide coins, which have on the obverse a portrait of Mauricius alone. One cannot speak of a sort of time-lag or retardation on the part of the Cherson mint in following Constantinople models, because Cherson will scarcely have been independent in minting in general and in the selection of coin types in particular.

Identifiying the three figures with Mauricius, Constantina, and Theodosius is also unconvincing. Koehne, for example, advanced well-founded objections against that attribution of the reverse figure (Theodosius's youth, he having been no more than six years old when proclaimed Augustus, whereas on the coins, as he sees it, there is re·resented an adult and bearded male; the presence in the figure's hand of a cross, not characteristic for members of the imperial family), and although his own explanation does not appear acceptable (Koehne, 1848, p. 167), the doubts nevertheless remain.

We consider that the prototype for the Cherson coins of the first series should be sought among the coins of Justin II (565-578) which have on the obverse the type of the imperial couple (Wroth, I, plate XI-XIII). It is under just this emperor that such a type, borrowed by all the mints of the empire, first appears. To our mind the Cherson series should also be dated to the time of Justin II.

The question as to who is represented by the figure on the reverse is rather complicated to resolve. The difficulty does not, however, lie in its being impossible to find a real person to whom it might correspond. Such a person might, in particular, be Tiberius, the future emperor, who was proclaimed Caesar in December 574 and who reigned as co-regent jointly with Sofia, the wife of Justin II, during the last four years of the life of Justin who was mentally ill (Wroth, I, p. XIX). But the presence of an identical type on coins of other series forces one to think that it most likely represents some symbolic figure or else a saint. One cannot fail to note that a cross of this shape is represented in the hand of Victory on the gold coins of this time.

Other and more numerous coins come in to take the places of these rare ones. They display a substantial difference in typology: a new designation of denominations—H and Δ instead of M and K; the name of the town is written with omicron (ΧΕΡϹΟΝΟϹ ; Plate XXII, 317-319). The exchanging of denomination indicators common to almost all the towns of the empire for others affords evidence that the pentanummion lies at the basis of the local monetary account. One cannot say that the currency of Cherson was not at some earlier time acquainted with any monetary unit smaller than the pentanummion: such small coins of the Vth—VIth centuries are constantly encountered among other coin finds on the town's territory. The most likely explanation is that from the time of Justinian I onward Cherson practiced the issuance of a unit equivalent to the pentanummion, something which had an influence on the way the local monetary account took shape.

As we have already said, the striking of coins of the second series was decidedly abundant, exhibiting a large number of variants. During its course the weight and size of the coin-flans diminish perceptibly. One may suppose that the striking of coins of this class, commenced under Justin II, continued under Tiberius II Constantine as well (578-582), but it does not appear possible to select out the coins that were struck in his reign.

It is only the third series that can be recognized as unquestionably belonging to the time of Mauricius Tiberius. It retains the typology of the coins of the second series, but the titulature of the emperor appears on the obverse instead of the name of the town (Plate XXII, 320, 321). Oreshnikov considered its belonging to the Cherson mint doubtful for two reasons: the absence of established finds of such coins on the territory of the town, and the possibility of attribution to Thessalonica, where such marks of value were also used (Oreshnikov, 1905, p. 4). Neither objection, however, can be of decisive significance. In the first place, find-sites are not always identical with mintage locations; in the second place, at Thessalonica the analogous mark (H) corresponded to a different denomination—not the follis, but 8 nummia, i.e. the fifth part of the follis. Koehne in his day (Koehne, 1848, p. 157) had already written about the difference between the denominations of the coins of Cherson and of Thessalonica.

In our view one must date the coins to the entire period of the reign of Mauricius Tiberius, i.e. 582-602), because it would be risky to construct a dating on the basis of recognizing the reverse figure as being an image of Theodosius, the son of Mauricius Tiberius.

We know of no Cherson coins for the time of the emperor Phocas (602-610), but under Heraclius (610-641) one again notes active functioning on the part of the local mint. Under him there were issued copper coins at a value of 8 pentanummia, having on the obverse a type of Heraclius and his older son by his first wife Eudocia, Heraclius Constantine who was born in 612, and the legend DD NN HER ET HERACON, on the reverse the image of still another standing figure, in whom people usually see Martina the second wife of Heraclius, and the mark of the denomination—H (Plate XXIII, 322).

Oreshnikov was cautious about considering them to be of Cherson, advancing the same reservations as regarding the preceding series of coins, and differing in this from other investigators (Murzakievich, p. 316; Tolstoi, issue No. V, 700; Bellinger, I, p. 38). One must indeed remark that such coins as this have as yet not once been encountered in excavations at the town. The titulature of the emperor shows the successorship of the coins of this series to those of the preceding one. Apparently the town was somewhat limited as to its rights under Mauricius Tiberius and Heraclius, something which was expressed in the disappearance of the town name. The denomination numeral—H—is the sole evidence, though a sufficiently weighty one, for their Cherson origin, reflecting the count by pentanummia customary for Cherson. The dating of this issue is based on comparison with the mintage of the Constantinople mint, where coins with the figures of the three persons referred to were issued from the 6th to the 19th year of Heraclius's reign, i.e. from A.D. 615/6 to 628/9 (Wroth, I, 206-209). Dating of the Cherson coins to A.D. 615-629 is also accepted by Grierson (Bellinger, I, p. 38).

After the reign of Heraclius the Cherson mint ceased operating for a long time. It has been held that it resumed work only in the days of the joint rule of Michael III and Basil (866-867). But among the cast coins of Cherson, both those known long since and those published only recently, there are some issues which must be assigned to an earlier period, in any case prior to the organization of the <u>theme</u>. They can be divided into two groups. The first consists of two issues imitating early types of coins of Cherson mintage but manufactured by casting.

The first issue copies the type of the Cherson half-folles of the end of the VIth century and the beginning of the VIIth (Plate XXIII, 323, 324). These coins have been known for a long time (Oreshnikov, 1911, plate V; Belova, 1941a, pl 328), and they have been dated to the time of Mauricius Tiberius. There has already been discussion of the unacceptable nature of this dating (Anokhin, 1968, p. 103), but the date we suggested earlier—the second half of the VIIth century—does not now seem convincing. The reform of Heraclius, which will be dealt with below, had the purpose of legitimizing the circulation at Cherson of a large quantity of alien coins, and for that reason a need for native issues will scarcely have been felt sharply enough in the second half of the VIIth century. At the beginning of the VIIIth century the town was destroyed by Justinian II, so that the issue of coins is not likely to have been among the town's first priorities for some time after that. In addition to this, the similarity of technique of manufacture in the case of these coins and those of the period when the <u>theme</u> was being organized forces one to put these two sets closer together in point of time. Unfortunately our lack of sealed complexes containing such coins prevents us from determining their date more exactly than as being the second half of the VIIIth century. But this dating, too, is arbitrary. One must point out that a large number of variants are known, distinguished one from another as regards the moulds in which they have been cast and also as regards size and weight, something which testifies to some duration of their issue. A special class among them consists of an unpublished coin in the State Hermitage collection (Plate XXIII, 325) having the symbol B on the obverse to the right of the figure. Unfortunately the significance of this letter is not to be explained satisfactorily.

The second issue consists of a unique and likewise not yet published specimen preserved at the Chersonesus Museum. This coin repeats the type of the early pentanummia of Justinian I (Plate XXIII, 326). It was brought to light among the undocumented finds from the pre-revolutionary Cherson excavations, so that its chronological placement is conjectural. It is plain that it was issued later than its prototypes, but it is hard to say by how much. Speculatively this coin is dated in the same way as the preceding ones, to the second half of the VIIIth century.

A second group consists of the coins from a hoard brought to light at Chersonesus in 1964 and published by Sokolova. The hoard of 45 whole specimens and two fragments consisted of coins of two sorts: with the letter Π on the obverse and reverse sides, and with the letters Π - Χ . The author notes the manufacturing technique for the coins, sets apart coins cast in the same mould, and indicates the rapid disintegration of the mould, in which, to her mind, there could be made no more than three to four castings (Sokolova, 1971b, p. 21).

The coins of the hoard, to use Sokolova'a words, illustrate the device of using coins as patterns for pressing types into soft (clay) moulds, which were then fired. This technical peculiarity, which in the author's opinion is not characteristic of the currency of Cherson at the time of Basil I (867-886) and the subsequent period, and also the absence from the hoard of coins with the initials MB, which she continues to regard as pertaining to the joint reign of Michael III and Basil I (866-867), force the investigator to date the hoard to A.D. 840-867. The letters Π - Χ she regards as a device for πόλις χερσῶνος, and she considers that it "could have been introduced only soon after the organization of the theme ," justifying this by saying that with the organization of the theme the town preserves certain features of self-government, for example the institution of archons (Sokolova, 1971b, p. 22).

Sokolova's arguments merit serious attention and will be examined later. But it remains unclear why, as she holds, the inscription πόλις χερσῶνος could appear only after the formation of the theme, and likewise why coins should have that inscription. For the theme was plainly created as a counterpoise to an increasing tendency of the civic authorities toward autonomy, in order to keep the town under the emperor's sway; and one evidence of Cherson's striving toward independence in the period prior to the organisation of the theme might in fact be the issuance of civic coin of its own.

The coins of the 1964 hoard with the letters П-X have nothing in common with the already known coins of the same class, to say nothing of the coins with the letters П-П . Whereas one might conceivably recognize the former as civic coin accompanying the issue of coins in the name of Theophilus, the latter find no analogy in even one of the classes issued after the organization of the theme, and for that reason they ought to be set before that date, i.e. before 834. The absence from the hoard of any of the coins we already know forces one to date it to a time before 834, and both the classes of coins represented in it fall to the very end of the VIIIth century or the first third of the IXth. Naturally one must also take into account the possibility Sokolova wrote about, to the effect that "they record a moment at which work was being done on the creation of a model, and on seeking of a type, for new coins of Cherson" (Sokolova, 1971b, p. 21).

2. The Structure of the Monetary Circulation Under Heraclius (610-641)

On Cherson folles of the time of Justin II and Heraclius one frequently encounters a countermark in the form of a monogram which is usually deciphered as the beginning of the name Heraclius (see Plate XXXII, a). The countermarking of coins at Cherson should be placed in conjunction with the mass overstriking of coins under the emperor Heraclius by all the mints that operated in his day—Constantinople, Thessalonica, Nicomedia, Cyzicus, Isauria, Constantia in Cyprus, and Antioch—with the exceptions of Alexandria, Rome, and Ravenna.

The fact that the countermark belongs to Cherson is determined through its being encountered preponderantly on coins of that town. But quite recently Golenko subjected this seemingly obvious fact to question (Golenko, p. 5-12). He assembled the designs of the countermarks on the various coins and brought to light the fact that they have diverse configurations, specifically that of a B, that of a monogram for Heraclius, and in a third case one apparently containing a letter kappa as an element but not containing a rho (Golenko, p. 6, 8). Taking as his point of departure the synchrony of the countermarks, Golenko sees a single meaning for them all, considering it probable that they convey a single symbol, a beta. But inasmuch as one of the countermarks, in the form of a beta, found on the Constantinople follis of Tiberius III Apsimarus (698-705) is the sole instance of its appearing on a coin that does not pertain to Cherson, this investigator considers it possible to date all the other countermarks, too, to the turn of the VIIth-VIIIth centuries. In examining possible variations on the decipherment of the letter B, Golenko comes to the conclusion that this is the initial for the name of the Bosporus, B B[ОСПОРО С]. Finds of such countermarked coins at Kerch and the absence of documented finds at Cherson enable one, in his opinion, to assert that the countermark pertains not to Cherson but to the Bosporus (Golenko, p. 9). Despite the externally convincing nature of this deduction, we cannot fall in with it.

The first thing to thrust itself upon one is the great gap in time between the Cherson folles, the very latest of which fall to the reign of Heraclius, and the Constantinople follis of Tiberius III Apsimarus. In the second place, it is quite apparent that the countermark on this last is, to judge by the photograph, distinctly different from all the rest—it does indeed remind one of a letter B (provided that the lower part of the countermark has not been damaged), whereas all the others represent nothing other than a monogram for the name Heraclius, more or less well preserved. The mass character of the countermarks on the Cherson coins and the unique nature of the countermark on the coin of Tiberius III, taken together with its being of a different design, prevent one from terming them identical and force one to think of a different significance and a different date of imposition.

Golenko's comment on the absence of finds of the countermarked coins at Chersonesus is decidedly significant, but to our mind it is not decisive for a deduction to the effect that the countermarking operation was carried out in the Bosporus and for the Bosporus, inasmuch as we have no assurance that the numerous countermarked coins in national and private collections do not come from Cherson. In addition, the undisputed belonging to Cherson of still another countermark of this same period confirms the old identification and obliges us to refrain from agreeing with Golenko's view.

The new type of countermark, in the form of a chrism, was found by the author on coins preserved in the Chersonesus Museum collection. This countermark of small size (see Plate XXXII, b) was imposed very carelessly indeed, so that it is frequently difficult to make it out. We did nevertheless succeed in revealing more than 30 different coins with such countermarks in the Chersonesus Museum collection (see table).

As one sees, the basic mass of the coins consists of Roman ones of the IVth-Vth centuries. In this list the thing most vital for us is the presence of a Cherson pentanummion of Justinian I and half-folles of Justin II (or Mauricius Tiberius, according to the generally accepted dating). The latter fall in the same series with folles bearing a countermark of a monogram for the name Heraclius, which enables one to regard the two countermarks as synchronous. In the present case we can come close to a resolution of the matter of their significance. The two countermarks, in accordance with the generally accepted view regarding the nature of countermarks in general, should be regarded primarily as official confirmation by the government of the circulation of preceding issues of coins. But this was apparently not the only purpose of the operation. It is not difficult to note that different countermarks were placed on coins of differing weights and sizes. Large ones got the countermark in the name of Heraclius, small ones (late Roman, early Byzantine Cherson ones of Justinian I, and even probably Chersonesus coins of the eleutheria) were countermarked with the symbol of the chrism. Accordingly what may be involved here is that by imposing the countermark the coins were divided into two denominations.

It would seem that the coins with the countermark of the name of Heraclius (folles) retained their denomination; no other types of coins with such a stamp have thus far been found. In that event, what denomination did the symbol of the chrism designate? The ones enumerated in the list of coins are of decidedly variegated sorts—they include both pentanummia and half-folles. The following observation helps to decide the question: The symbol of the chrism is encountered as an obverse type on a range of coins of the early Byzantine empire. Best known are coins of the Constantinople mint

Number	Description of Coin	Inventory Number
1	Rome, IVth century	Field No. 11, 086, 1968 excavations
2,3	Theodosius (379-395)?	No. 5017; undocumented
4	Arcadius (395-408)	Undocumented
5-10	Leo I (457-474)	No. 750/3; 2431; 2500/3; 3756; from 1969 hoard; undocumented
11	Verina	No. 5538
12-27	IVth-Vth centuries	No. 4272; 9658; field No. 337, 1970 excavations; from 1969 hoard (two); undocumented (eleven)
28	Chersonesus? Dupondius of end of IInd century A.D.?	No. 1008
29	Cherson. Pentanummion of Justinian I (527-565)	Undocumented
30-31	Cherson. Half-follis of Justinian II (565-578)	No. 1248; undocumented

under Justin I (Wroth, I, plate III, 10). The numeral Є accompanying the chrism indicates that the denomination is a pentanummion. The coins with the chrism (and the numeral Є) of the Constantinople mintage of Mauricius Tiberius (Wroth, I, plate XVII, 14-15) are such pentanummia. An instance of using the chrism as a reverse type is also encountered on coins of Heraclius struck by the Ravenna mint (Wroth, I, plate XXX, 11); these too can perhaps be defined as pentanummia. Thus we may with full justification assert that the symbol of the chrism coincides with a specific denomination, the pentanummion, and that accordingly the coins of Cherson countermarked with that symbol ought also to be considered pentanummia.

But an operation of countermarking coins of various denominations with different symbols would not of itself have had much sense if the coins in circulation had been of a single sort. Yet to judge by the 1969 hoard from the Chersonesus district (unpublished) and the series of coins with the chrism countermark (see table), in the VIIth century the monetary circulation of Cherson consisted of an exceedingly heterogeneous mass of coins from various periods. Thus in the composition of the 1969 hoard there were, over and above the countermarked coins that have been listed, late Roman coins of Flacilla, wife of Theodosius I (379-395); Gratian (375-383); Theodosius II (408-450); Zeno (474-491); a dekanummion of Justinian I (527-565); staters of the Bosporus for the years 590, 592, and 623, plus ones with erased dates; and also a Roman provincial coin in poor state of preservation.

Plainly such a motley mass of coins could not satisfactorily perform its intended function as a circulation medium, a means of payment, a measure of value, etc., inasmuch as it was constantly in need of being recalculated in a new scale of monetary units. The countermarking operation that was carried out was, in our view, nothing other than a monetary reform sui generis, as a result of which every sort of coin circulating at Cherson was made equivalent to the smallest of the denominations which had arisen after Anastasius—the pentanummion. With that as our basis we can reach the following conclusions.

In the late ancient and early Byzantine period the money market at Cherson did not eliminate earlier issues from circulation. Any coin retained buying power no matter when it may have been struck. The constant replenishment of the money mass with new issues, despite the absence of a local coinage, ensured saturation of the market with a quantity sufficient to maintain monetary circulation at the previous level or at one even higher. Consequently there are no grounds for claims that trading and monetary exchanges petered out or fell off at Cherson in the IVth-VIIth centuries. What is more, the unification of the coins in the first half of the VIIth century was unquestionably dictated by requirements for intensification of monetary circulation which had slowed down through the inadequacy of the circulating medium (in view of insufficient entry into the market of local and imported coin). The deficit was covered by earlier emissions which will scarcely have had a firm, governmentally established rate of exchange vis-a-vis the system of denominations currently in effect.

3. Historical Sketch

Toward the middle of the Vth century, when the tidal wave of miseries associated with the onslaught of the Huns had begun to recede, the situation of Cherson was reasonably stable. The status as a free city, specific trading privileges, freedom from imposts for the citizens and vessels of Cherson, the annual grant of a thousand rations to the soldiers of the local garrison, the concern of the emperors for the fortunes of the town as one of the main strongholds in the Tauris, and finally to a certain extent the remoteness of Cherson from the empire created favorable conditions for preservation of its political independence and an improvement of its economic level.

During the period of the emperor Zeno (474-481) the town made use of imported coin. Thus during excavations at the town more than 3,500 coins of the IVth and Vth centuries have been found (Gilevich, 1968, p. 56), which exceeds by a great deal the volume of Chersonesus's own coinage in the Ist-IIIrd centuries. So it would be radically wrong to speak of any decline in trading and monetary exchange during this period merely on the basis of the non-existence of a local coinage.

The first Cherson coins (Zeno and Justinian I) wholly preserved the appearance of empire-wide ones, with the exception of the fact that the place of mintage was not indicated upon them. Under Justinian, however, the town issues a class of polis coins, differing from all the other coins of this emperor, which has a monogram for the name of the town. The importance of this fact must nevertheless not be overemphasized. During subsequent reigns the typology of the coins gradually loses its vividly expressed polis character. One should note the existence at Cherson of a special monetary account—the basic unit among the copper coins was the pentanummion, one-eighth of a follis.

At the beginning of the VIth century Byzantium enacts a range of measures designed to re-establish its sway in the Crimea. According to a notice of Procopius, Cherson was surrounded by Huns and Alt-tsyagirs. The Huns were fully masters of the situation in the Bosporus, but under Justinian I Byzantine authority was reinforced there as well as elsewhere. During the time of Justinian I great construction is carried on everywhere in the Crimea—new fortifications are erected and the defensive structures of the old towns are restored.

We know that under Justin II (565-578) there was a ducas at Cherson—a military commander under whose charge the frontier forces were marshalled. Under the same emperor Cherson and the Bosporus were freed from the duty of furnishing ships (A.D. 575). All this, taken together, recalls to mind the beneficient policy of Diocletian and Constantine the Great. These measures evidently played a part to some extent during the next onslaught of the barbarians—that of the Turks. In A.D. 575 the Turks seized the Bosporus, and seven years later they threatened Cherson but could not gain possession of it. In 589, however, a peace was concluded with them and relative calm once more made its appearance in the Crimea. Stratilarius Eupaterius, ducas of Cherson, set up a palace in the Bosporus in 590.

Data on Cherson in the VIIth-VIIIth centuries are so fragmentary that it is a complicated matter to formulate any distinct idea of the history of the town during this period. Some light might have been thrown on the matter by coins, but their production ceases under Heraclius (610-641). During the reign of Heraclius measures were enacted at Cherson to set monetary circulation in order; mass countermarking of the coins in use was carried out. Countermarks of two classes are known—a monogram of the name Heraclius, and a chrism. The first is encountered only on large coins having a value of 40 nummia, the other on Cherson coins of 5 nummia, and likewise—something which is very important—on Roman coins of the IVth-Vth centuries. The aim of the reform consisted in placing on a uniform basis all the heterogeneous classes of coins that had become current in the town after the cessation of its own coinage, converting them into a denomination of 5 nummia. Thus by conferring upon these coins the status of a legitimate monetary unit the town to a certain extent satisfied its requirements for coinage. The actual reform was perhaps carried out because of the termination of the issuance of local coin, the need for which now became less acute.

The reform ensured stability of monetary circulation over a prolonged interval of time, and making coins of early issues equivalent to pentanummia created great opportunities for replenishing the monetary mass. Under Heraclius the Heracleia mint ceased operations for a long time. It is not out of the question that at a certain stage a part was played by events at the beginning of the VIIIth century, when the town became the victim of a cruel revenge on the part of Justinian II and was subjected to devastation. With this exception, any serious alterations in the economic position of Cherson will scarcely have come about, and the circumstance of termination of the local mintage cannot be used as an argument in favor of a thesis claiming decline in the town's economy (Yakobson, 1959, p. 35). The political position of the town also remained in all likelihood what it had been earlier. True, the presence in the town of a representative of the Khazars—the Tundun—affords seeming evidence of dependence, of subordination of the town to the Khazars (Artamonov, p. 197), but this is unlikely. The fact that even in the VIIIth century and the beginning of the IXth Cherson continues to serve as a place of exile for fallen figures of the empire shows that it remained subject to Byzantium. Thus in A.D. 655 Pope Martin was exiled to Cherson; in 685, the deposed emperor Justinian II, then his rival Vardanus; in 775, the brothers of the emperor Leo VI the Khazar, who had taken part in a plot against him, along with some other figures.

From the communications of Constantine Porphyrogenitus and other sources we know that the town preserved self-government. At its head was the protopolitus, "first over the city," the institution of which goes back to the ancient period. Unfortunately information on the town is of a fragmentary nature, One may hope that archeological investigation of Cherson will provide new materials that may throw light on the history of this period, which has quite deservedly received the appellation of "dark ages" in the literature.

CHAPTER II

THE THEME PERIOD
(A.D. 834—Beginning of the Twelfth Century)

The occasion for the establishment of a theme at Cherson was afforded by the events associated by the Byzantines' erection of the fortress of Sarkel at the request of the Khazars. The spatharokandidatos Petronas Kamatiros, brother of the emperor's wife, was sent out via Cherson in 834 to construct the fortress. After he had accomplished his principal mission and upon having become acquainted with the state of affairs at Cherson he counselled Theophilus to appoint a strategos at Cherson and to place no trust in the Cherson elite. Theophilus acceded to this suggestion and named Petronas as strategos. In this way the theme of the Climates was created—a military and administrative district with its center at Cherson. The town, however, preserved certain features of self-government—it is administered by archons, and one may even speak with more or less assurance of retention of the institution of the "preeminent" or proteuousoi (Yakobson, 1950, pp. 19, 20).

Over a prolonged stretch of time the town was regularly confirmed by the emperors in the right to issue coins. The Cherson coins of the theme period are appreciably distinguished from the output of the other mints of the empire through technique of manufacture, external appearance, and likewise a range of other peculiarities. In a majority of cases attribution of the coins gives rise to no doubts, inasmuch as they are furnished with the first one or two letters of the emperor's (or emperors') name or with his monogram.

Before we pass on to examination of the chronology of the coin issues, we should pause to consider the technique of manufacture of the coins, which is linked with problems in dating them.

1. The Technique of Manufacturing the Coins

Commencing perhaps as early as the second half of the VIIIth century the main method for producing coins becomes that of casting. Only a few classes of civic coins of the time of Michael III (?) were made by striking. There were probably several reasons for the shift to casting: a drop in the range of technological facilities available to the Cherson moneyers, the comparative simplicity of casting, speeding of production through elimination of die-cutting operations and shortening of the actual process of mintage. Casting had even before this constituted an indispensable first stage in the process of making coins: it was by casting that the blank disks going on to the strikers were manufactured. But now the whole process was comprised in this first stage.

The moulds for casting the coins were unquestionably of clay. At one time there was another view, to the effect that the material for the moulds consisted of talc (Kadeyev, p. 48), but this was overthrown through well-founded critical analysis (Sokolova, 1968, p.88). Indeed, a number of defects in the types on the coins, and in particular the use of a few moulds with defective design, slippage of images represented, and also other cases, convince one that the moulds were made of a soft material (clay), and that the types were impressed into them with stamps, after which they were fired and were put to work.

Such moulds could not have a long working life. Sokolova holds that moulds used for manufacture of the coins in the 1964 hoard could stand up to only three to four pours (Sokolova, 1971b, p. 21). It is true that what was involved here was poorly fired moulds or even ones not fired at all, but even a well-fired mould would scarcely last out more than a couple of dozen pours. Even so, the majority of coins of a single sort produce the impression of having been manufactured in the same mould, something which points toward mass production of moulds, the designs in these being impressed by a single pair of stamps. One could place approximately 70-80 impressions on each mould, since on account of the rapidity with which the metal cooled one would not manage to fill any larger number of recesses (Kościuszko, p, 169).

It is curious to note that this sort of mass production of moulds nowhere comes to light, despite the scope of archeological investigations at Chersonesus. Apparently the moulds were strictly accounted for and were destroyed after wearing out; this is just what happens with dies for striking coins, finds of these in ancient townsites being exceptionaly rare.

It was necessary to key precisely to each other the faces of several dozens of obverse and reverse moulds for coins that had been pressed into two moulds. Coins with obverse and reverse faces that are off-center to each other are quite rarely encountered. Accuracy was apparently achieved by prior measuring off of the face-positions on the blanks for two clay moulds.

The stamps were most likely made of clay or of soft metal (lead). The use of coins of earlier issues as stamps is of particular interest. Coins made in this way are distinguished through somewhat smaller dimensions by reason of shrinkage of the clay mould during drying and firing, but they preserve all the features of the design. Sokolova drew attention to this method in her study of the coins in the 1964 hoard. We may note that in accordance with our own observations the coins in question do not exhibit signs of reduction in size and that in this instance there can be involved only a gradual and comparatively rapid wearing away of one and the same mould. Sokolova is also not right in saying that the use of coins as stamps is not characteristic for the currency of Cherson commencing with the days of Basil I (Sokolova, 1971b, p. 16). It is just the reigns following thereafter that provide us with many convincing examples of the use of coins as stamps. It is interesting to observe that this practice is followed not only for reigns of prolonged duration, such as for example that of Leo VI (886-912) or Constantine Porphyrogenitus (913-959), but also for relatively short ones: among the coins of John Zimisces (969-976) one can distinguish with confidence at least three such issues.

It is not difficult to see that the use of coins as stamps offers exceedingly rich opportunities for the study of the process of coin production at Cherson under each of the emperors and enables us to work out narrower dating limits for issues within the confines of each reign. But first of all we must determine the causes occasioning the rise of this sort of method of making moulds. In our view two different approaches are possible, based upon recognition of the coins made through the use of other coins as mould stamps (we shall call these "secondary issues") as being lawful or governmental, or alternatively as private or unlawful.

If these issues were official emissions, technological or political considerations may have operated. Among the technological ones we may cite an attempt to simplify and speed up the manufacture of moulds, thereby saving time necessary for the manufacture of stamps. It is also possible that stamps wore out quickly when there was a large volume of production, and that instead of making new ones they used coins of preceding issues for this purpose. It is possible that with time some further explanations will also turn up in connection with the technique of coin manufacture.

The appearance of "secondary" issues may also depend on causes of another nature. There is no doubt that starting at least with the moment of the establishment of the theme the civic coinage depended upon the emperor, who after ascending the throne granted permission for the issuance of coins or cancelled it. The volume, the period of production, the sorts of coins, and other basic data of emission were determined, as it would appear, by someone among the representatives of the Byzantine administration at Cherson. Authority to check upon the issuance of coins most likely also fell to him. One may suppose that stamps or even the actual moulds were under a system of strict accountability. This is evidenced by the circumstance that, despite the enormous volume of the coin output of Cherson, which likewise presupposes a great quantity of casting moulds (it is calculated that each of these might serve for approximately a score of pours), not one such mould or even a single fragment of one has been found during excavation of the town, And if the town authorities and moneyers found that the volume which they had prescribed for an issue was too small, they might proceed to expand the issue on their own, using coins of the first, official, issue as stamps for this purpose.

The explanations presented as regards the possible causes of the appearance of "secondary" issues stem from the theory that these were produced at the Cherson mint and ought thus to be regarded as governmental emissions. But one may take it that all or the greater part of the "secondary" issues were the unlawful production of local artizans. The extreme ease of manufacturing the coins might very well draw the attention of "interested" parties. In order to ensure exactitude of copying they made use of coins in circulation, with the result that their product, actually their forgery, is to be recognized through its reduced dimensions.

Both hypotheses regarding the origin of the "secondary" issues seem to be equally acceptable, because there has thus far been no success in finding decisive proofs in favor of one or the other. One may hope that further study of the cast coins of Cherson will allow us to come closer to a solution of this important question.

2. The Chronology of the Coin Issues.

Until recently the earliest coins of Cherson issued after the organization of the *theme* were considered to be coins with the letters MB, assigned by all numismatists to the period of the joint reign of Michael III and Basil I, i.e. to A.D. 866-867.

In a brief survey of the currency of medieval Cherson we assigned to the time of Theophilus one class of Cherson cast coins that had been unattributed (Anokhin, 1968, p. 104). Since that time new material has appeared which permits us to fill in with adequate assurance the interval of time falling between the organization of the *theme* and the commencement of the issuance of coins.

The coins of Theophilus have on the obverse the letters DN/TH, which in our opinion are to be deciphered as an abbreviation of the title and name of the emperor (DN THEOFILVS), and on the reverse Π°Λ , i.e. πόλις χερσῶνος. A coin of this class was first published by L. N. Belova (Belova, 1941a, No. 8). Sokolova considers our deciphering of the inscription to be hypothetical on account of the Latin form of the name of Theophilus (Sokolova, 1971b, pp. 21-22). We have earlier offered an explanation of this state of affairs, so there is no need to repeat it here. Despite all misgivings, both the actual coins (several of them are known by now) and the Latin language of the inscriptions are unquestionable realities. One should date these coins to the interval of time between the establishment of the *theme* and the end of the reign of Theophilus, i.e. between A.D. 834 and 842.

Coins of Cherson for the time of Michael III are of great interest to numismatists and historians. Only a few years ago the issuance of coins under him was open to question, but by now we are acquainted with a large quantity of coins of various classes which can be dated with conviction to his reign.

The largest group of coins, with the letters MB on the obverse and ΠX on the reverse, has ordinarily been assigned to the brief joint reign of Michael III and Basil I. Doubts are aroused by the exceptionally abundant character of the issue. According to A. M. Gilevich's calculations, 249 specimens would have fallen to the one year of the reign (Gilevich, 1974, p. 93). Such intensiveness did not occur at any other time. It is also strange that the mintage should have commenced only when Michael III and Basil I came to reign jointly. Of course we do not know so much about Michael III's monetary policy with respect to Cherson, but so decisive a shift in it at the end of the reign still looks unexpected to say the least.

The discovery of coins of Theophilus also brings into question the earlier attribution of the coins with the letters MB, since granting of the right of issue to the town by Theophilus, and withdrawal of this right by Michael III, reversed only a year before his demise (by violence, it is true), have to be explained by some sort of exceptional events. Assigning the coins with the letters MB to the sole reign of Michael III allows one to resolve satisfactorily all the problems associated with their abundance. The coins of Theophilus, those of Michael III, and those of the first issues of the sole reign of Basil I relate to a single typological order. They have a reverse in common, and they also have approximately uniform diameters and weights.

The only matter requiring explanation is the presence of the supplementary letter B after the initial for the name of Michael III. We suggest that it be considered the initial for the title βασιλεὺς. Koehne in his day had already examined the possibility of such a decipherment, and he had rejected it on the ground that "this title is not met with alongside the name on a single one of the subsequent Cherson copper coins" (Koehne, 1848, p. 184). Sokolova upholds Koehne's opinion and considers incomprehensible "a renunciation of titles on the coins of Basil I and his successors" (Sokolova, 1971b, p. 22).

We have the following to say on this matter. In the first place, the title DN appears on the coins of Theophilus, the predecessor to Michael III, and accordingly we can understand the reason why the Cherson moneyers retained it on the coins of Michael as well. In doing so they made use of the Greek word βασιλεὺς which was more familiar to them. In the second place, one need not accord great importance to the renunciation of titulature on the coins of subsequent rulers. The numismatics of Cherson offers so many examples of changes of classes, inscriptions, and the like that an explanation for any one of these may seep away into hypotheses and unconfirmed conjecture. As for the present case, the cause consisted to our mind in the fact that the technique of casting did not permit the placement on the small disk of more than one or two letters and the abandonment of the supplementary letter indicating the title may have been dictated first and foremost by technical considerations. There may also have been some significance in the fact that the letter M was primarily comprehensible to all as a mark of value, the symbol for the follis, and on that account in this instance, in order to prevent that idea of its meaning from developing, it was supplemented by the initial letter of the title. Eschewing placement of the indication of the title may also have been evoked by a situation where at that time the population was becoming persuaded that the letter on the obverse corresponded to the initials of the emperors, and for that reason it had become superfluous to include the title.

Thus the arguments of the opponents of attribution of the coins with the letters MB to the period of the reign of Michael III do not appear convincing to us, even if we do not take into account two of his coins of a new class that have recently become known. On the obverse they have the letter M, and on the reverse a cross (Plate XXIII, 331, 332). Both coins are preserved in the cabinet of the Sebastopol collector V. N. Orekhov. (*) That both coins belong to Michael III is something that can scarcely give rise to any serious objections.

The shape of the cross differs on the two coins: a simple one (Plate XXIII, 331) and a more ornate one (Plate XXIII, 332). Each of the ends of the ornate cross finishes in a short transverse bar, and this in particular keeps one from seeing in it a letter X. This shape of cross is also found on other Cherson coins—these, however, being distinguished by a different letter on the obverse, a Π or an A (Plate XXIII, 333, 337).

(*) We express our gratitude to V. N. Orekhov for permission to make use of casts of the coins in the present study.

Coins of the Π and cross type were known to Oreshnikov, who dated them to A.D. 866-867. Yet the shape of the cross allows one to refer them also to the time of Michael III. It is curious that the coins with the letter Π on the obverse offer the same sorts of crosses on the reverse as do the coins of Michael III (Plate XXIII, 331 and 335, 332 and 334), something which testifies to parallellism of their issues.

A coin with the letter A on the obverse, formerly assigned to the time of Alexander (Oreshnikov, 1911, plate B, 13) is unquestionably contemporaneous with the coins of Michael III having the compound cross, and also with the coins bearing the letter Π . Neither in accordance with the shape of the cross, nor in accordance with its dimensions, can this coin by any means be dated to the period of the reign of Alexander (912-913).

Thus we can put on record a parallel issuance at Cherson of three sorts of coins: with the letter M, which should be understood as the initial for the name of Michael III; with the letter Π ; and with the letter A. The classes are all brought together by the uniform shape of cross.

In examining the next group of coins we bring the same picture to light. Coins with the letters MB have on the reverse no longer a cross, but the letters Π°X (Plate XXIII, 338-344), which should be understood as an abbreviation of the words πόλις χερσῶνος . Coins with the letter Π also have on the reverse not a cross, but the letter X (Plate XXIV, 345-348). And finally, one should include in the same series with these another sort of coin, with the letter A, which has also been dated earlier to the period of the reign of Alexander (Plate XXIV, 349). The letters Π°X , appearing on the reverses of these coins, strike one as a complete anachronism for the period of the reign of Alexander—such an inscription is found only on coins of Michael III and the very earliest issues of Basil I. On the later issues of Basil I and on all issues of Leo and Alexander (886-912) they are supplanted by a cross or a portrait. Accordingly this group of coins also affords evidence of a parallellism of three issues of coins—those with the letters MB, Π , and A. Both groups should be dated to the time of Michael III (842-866).

A unique coin in the collection of V. V. Pereplesnin (Plate XXIV, 350) perhaps falls to this same time. On the obverse of the coin there is a symbol which may with pronounced reservations be taken for the Greek letter mu (M). On the reverse there are the letters Π° and a cross to the right, characteristic for early coins of Basil I. One will be able to speak more concretely about this mysterious coin once a further specimen in a better state of preservation has been found.

Coins of two sorts were issued under Basil I. The early ones have on the reverse a letter B and a cross to its right, on the reverse the letter Π° (πόλις), with crosses to either side or to its right (Plate XXIV, 352-356). Some variants of these coins are known which exhibit deviations from the underlying type (Plate XXIV, 357-359). Of particular interest is a specimen published by Oreshnikov, with the letter B and a cross of the same shape as on the early coins of Michael III (Plate XXIV, 351). One perceives around the cross the traces of a circular inscription which unfortunately is illegible.

The later group of coins has a different design—on the obverse there is a letter B, on the reverse a cross. This class of coins of Basil I is represented by a large number of variants, something which was associated with the manufacture of a considerable number of stamps both for obverses and for reverses (Plate XXIV, 360-364; XXV, 365-375). As a rule the type was not changed, but varieties are found with a single dot placed within the lower loop of the letter B (Plate XXV, 376), and with two dots placed to either side of the letter (Plate XXV, 377-383). Inasmuch as the coin varieties with the dots exhibit more distinct features of degradation (the weight and diameter of the coins fall off in particular), it is precisely these which may be allocated to the concluding issues of Basil I. It is difficult to justify exact chronological boundaries for each of the groups listed, although apparently their being dated generally to the period of the reign of Basil I can give rise to no doubts. The abundance of the varieties of the coins, arising from the use of a corresponding number of new dies, show that in the days of Basil I the method of preparing moulds through the use of actual coins was either not known or was not exploited on a large scale. This practice commences to be widely resorted to only during the period of the reign of Leo and Alexander (886-912), which affords us an opportunity to establish a range of chronological groups within the limits of their reign.

The coin issues of Leo and Alexander are represented by four classes of coins: with the letters Λε on the obverse and a cross on the reverse; with the letters Λε separated by a cross on the obverse, and a portrait on the reverse; with the letters ΛA on the obverse and a cross on the reverse; and with the letters ΛA , separated by a cross, on the obverse, plus a cross on the reverse.

We had earlier believed it possible to divide the issues into two chronological groups covering the whole period of the reign of the two emperors (Anokhin, 1968, p. 107). Detailed study of the coins has made it possible to establish even more precisely the relative dating of the individual classes and variants.

Changes from the first class have been set at the basis of the chronology of the currency of the entire period. This class is represented by seven variants at different stages of reduction. The indisputable nature of the argument to the effect that these are a range of sequentially issued variants rather than of ones issued in parallel is demonstrated by the fact that coins of preceding issues are used as stamps. By superimposing upon the gradually deteriorating succession of coins with the letters Λε all the other classes we get a very sturdy framework for the coinage as a whole.

The initial issue is represented by a single coin in poor state of preservation, with the letters Λε on the obverse and a cross on the reverse (Plate XXVI, 385). Its diameter is 21 mm, which greatly exceeds the dimensions of the remaining coins. A coin of this type served as a stamp for making moulds of the second issue (Plate XXVI, 386). The diameter of the new coins now comes to 19 mm. Third-issue coins of this class have smaller diameters, around 17 mm; fresh obverse and reverse stamps were used to make them (Plate XXVI, 387, 388). To our mind simultaneous with these are coins with a new obverse type, the letters ΛA (Plate XXVI, 389), showing that they were issued in the name of the two co-rulers, the brothers Leo and Alexander. The reverse stamp is the same as for the coins with the letters ΛЄ. Coins likewise issued in the names of both brothers belong to the fourth issue. For these a new obverse stamp was prepared, but the same one continued to be used for the reverse (Plate XXVI, 390). Subsequent coins, right down to the end of the reign, were issued only in the name of Leo. Thus for coins of the fifth issue new obverse and reverse stamps were made (Plate XXVI, 391). One may regard as contemporaneous with these the coins with the portrait of Leo (Plate XXVI, 392). Coins of both varieties were used as stamps in issuing the sixth group (Plate XXVI, 393-394), which was in our opinion supplemented by coins issued in the name of Constantine VII Porphyrogenitus (Plate XXVI, 395). One should assign to a seventh and last issue coins of Leo, stamps for which were provided in the form of coins of his preceding group (Plate XXVI, 396). The framework we have presented for the coin issues of Cherson in the period of the reign of Leo and Alexander is the first stage for establishing an absolute dating of the individual classes of coins. Failure to clear up certain problems, in particular the causes of the use of coins as stamps, obliges us to limit ourselves to this first stage for the time being.

The brief sole reign of the emperor Alexander (May 912-July 913) has in all likelihood left no trace in Cherson numismatics. The coins ascribed to him actually relate to an earlier period.

The sequence of the Cherson coin issues for the period of the prolonged reign of Constantine VII Porphyrogenitus is one of the most complicated of our problems. The reason is that he had two co-rulers of the same name—Romanus I (920-944) and Romanus II (945-959), the former of these having for practical purposes kept the young Constantine out of the administration of the empire.

Two of Sokolova's monographs are devoted to study of the chronology of the coin-issues for this period. In the first she examines coins issued in the opening years of the reign of Constantine VII Porphyrogenitus and Romanus I (Sokolova, 1965, pp. 116-120). Sokolova assigns to the period of the reign of Constantine VII under the regency of his mother Zoë some rare coins with two portraits, in which she sees those of the son and the mother, and which she dates to A.D. 913-919. Sokolova assigns to the beginning of the rule of Romanus I, prior to the coronation of his sons Stephen and Constantine, i.e. to A.D. 920-924, coins having a portrait on the obverse and a monogram for the name Romanus (ł) on the reverse. And finally, she dates to the period of the coronation of Christopher (A.D. 921) coins having portraits on both sides and letters ρ-ο and Χ-ρ. In her opinion, moulds or stamps of preceding issues were used in the casting of these last—the female portrait from the coins of Constantine and Zoë, the male portrait from the coins of Romanus I (Sokolova, 1965, p. 120).

In a second study she defines more closely the dating of two groups of coins of Constantine—those with portrait and cross (Sokolova, 1968, pp. 87-89). She assigns the first group to the brief sole reign of Constantine VII Porphyrogenitus between the expulsion of Zoë and the coronation of Romanus I, i.e. to A.D. 919-920; the second she assigns to the equally brief reign of Constantine VII after the relegation of Romanus I in a monastery and prior to the coronation of Constantine's son Romanus II, i.e. to A.D. 944-945.

Sokolova's general dating of the coins with the portrait types gives rise to almost no objections, although the sequence of a few groups might be presented in another fashion. Thus the basis for the dating of all the classes of coins with portrait types should apparently be the coins with the letters $\rho - o$ and $X - \rho$, which are only to be understood as the names of Romanus I and Christopher. Dating them to A.D. 921 or to years immediately after that date will scarcely evoke doubts. Furthermore, one of the portraits is unquestionably female, something to which Sokolova has drawn attention. But we find difficult to understand and even enigmatic the demonstration which she undertakes as regards the borrowing for coins of Romanus I and Christopher of the stamp for coins of Constantine and Zoë: if one follows her dating, this stamp had already been out of use for two years, with coins in the names of Constantine VII and Romanus I having been issued in the interim. We may moreover note, so as not to have to return to the problem of the use of an old stamp, that the two portraits, although close to each other, are not identical. The enlarged illustrations Sokolova has published confirm this in sufficiently obvious fashion—on the coin of Constantine VII and Zoë (as she identifies it) the female portrait has to the right of the face three points forming a triangle with the apex upward, whereas on the coin of Romanus I and Christopher the three points form a triangle with the apex downward (Sokolova, 1965, plate I, 10).

One can accept the dating proposed by Sokolova only on condition that one concedes that Cherson was copying exactly an issue of coins at Constantinople. That is an idea which has weighed upon all investigators who have concerned themselves with the Cherson-Byzantine coins to any extent. As we see, Sokolova has not escaped from its toils either. And yet it would be mistaken to concede such a possibility. In our opinion, a considerable difference existed between the situations of the mints of the capital and of Cherson. The former would have to react sensitively to every change in the composition of the royal house, inasmuch as one of the principle meanings a coin had was that of a political nature, and this was a meaning no one could afford to spurn under the stormy circumstances of life in the capital. The situation of the Cherson mint, however, was different. Every change on the throne might bring in its train an alteration in the policy of the new ruler toward Cherson, and on that account in each such instance they apparently awaited some sort of special directives concerned with the activity of the mint, which certainly will not have operated without supervision. That which was obligatory for Constantinople might not always have been extended to Cherson. Of course it is indispensable to use the data for the Constantinople mint in studying the currency of Cherson, but one may not fit the latter into the frame of the former. Thus, for example, from the formal point of view Sokolova is right in assigning the two sole classes of coins of Constantine VII Porphyrogenitus (with portrait and with cross) to the two periods of his sole reign, to A.D. 919-920 and to 944-945. With that sort of dating it turns out that over the remaining period of more than forty years no coins at all were issued at Cherson in the name of Constantine VII. We know that Romanus I totally set Constantine VII aside from affairs of state, but he was not in a position to deprive him of the right of coinage. An analogous situation existed under Leo VI as well. His brother and co-ruler Alexander was actually not up to his task, but Cherson issued coins in his name too (not as sole Emperor, to be sure).

We can conceive of the sequence of the coin issues for the period of Constantine VII in the following form. The earliest are the coins with the letters Kω and the portrait of Constantine VII (Plate XXVII, 397-400). They are reasonably numerous and they run to a number of variants distinguished through the reciprocal positioning of the letters and through the configuration of these. It is not out of the question that coins of the initial classes served as stamps for some of the variants. This issue may be dated with more or less confidence to A.D. 913-919. The next issue is represented by the coins with two portraits in which, in our opinion, one should see portraits of Constantine himself and his wife Helen (Plate XXVII, 401, 402). The coins are relatively rare, and this may correspond to the brevity of their issuance—they are assigned to A.D. 920. After these one should place the coins issued in connection with the coronation of Christopher (A.D. 921). They copy the preceding issue with the single difference that the male portrait was supplemented with the letters Ρ-Ο, and the female one with the letters Χ-Ρ (Plate XXVII, 403). Sokolova considers that old moulds were used for this issue, but this is something which is doubtful. In her view the coins were issued in the names of Romanus I and of Christopher (Sokolova, 1965, p. 117), but the presence of a female portrait runs counter to that explanation. To our mind this coin was issued in the names of four figures—Constantine VII, Helen, Romanus, and Christopher, thus reflecting the entire muster of the royal family in 921. The rarity of the coins indicates the extraordinary nature and the brief duration of the issue. Subsequent issues may be dated only to the whole duration of the reign of Romanus, although thanks to the utilization of several classes of coins as stamps one can distinguish a range of emissions sequentially succeeding one another, the coins being issued both in the name of Romanus I and in the name of Constantine VII, but in decidedly uneven proportions. Thus the fourth issue of coins with the portrait of Romanus I (Plate XXVII, 404-407) does not in our view have a contemporaneous issue of coins of Constantine VII, although such a possibility should not be excluded. The fifth and sixth issues were also struck in the name of Romanus I, with a monogram for his name and a cross (Plate XXVII, 408-412). Characteristic of both issues is the use of a single stamp for the reverse—the cross has an easily distinguishable defective right shoulder. In the seventh issue one can set apart coins of Romanus I (Plate XXVII, 413) and of Constantine VII (Plate XXVII, 414-418) which are conjoined by a single practice—the use of both sides (for the issues of Romanus I) or of one side (for the issues of Constantine VII) of coins of the sixth issue as stamps. The diameter of the coins and the size of the types are reduced, but it is not difficult to recognize the defective cross we have mentioned above. The eighth issue consists of coins of Romanus I with a somewhat revised design of the same monogram (Plate XXVIII, 419-421), and of coins of Constantine VII (Plate XXVIII, 422). One should assign to the time of Romanus I the small coins with a monogram of his name (Plate XXVIII, 423-424, 426). Sokolova associated them with other more widespread coins having a monogram closely similar in design, regarding them as a special small denomination (Sokolova, 1968, p. 90), but this is not right. The shape of the monogram on these coins, when one compares it with the evolution of the standard "rho" monogram (bb) on the larger coins, does not allow one to consider the one and the other to be related genetically. Two of the three classes of these coins, together with coins of Constantine

VII, may be brought together in a ninth issue (Plate XXVIII, 423–425); the third class, to which coins of Constantine likewise correspond (in size), in a tenth issue (Plate XXVIII, 426, 427). It is curious that the coins of Constantine VII (Plate XXVIII, 427) have on the reverse the image of the cross with the defective right shoulder, its size having been reduced by three or four millimeters (Plate XXVII, 416); this allows one to guess that three or four intermediary stages of reduction existed.

One may assign to the joint rule of Constantine VII and his son Romanus II, i.e. to A.D. 945-959, coins with monograms for the names of both emperors, totalling no less then three varieties (Plate XXVIII, 428–430).

Romanus II reigned from November 959 to March 963. In our opinion there are no coins that can be assigned to the sole reign of this emperor among the known classes of Cherson-Byzantine coins. This circumstance might offer evidence that the question of the issuance of coins at Cherson had not been resolved in the first half-year of his reign. But we are acquainted with coins issued in the name of Romanus II and of his elder son, Basil II, which bear monograms for both the one and the other (Plate XXVIII, 431). They can be dated between April 960 and April 961, that is to say the period between the coronation of Basil II and that of his younger brother Constantine VIII. Despite the brief duration of the issuance of these coins one notes their being used as stamps (Plate XXVIII, 432). A second issue which we likewise assign to the time of Romanus II consists of coins with the letters BA and KωT (Plate XXVIII, 433, 434). The rarity of the coins affords evidence that they will scarcely fall to the prolonged period of the joint rule of Basil II and Constantine VIII (976-1025); they should most likely be dated to 961-963.

Under the emperor Nicephorus (963-969) coins were issued with a monogram for his name on the obverse and a monogram for the title δεσπότης on the reverse (Plate XXIX, 435–437). Likewise beyond question is the dating of the coins of the emperor John Zimisces (969-976)—they have a monogram for his name on the obverse, and on the reverse a monogram for the same title but in another configuration(Plate XXIX, 438–440). The three varieties of his coins exhibit a gradual diminution of sizes with retention of all the peculiarities of the design of the monograms, which testifies to use of the coins themselves as stamps.

Two classes of coins are ordinarily assigned to the joint rule of Basil II and Constantine VIII (976-1025)—one with monograms for the name of Basil II and for the title of despot, the latter being analogous in design to the monogram on the coins of John Zimisces (Plate XXIV, 441–444); and the other, the coins with the initials for the names of both brothers which have already been mentioned. We have already spoken about the attribution of these latter. Therefore it would seem most likely that for the whole period we have issuance of coins only of one type, the first one mentioned above. These coins are found in hoards the burying of which is associated with the siege of Cherson by the Kievan Grand Prince Vladimir in 988-989. Accordingly they were issued before that date, and the remaining part of the rule of Basil II and Constantine VIII actually remains without coins. Until recently it was held that the currency of medieval Cherson ended at this point.

In studying hoards of Cherson-Byzantine coins of 988-989 A. M. Gilevich noted that there were amid their compositions no coins with a "rho" monogram dating to the reign of Romanus I (920-944) even though coins of the other emperors of the Xth and even the IXth centuries are represented by a great quantity of specimens save for certain rare classes (Gilevich, 1964, p. 158). This seemed the more strange in that the coins with the "rho" monogram are among the most widespread coins of Cherson.

Later Sokolova addressed herself to this question, confirming with certain archeological data the observations of Gilevich regarding the composition of Cherson hoards. For one thing she drew attention to the absence of coins with the "rho" monogram among Sarkel and Tmutarakan finds, even though other Xth century Cherson coins and Xth-IXth century Byzantine coins are regularly encountered there. And on the other hand such a coin was brought to light at the Izyaslavl townsite, where in her words "not a single object earlier than the XIIth century had been found." She brought in several Byzantine XIIIth-XIVth century analogies to the monogram for the title "despot" and to the image of a lily (?) appearing on some types of coins with the monogram "rho", and she dated the latter to the XIIth—XIIIth centuries. Sokolova tried to classify the coins in question, segregating among them nine classes which in her opinion corresponded to three different denominations (Sokolova, 1968, pp. 90, 93, 98).

Basically the argument regarding the late origin of the coins with the "rho" monogram appears indisputable. This is confirmed in particular by the shape of the coins under examination. Many of them (and also some coins of the Xth century) are scyphate like Byzantine coins. None of the investigators has drawn attention to this circumstance hitherto, all of them presumably having considered it a random pehnomenon. Even the most casual counts show that no less than half of all the coins with the "rho" monogram, especially the early ones, are scyphate. Such coins as a rule bear traces of the blows that gave them the scyphate form; in the process many of the coins have been cracked. It is quite obvious that the operation giving the coins the form of a cup was of a preconceived nature and that it assumed massive proportions. The issuance of scyphate coins commenced at the middle of the XIth century in Byzantium. The Cherson moneyers could not produce scyphate coins with the casting process, and on that account they were evidently forced to give their output the appropriate form through a secondary operation. It is not out of the question that that operation was performed during the period when they were already in circulation. This observation provides us with supplementary data for dating the coins with the "rho" monogram to a later period then the Xth century.

Despite the coincidence in outlook, the classification and dating proposed by Sokolova for the coins with the "rho" monogram appears to us unacceptable. Thus it is methodologically incorrect to regard the coins described as being a single typological group—they are distinguished as to configuration of monograms and as to class of reverse (blank, cross, letter X, monogram for title "despot", etc.). Furthermore, one cannot argue for nor justify setting rare or unique coins apart as separate classes, and in her classification system six cases out of nine are of this sort. Where should one rate their specific gravity if their total number in all the soviet collections fails to exceed some dozens of specimens, while the remaining three (?) classes are represented by thousands of coins?

Nor does Sokolova's separation of three denominations stand up to any criticism. It would have been impossible to distinguish them in circulation, since with only one sort of monogram the coins exhibit a broad range of weights and dimensions. We are aware that the concept "coin" disappears at once upon money's commencing to be weighed or measured out. In studying the coins of Cherson, moreover, it is scarcely possible to assign decisive significance to Byzantine parallels. Their typology and external appearance, determined by the differing method of manufacture, are so idiosyncratic that any elements of resemblance must be merely of a chance nature. And it is surely quite impossible, once more from the standpoint of methodology, to base a dating of a record so limited chronologically as is the coin by means of the phenomenon of a monetary circulation extending over no more than two generations, these being moreover neither successive nor within the same ethnic milieu. Archeological data may be of some importance in instances where numismatic methods are powerless; but the inherent possibilities for dating the coins with the "rho" monogram are still far from having been exhausted. Let us pass on to examination of the actual material.

Starting from hoard analysis, the coins with the "rho" monogram did not participate in the monetary circulation of Cherson in the Xth century. The same is to be said of the coins with the letters κBω, ordinarily dated to the reign of Basil I and his son Constantine (869-879). Other coins of Basil I are found in the hoards, for which reason the absence from these of coins so widespread cannot be explained by their having fallen out of circulation or of their being rare.

The letters κBω can be understood in two senses—as an abbreviation of the names Basil and Constantine (in the present instance only Basil II and Constantine VIII), or as an abbreviation of the name and title ("basileus") of some one of the Constantines (sole rule of Constantine VIII, Constantine IX Monomach, or Constantine X Ducas). To our mind, the selection should fall to the first of these possibilities. As we are aware, all the IXth-Xth century coins of Cherson, commencing with the second half of the reign of Basil I, have approximately uniform dimensions and average weights. Only the coins with the letters κBω and the initial variants of the coins with the "rho" monogram stand out sharply through greater average weight and dimensions. Increase of the weight of coins is observed in the Constantinople coinage as well: it dates to the time of Basil II (Bellinger, III, p. 265), and on that account one should assign the issuance of the coins with the letters κBω to the time of Basil II too. One could not reasonably claim that at Cherson they had gone over to a different and larger denomination. It is impossible to say such a thing for the Constantinople coinage, because the coin class (anonymous folles) remains as before.

Any closer dating of the coins with the letters is obscure, inasmuch as the political status of Cherson after the events of 988-989 continues to be unknown. It is only from A.D. 1016, after the suppression in the Crimea of the rising headed by George Tzoula, which was accomplished by a Byzantine expedition, that one may speak of outright incorporation of the town into the composition of the empire. Apparently the issuance of the coins with the letters κBω should be assigned to the concluding years of the joint reign of Basil and Constantine, which is to say to A.D. 1016-1025.

Let us examine the coins with the "rho" monogram. Among their number there are two varieties, conjoined by a special configuration of the monogram (z), but diverging as to reverse type: on the one, a monogram for the title δεσπότις in several variants (Plate XXX, 449-452), on the other a cross (Plate XXX, 453). The two varieties are united not only by the monograms, but also by a uniform type orientation (↑↓).

Two circumstances are of importance for attribution of the coins under examination. In the first place, the cross on the coins of the second variety has been impressed, unquestionably, by the same stamp as that used for the coins with the letters κBω (Plate XXIX, 445; XXX, 453), only smoothed away a little; accordingly the two must be close to each other in time. In the second place, the presence of the "despot" title on the coins of the first variety draws in its train recognition of the "rho" monogram as being a monogram for the name Romanus, who must beyond question be only Romanus III Argyros (1028-1034); and this is what enables one to refute categorically the opinion of Sokolova as to the anonymous nature of the coins with the "rho" monogram, inasmuch as the title must be associated with the name of an emperor. Also of some interest is a coin with two "rho" monograms of differing configurations, which perhaps owes its origin to a chance combination of moulds for the first and for the second varieties (Plate XXX, 454).

Next in time are heavy coins with a monogram for the name Romanus, different in shape, on the obverse and with a cross on the reverse (Plate XXX, 456-457; XXXI, 458-464). These are perhaps preceded by a short-lived issue of coins with a monogram for the title of "despot" on the reverse, the existence of which one may judge by the unique specimen published by Oreshnikov (Plate XXX, 455). Thus one cannot consider the monogram "rho" of the new type to be anonymous either. Yet after Romanus III Argyros there was only one Byzantine ruler who bore the same name—Romanus IV Diogenes (1067-1071), to whom in our opinion one should in fact ascribe the coins of the new class.

On the basis of what has been said we may place it on record that between the reigns of Romanus III and Romanus IV Cherson was deprived of the right to issue coin of its own. This circumstance to some extent explains the abundance of coins of Romanus IV. During those four years a large number of "rho" monogram stamps were in use, although there was probably only one stamp for reverses (the cross), perhaps the same one as under Romanus III. It has been heavily worked over and the greater part of the coins manufactured through its use have the cross image in low relief.

The diameter of the coins dated to the time of Romanus IV comes to 25-26 mm. Moulds for these were prepared with the help of special stamps. All the other varieties of coins with the "rho" monogram (Plate XXXI, 465-471; XXXII, 472-480) were most likely issued after the reign of Romanus IV. They are represented by two categories of coins. The coins of the first category were made through the use of coins of preceding issues as stamps—they are so-called "secondary issues". In this process coins of almost every preceding stage of reduction were copied, something which affords us the opportunity of laying out a range of approximately ten successively diminishing coins. The cross on these gradually disappears and the reverse side becomes smooth and without type. Coins made through the use of special stamps for the monogram "rho" belong to the second category. These, in our opinion, should be distributed among the coins of the first category in accordance with diameter and weight. Inasmuch as the same type of monogram as on the issues of Romanus IV is retained on the majority of the variants, both categories of coins may be regarded as immediately contiguous to his reign.

Let us try to define the chronological range of this concluding issue. In our opinion this cannot have been particularly great. For example, during the seven years of the reign of John Zimisces one underlying issue and two "secondary" ones were cast. Thus each issue might correspond to a matter of two or three years. The concluding group of coins with the "rho" monogram comprises no less than 14 variants. Thus the overall duration of their issuance ought to come to approximately 30-50 years or even less, since it is quite plausible that issuance of coins of the first and of the second category should have run in parallel. The upshot is that the concluding group of coins with the "rho" monogram, and along with this the close of the history of the Cherson currency lasting over many centuries, may be placed at the end of the XIth century and the begining of the XIIth, and hardly later than the first quarter of the XIIth century.

3. The Organization of the Currency

It is first and foremost the coins themselves that are the fundamental source for study of the organization of the Cherson currency during the theme period. As the issues examined above show us, the coins bore as a rule the initials of the emperor's name or a monogram for the name, sometimes in conjunction with a monogram for the title Βασιλεὺς or δεσπότις.

The only exceptions are a few issues fairly confidently dated to the time of Michael III (842-866). Two chronological groups may be distinguished among these. To a first one, most likely the earlier, there are assigned coins of the following types: M—cross (Plate XXIII, 331, 332); Π —cross (Plate XXIII, 333-336); and A—cross (Plate XXIII, 337). To a second: MB—Π°X (Plate XXIII, 338-344); Π —X (Plate XXIV, 345-348); and A—Π°X (Plate XXIV, 349).

In this way we get a distinct picture of a parallel issuance of coins in the names of three personalities designated by the letters M (or MB), Π , and A. Clearest of all is the question of the meaning of the first letter M (MB), which can be acknowledge to be the initial for the name of Michael III on the first issue, supplemented with the initial letter of the title on the coins of the second issue. Inasmuch as he had no other co-rulers than Basil I, the thesis that the letters Π and A ought to designate the highest offices of medieval Cherson, those of archon and of proteuon, should occasion no surprize. We are convinced of the correctness of this deduction first and foremost by the circumstances under which the theme was created. As we are aware, Petronas named the archons and prōteuousoi who stood at the head of the civic government, and counselled the emperor Theophilus to place no trust in them and to subordinate them to officials who should be sent from Byzantium. Both titles are mentioned in other literary sources as well; and archons of Cherson are mentioned in a Byzantine table of ranks (Uspenski, p. 124) and on seals (Sokolova, 1973, p. 208).

It is true that the letter Π has been interpreted more often as πόλις, and Π –X as πόλις χερσῶνος. This explanation appears doubtful to us. In the first place, there is Π°Λ for πόλις on coins of Theophilus, and Π°X or Π° on coins of Michael III and Basil I. In the second place, we are acquainted with coins having two letters Π (Sokolova, 1971b, plate I) still falling, in all likelihood, to the period prior to the formation of the theme, when the prōteuousoi were the sole authority in the town that was entitled to issue coins. In our opinion one ought more probably to expect an indication of the person in whose name coins were struck rather than the simple statement "polis". In the third place, given the parallel issue of coins with the letter A, which can only indicate an archon, the letter Π should rather be understood as a designation of the office of proteuon. Thus in our opinion the letter Π should in all cases be taken as an abbreviation of the word πρωτεύων and not of the word πόλις.

Let us adduce a further indirect consideration concerning the special reverse of coins of the Π –X type. The coins of the MB—Π°X and A—Π°X types, parallel to these, are to be understood as coins "of king Michael, of the polis of Cherson" and "of the archon of the polis of Cherson". Inasmuch as coins of Michael III were issued in various towns, and as there were also archons in various towns, in just such measure was the explanatory inscription indicating the place of issuance necessary. It was another matter when coins of a proteuon were involved (the very concept of "proteuon" embodies an indication of the polis character of the town's organization), and on this account an analogously constructed inscription—a coin "of the proteuon of the polis of Cherson"—would contain a certain element of tautology. Thus for the coin type to be complete the expression Π –X would be quite sufficient—i.e., a coin "of the proteuon of Cherson."

The data that have been cited characterize the status of the town during the early days of the existence of the theme in a new way. Apparently at the start the sovereignty of the town was not affected, something which must have been intended to ward off the complications to be associated with an incorporation of Cherson into the empire. Probably the ancient merits and privileges of Cherson will have played no small part in this connection. What strikes us most of all is unquestionably the renewed flowering of the currency: side by side with imperial coins the town issued coins in the names of the superior office-holders of Cherson, the proteuousoi and the archons. This circumstance sets Cherson apart from other towns of the empire which do not have such rights and which at best issue coins of empire-wide pattern.

But the first step toward the liquidation of self-government had been taken. As the coins testify, this state of affairs, abnormal from the standpoint of autocratic authority, was preserved only under Michael III. Only at the very start of the reign of Basil I are coins still issued in his name with the letters Π° (πόλις) on the reverse, but issues in the names of the archons and proteuousoi have already been abolished. The main bulk of the coins of Basil I lacks mention of the polis, as do the coins of all the succeeding emperors. True, the issuance of coins by Cherson does continue, while not one other city of the Byzantine empire any longer had such rights.

The existence of a special organisation of the currency of Cherson at the middle of the IXth century permits one to advance a suggestion as to the nature and dating of a still further sort of local coin, that with two crosses (Plate XXV, 384). The notion that this class of coins should have arisen by chance (for example, through mistaken use of two reverse moulds) should be abandoned—the crosses are of different shapes, one of them having a hemispherical base rather than one consisting of three steps, and this one is never encountered again on coins of Cherson. May one not suggest that this special sort of coins was issued by the eparchy of Cherson? Such an attribution seems altogether admissible against the background of relative freedom in the field of the coinage under Michael III. It is in order to recall here the temple issues of Chersonesus, which were struck side by side with civic ones from the Ist century B.C. to the middle of the IInd century A.D. It is not out of the question that the Chersonites of the middle of the IXth century should have derived support from the ancient practice in justifying the rights of the church to monetary regalia.

One should point out that the coins with two crosses are unquestionably of later date than the coins of the archons and proteuousoi. They can be dated approximately to the second half of the reign of Basil I or to the beginning of the reign of Leo VI and Alexander. What we see is that the church commenced to issue coins at the moment when the polis coinage had just been abolished. It is possible that an issuance of coins by the eparchy will have been a transitional stage in the way toward total prohibition of any emissions other than imperial ones, or that a part may have been played here by other causes, which we can only guess at.

Definitive disappearance of polis features in the currency of Cherson took place under Basil I, something which is most likely to be associated with the reformation of the theme of Climates, as it is called in the "table of ranks", and its conversion into the theme of Cherson. Where earlier the civic authorities had enjoyed a certain sovereignty, and the sway of the strategos bore in full measure only upon the Cherson district, now the town was probably subordinated to him as well. On the basis of sphragistic data Sokolova assigns the reformation of the theme to the end of the 60's or to the 70's of the IXth century (Sokolova, 1975, p. 11), although the coins indicate a later period—the 70's to 80's,—inasmuch as at the beginning of the reign of Basil I, as we have already remarked, coins with the letters Π° on the reverse are still being issued.

4. Historical Sketch

From what Constantine Porphyrogenitus tells us we know that prior to the creation of the theme all business at Cherson was dealt with by the so-called "pre-eminent" together with persons styled "fathers of the city" (Const. Porph., De adm. imp., 42), although the town was probably under the control of Byzantium. Apparently a certain political apartness of Cherson led the Byzantines toward the idea of a need for strengthening imperial authority in that town, this in fact having found expression in the organization of a special _theme:_ a military and administrative district headed by a strategos appointed by Constantinople. It is quite possible that a certain part was played in the strivings of Byzantium to reinforce its influence in the Tauris by the appearance in the northern Black Sea littoral of a new military and political force, that of Kievan Rus.

The creation of the _theme_ was linked with construction by the Byzantines of the fortress of Sarkel on the Don at the request of the Khazars. The construction work was carried out by the _spatharokandidatos_ Petronas, who recommended to the emperor after the operation had been completed that a strategos be appointed at Cherson if he wished "to hold mastery over Cherson and its region for any appreciable time and not to lose these from beneath his hands." The advice was accepted by the emperor, and Petronas himself became the first strategos of the town.

Simultaneously with the organization of the _theme_ Cherson received the right to strike coins, the first issue of these falling to the time of Theophilus (829-842). But it is the Cherson coins of Michael III that are of the greatest interest. During his reign three classes of coins were issued, those with the letter M (or MB), Π , and A on one side and the image of a cross, uniform for all three classes, on the other. These three classes are issues of Michael III himself, but also of the _proteuon_ and of the archon of Cherson, demonstrating the retention of the important function of representatives of local self-government under that emperor. But under Basil I coins in the name of the archons and the _proteuousoi_ already cease to be issued, although the existence of both the one office and the other in Cherson in the IXth and Xth centuries is confirmed by literary sources and seals.

The political events which took place in Cherson during the IXth and Xth centuries are almost unknown. The most systematic source—the coins—testifies that mintage was carried out regularly from reign to reign. Coins were issued both in the name of the emperor and in the name of his co-ruler if there was one, the coins of the person occupying the main position being as a rule more various as to types and being represented by a greater number of specimens. Yet at the same time the Cherson mint did not react with equal sensitivity to changes in the composition of the ruling family—coins of many co-rulers were not issued at Cherson even though we know of their being struck at Constantinople. Side by side with this one should note an abundant issue at Cherson in the name of Constantine Porphyrogenitus, who had actually been eliminated from rule by his wife's father Romanus I.

The most important source for the history of Cherson is the work of Constantine Porphyrogenitus "Concerning the Administration of the Empire," which was composed between 948 and 952 as a guide for his son, the future emperor Romanus II. In it there are brought together information of a historical nature, and data on the town's position which were contemporaneous with Constantine Porphyrogenitus. From these, in particular, we find that Cherson received from the treasury 10 litrae of gold, in which connection we should recall the annual apportionment to Chersonesus of a thousand rations for the ballistarii by Constantine the Great. Constantine Porphyrogenitus provides important advice as to how one should proceed against Cherson in the event of its moving against the emperor. It is interesting that principal reliance was placed upon economic blockade—the Chersonites could not exist otherwise than by buying up merchandise among the Pechenegs and by selling it to the coastal towns of the empire.

As we see, Cherson's native economic base was weak or even non-existent, something which is by the way not surprising—nomads were constantly lurking about the town and missing no opportunity of making a living at its expense. It was this recourse to middleman trade, unquestionably of necessity, which in fact brought about the impoverishment of Cherson in the XIIth-XIIIth centuries, when trade on the Black Sea passed into the hands of Genoese merchants.

The ever more frequent campaigns of the Russian princes against Byzantium in the Xth century affected the interests of Cherson as well, and for that reason in treaties of 945 and 952 with Byzantium, The Rus undertook not only not to fall upon Cherson, but even to protect it against possible attacks. Yet this did not save Cherson from sack. In order to compel the emperor to carry out his undertakings Vladimir besieged and took the town in 988-989. The damage inflicted upon the town was great: in excavations we note everywhere a conflagration stratum of the Xth century. It is with just this incident that one should associate the accumulation of a range of coin hoards which constitute an exceptionally important source for study of the composition of the monetary circulation at the moment of the siege. They have been of assistance, in particular, in scrutiny of the chronology of the coins with the "rho" monogram.

Cherson was restored to the empire, but its further fate in the next few decades is not altogether clear. We know that in A.D. 1016 an expedition of the Byzantine fleet suppressed a rising in the Crimea headed by George Tzoula. We are also acquainted with a few seals bearing the name of Tzoula and supposedly belonging to the same individual (Sokolova, 1971). On one of the seals Tzoula is called protospatharios and strategos of Cherson. It is possible that Cherson rose against the emperor, on which account it suffered at the hands of the Rus together with its strategos (Skrzinskaya, pp. 266-267). George Tzoula was slain and the authority of Byzantium was restored.

After the events of A.D. 988-989 Cherson issued coins in the names of the two emperors Basil II and Constantine VIII; but it is difficult to say whether these were issued before 1016, or after that year. These coins begin an output of new coins larger in dimensions and weight than the coins issued in the IXth-Xth centuries. Dating them to the time of Basil II, rather than to that of Basil I as was held earlier, helps one to establish the relative and absolute chronology of the concluding coins of Cherson (with the "rho" monogram).

Thus among them there is singled out a group of coins of Romanus III Argyrus (1028-1034), and also one of Romanus IV Diogenes (1067-1071). The concluding issues of coins with the "rho" monogram copy the types of the coins of Romanus IV. The duration of their emission is not to be established with satisfying exactitude, but study of the technological peculiarities of the production of the coins, in particular the use of actual coins as stamps, allows one to speak of a relatively limited interval of time not exceeding a few decades.

Events of the end of the XIth century permit one to sketch out with an adequate measure of plausibility the concluding phase of the history of the Cherson currency as well. The domestic policy of the Byzantine government under the successor to Romanus IV, Michael VII (1071-1078), was distinguished by particularly far-reaching measures for pumping money out of the population. A monopoly was established over the grain trade, and this brought on a sharp rise in the price of grain associated with harvest shortfalls. In the overall chain of the new emperor's measures there was apparently included that of depriving the towns of the Crimean coast, including Cherson, of the trading privileges one must assume they had for long enjoyed. In addition Cherson was evidently refused the right to issue its own coin. In the XIth century this had already become a commonplace: coins were not issued between 1034 and 1067.

The deprivation of trading privileges evoked disturbance in the town. To understand how miserable was the situation in which Cherson found itself one should recall the words of Constantine Porphyrogenitus concerning the decisive role of middleman trading in the economy of Cherson. As a result Cherson rose and separated itself from the empire. The rising was of a protracted nature, inasmuch as Byzantium was forced simultaneously to carry on a struggle against Bulgaria, where a revolt had also broken out in 1072.

According to V. N. Tatishchev (Tatishchev, pp. 91-92), Michael VII turned to the grand prince Svyatoslav for aid, asking him to come forth against the Bulgarians and the Korsunians. A campaign against Cherson was initiated, but after the death of Svyatoslav (1076) and the news of the deposition of Michael VII (1078) the force was withdrawn. We do not know how the rising came to an end, but after some time a reconciliation was apparently achieved, since under Alexius Comnenus (1081-1118) Cherson was again serving as a place of exile for figures perilous to the empire. We know that around 1092 there was sent to Cherson under guard a certain pretender who represented himself as being Leo the son of Romanus IV Diogenes. One must assume that the earlier trading status was re-established as well. It is interesting to note that the pretender managed to flee from Cherson with the help of the Kumans, who had thronged thither in order to trade. But this time the town had lost the right of coinage for good. Evidently this did not weigh too much upon Cherson—they simply continued to issue coins with the "rho" monogram, copying the last lawful class, which was in addition probably the sole one remaining in circulation. The residents of Cherson doubtless counted upon a change in the situation in the future, yet this did not come about, and the coins we have mentioned proved to be the last in the history of Cherson. Such emissions could not provoke reproaches on the part of the Byzantine administration. Perhaps this is how one should explain the enormous quantity of the coins with the "rho" monogram; it will scarcely have fallen short of the total volume of the coin production of the IXth-Xth centuries. Such a mass of coins must have sufficed for many years of the domestic monetary circulation of Cherson even if it was of an intensive nature. But the overall economic balance was already becoming a deficit one. Under Alexius Comnenus Venetian merchants received extremely important trading privileges in the Black Sea. In the middle of the XIIth century it was the turn of the Genoese, who founded a network of trading factories in the Crimea. The town was not in a position to compete with these either in a military or in an economic sense. It was doomed, and the complete cessation of its existence was merely a matter of time.

CONCLUSION

In this study we have assembled and interpreted all the available numismatic material of ancient and medieval Chersonesus. Principal attention has been devoted to facts which define the activity of the local mint, that is to say the emissions of individual denominations or series of coins, but also to countermarks and restrikes. The quantitative parameters of emissions (counting the numbers of dies and of surviving coins) have been taken into consideration only to the extent that this has been necessary in order to bring out the peculiarities of an issue and in the last analysis to date them. Thus we have gained an idea of all the operations of the Chersonesus mint over the period of almost fifteen hundred years of its existence, and this has provided an opportunity, by making use of data regarding relative chronology and of a number of exact absolute dates, to establish an absolute dating for each operation within limits of up to one decade. The issue-dates secured in this way do not run counter to the iconographic, paleographic, or stylistic features of the coins. What is more, these dates are considerably more exact and narrower than those which one would have been in a position to cite by relying upon the features referred to.

The advantage of studying numismatic material covering a broad chronological period has become manifest through the fact that it has become possible for the first time to trace out with respect to Chersonesus the organization of the currency, and in particular to follow the evolution of the monetary magistracy. During the early period of the town's existence, that of autonomy, the functions of monetary magistrates pertained to a college of _nomophylakes_ consisting of three persons. This was one of the most important colleges of the municipal government, one which offered legislative proposals to the national assembly. For reasons with which we are unacquainted in detail the _nomophylakes_ gradually ceased to carry out the function of monetary magistrates, which became concentrated in the hands of a single figure. This was happening from time to time as early as the IInd century B.C., but the process was finally accomplished only during the period of Mithradates Eupator. One can also define with a greater or lesser degree of plausibility the figure to whom the functions of monetary magistrate pass—this is the _dioikētēs_, i.e. "he who stands at the head of the administration." The _dioikētēs_ retains this function throughout the entire period of Bosporan influence, which is most distinctly to be traced via literary, epigraphic, and numismatic sources. At the middle of the Ist century A.D. the functions of monetary magistrate pass to the first archon, who had concentrated not only military and political power, but economic power as well, in his own hands.

This last circumstance coincides in time with a pronounced debilitation or indeed even a complete elimination of Chersonesus's dependence upon the Bosporus. But this did not bring liberty to Chersonesus—the town apparently passed into direct dependence upon Rome. Where up to this moment Chersonesus had in practice enjoyed complete sovereignty in the field of currency, from the middle of the Ist century and until the end of the XIth century the issuance of coins was dependent wholly upon the policy of the Roman and later on the Byzantine emperors, who offered, confirmed, or withdrew the right of coinage.

The devices resorted to by the Chersonesites in getting around imperial prohibitions against the issuance of coins are of great interest. They practiced the striking of coins dated to the last year of the reign of the emperor under whom the issuance of coins had been permitted. This curious state of affairs in a way reminds one of the posthumous issues of talers of Maria Theresa dated 1780, i.e. the last year of the empress's life, an issuance which continues to this very day.

The same practice is to be sensed in medieval Chersonesus as well. The exceptional abundance of coins with the "rho" monogram, side by side with their marked and rapid degradation in size and weight, can only be explained as a result of a short-lived copying of coins of the last lawful issues of coins of the same class under Romanus IV Diogenes.

Chronological processing of a numismatic source is possible thanks to the fact that coins, like other records of material culture, have changed along with the socio-economic structure of the society in which they flourished. But coins, being records of state, reflect considerably more than do other categories of material things the political and historical events of their day. It is just for this reason that numismatics, a historical discipline, seeks also to elucidate those political events which lie behind one or another set of peculiarities appearing in numismatic material. Study of the coins of Chersonesus has provided decidedly positive results in this field as well.

First of all it has been possible to determine that at the middle of the IVth century B.C. an oligarchic coup took place at Chersonesus and that the oligarchs remained in power for eighteen years. This event most likely served as the cause of the creation of that very important document, the oath. There have also been clarified the circumstances under which the town commenced, at the middle of the Ist century A.D., an unprecedented striking of gold—it receives this right as an ally of Rome in a victorious war with the Bosporus.

The fact that the functions of monetary magistrates were performed on a periodic basis at Chersonesus by priests of the Maiden-goddess is of extreme importance for the numismatics of the whole northern Black Sea littoral. The temples, being endowed with considerable riches, could come forward as legitimate issuing authorities at moments when the town was experiencing shortage of coinage.

The elucidation of the reform carried out under Heraclius is of special importance for an understanding of the problems of the currency in medieval Chersonesus. As a result of this reform all coins which had circulated hitherto in Chersonesus, all the way back to coins of the ancient period, were adjusted in value to pentanummia. Thus the town was enabled to fill out the composition of the coinage through the use of early issues, something which made the problem of issuing coin of its own less acute.

Finally, it is difficult to overestimate the importance of the fact that coins were put out by representatives of the municipal government and by the local eparchy in the first decades of the existence of the theme. Let it suffice to say that no other city of the Byzantine empire ever possessed such rights.

These and other data, valuable for the history of the town, have been established thanks to new numismatic finds, and also to re-classification of older and quite familiar material. One cannot fail to recall the optimistic words of the distinguished numismatist A. L. Bertier de la Garde: "There is much hidden information in the soil of the Tauris," he wrote, "and it will be a long time before this source of instruction for archeologists and numismatists dries up. These last have assembled and described extensive collections; it would seem that all has become known, but new coins continue to be discovered, and explaining them often calls for reconsideration of what has been described earlier, and for a new way of understanding it all. Not with us did such a state of affairs begin, and not with us will it come to an end—to the general delight both of scholars and of amateurs" (Bertier, 1912).

CATALOG OF THE ANCIENT AND MEDIEVAL COINS OF CHERSONESUS

Series of about 390-380 B.C.

1. Obv: Head of the Maiden left, wearing kekriphalos.
   Rev: XEP. Fish and club right.
   Silver. Tetrobol. 3.55 g. State Hermitage.

2. Obv: Same.
   Rev: Same.
   Silver. Diobol. 2.01 g. 12 mm ↖ . V. V. Pereplesnin collection.

3. Obv: Same.
   Rev:
   Silver, Hemiobol. 0.49 g 7 mm, ← . British Museum.

4. Obv: Same.
   Rev: Same.
   Copper. Chalcon. 3.94 g 16 mm. ↗ . D. I. Moshnyagin collection.

5. Obv: Same.
   Rev: XEP . Same.
   Copper. Chalcon. 3.75 g 14 mm. ↓ . L. de Hirsch collection (Naster, No. 850).

6. Obv: Same.
   Rev: XEP. Same
   Copper. Lepton. 0.65 g, 7 mm, ↓ . D. I. Moshnyagin collection.

7. Obv: Same.
   Rev: XEP. Fish and club left.
   Copper. Lepton. 0.72 g, 10 mm, ↖ . State Hermitage, No. 8.

Issue of about 380-370 B.C.

8. Obv: Maiden seated on cippus right, holding arrow; to the right of a hind.
   Rev: XEP. Butting bull on club left.
   Copper. Dichalcon. 8.07 g, 24 mm, ↖ . State Chersonesus Museum. No. 28.

Issue of about second quarter of IVth century.

9. Obv: Facing head of bull decorated with garland.
   Rev: XEP. Fish and club right.
   Copper. Dilepton (?). 1.58 g, 11 mm, ↙ . State Historical Museum, unnumbered.

10. Obv: Same.
Rev: Same. Fish and club left.
Copper. Dilepton (?). 1.40 g, 11 mm, ↖ . State Hermitage, No. 137.

11. Obv: Same.
Rev: Same.
Copper. Dilepton (?). 1.32 g, 11 mm, ← . State Hermitage, No. 136.

12. Obv: Same.
Rev: Same, fish and club right.
Copper. Dilepton (?). 1.08 g, 10 mm, ↙ . State Hermitage, No. 141.

13. Obv: Wreathed head of Maiden right.
Rev: Wreath, within it a club right, above it a symbol Δ , beneath an inscription XEP.
Copper. Tetralepton (?). 2.39 g, 13 mm, ↓ . State Historical Museum, No. 1.

14. Obv: Same.
Rev: Same, no symbol.
Copper, Tetralepton (?). 2.31 g, 13 mm, ↖ . State Historical Museum, No. 4.

15. Obv: Same, left.
Rev: Wreath, within it club vertically, above this three points, to left an inscription XEP.
Copper. Trilepton (?). 2.26 g, 13 mm, ↗. State Historical Museum, No. 3737.

16. Obv: Crowned head of Maiden right.
Rev: XEP. Fish right, club left.
Copper. Dilepton (?). 1.00 g, 11 mm, ↖ . State Historical Museum, No. 1629.

17. Obv: Wreathed head of Maiden right.
Rev: XEP. Dolphin right.
Copper. Lepton. 0.38 g, 8 mm, ↑ . State Historical Museum, No. 1700.

18. Obv: Same.
Rev: ꟼƎX. Same, left.
Copper. Lepton. 0.38 g, 8 mm, ↙ . State Historical Museum, No. 1697.

19. Obv: Krater.
Rev: Wreath, within it club vertically downward, to left and inscription XEP.
Copper. Dilepton (?). 1.33 g, 11 mm, ←. State Hermitage, No. 134.

20. Obv: Same.
Rev: Same, inscription to right. Copper. Dilepton (?). (Giel, 1896, plate XVIII, 20).

21. Obv: Dolphin.
Rev: XEP. Club left.
Copper. Dilepton. 0..87 g, 11 mm, ↓. State Historical Museum, No, 1705.

22. Obv: Same.
Rev: Same, club left.
Copper. Dilepton (?). 0.61 g, 10 mm, ↑. State Chersonesus Museum, No. 9808.

Series about 370-364 B.C.

23. Obv: Head of Maiden with short wavy hair, three-quarters left.
Rev: XEP. Butting bull on club, fish beneath, all left.
Silver. Octobol. 6.58 g, 18 mm, ↘. State Historical Museum, No. 9122.

24. Obv: Same.
Rev: XEP. Protome of bull left, beneath a bow with string upward.
Silver. Tetrobol. 3.44 g, 12 mm, (Bertier, 1906a, plate I, 3).

25. Obv: Same.
Rev: XEP. Protome of bull on club, beneath a fish, left.
Silver. Diobol. 1.68 g, 13 mm, (Bertier, 1906a, plate I, 2).

Issue of about 364-350 B.C.

26. Obv: Head of Maiden right, wearing kekriphalos.
Rev: XEP. Facing muzzle of lion, beneath a club left.
Copper. Dichalcon. 6.75 g, 21 mm, ↙. State Historical Museum, No. 1778.

Issue about the middle of the IVth century.

27. Obv: Head of lion right.
Rev: Five-pointed star, between its rays five points.
Copper. Lepton. 1.07 g, 10 mm, State Hermitage, no. 52.

28. Obv: Same.
Rev: Same, between the rays an inscription XEP.
Copper. Lepton. 0.98 g, 10 mm, ↙. State Hermitage, No. 26.

29. Obv: Same.
Rev: Six-pointed star, between the rays the inscription XEP and three points.
Copper. Lepton (Giel, 1896, plate XVIII, 23).

30. Obv: Same.
Rev: Same, between the rays the inscription XEP and a letter Π.
Copper. Lepton (Giel, 1896, plate XVIII, 25).

31. Obv: Same, left.
Rev: Same, between the rays an inscription XEb.
Copper. Lepton. 0.74 g, 9 mm, ↓. State Hermitage, No. 43.

32. Obv: Same.
Rev: Same, between the rays the letters XE.
Copper. Lepton (Giel, 1896, plate XVIII, 33).

Issue about 355 B.C.

33. Obv: Head of Maiden left, with short hair bound by fillet.
Rev: XEP. Butting bull on club, right. Beneath a letter K.
Silver. Didrachm. 9.38 g, 25 mm, (?) (Bertier, 1906a, plate I, 4).

34. Obv: Same.
Rev: Same, beneath a name ΖΩΠΥΡΟ.
Silver. Didrachm. 9.90 g, 22 mm, ←. British Museum.

Series of about 350-330 B.C.

35. Obv: Quadriga right, the Maiden standing in the chariot with a torch.
Rev: XEP. Nude kneeling warrior left, with shield and spear, helmet on head.
Copper. Dichalcon (Bertier, 1912, p. 47).

36. Obv: Same, above the letters HP.
Rev: Same.
Copper. Dichalcon. 6.13 g, 20 mm, ↗. State Historical Museum, No. 4628/1.

37. Obv: Same, letters ΛΥ.
Rev: Same.
Copper. Dichalcon. 6.10 g, 20 mm, ↗. State Chersonesus Museum, No. 9.

38. Obv: Same, letters ΣΑ.
Rev: Same.
Copper. Dichalcon. 5.41 g, 19 mm, ↑. State Historical Museum, No. 1668.

39. Obv: Same, letter A.
Rev: Same.
Copper. Dichalcon (Bertier, 1912, p. 47).

40. Obv: Same, letter B.
Rev: Same.
Copper. Dichalcon. 6.36 g, 21 mm, ↓. State Historical Museum, unnumbered.

41. Obv: Same, letter Γ
Rev: Same.
Copper. Dichalcon. 5.91 g, 20 mm, →. State Hermitage, No. 94.

42. Obv: Same, letter Δ
Rev: Same.
Copper. Dichalcon. 6.61 g, 19 mm, ↑. State Historical Museum, unnumbered.

43. Obv: Same, letter Ε
Rev: Same.
Copper. Dichalcon. 6.53 g, 20 mm, ↓. State Hermitage, No. 98.

44. Obv: Same.
Rev: Same, letter Ζ
Copper. Dichalcon (Zograph, 1927, p. 382).

45. Obv: Same.
Rev: Same. letter H.
Copper. Dichalcon. 6.15 g, 20 mm, ↙. State Chersonesus Museum, No. 4628/2.

46. Obv: Same.
Rev: Same, letter Θ
Copper. Dichalcon. (Bertier, 1912, p. 47).

47. Obv: Same.
Rev: Same, letter Ι
Copper. Dichalcon. 6.94 g, 20 mm, ↗. State Hermitage, No. 100.

48. Obv: Same.
Rev: Same, letter K.
Copper. Dichalcon. 5.70 g, 21 mm, ↘. State Chersonesus Museum, No. 31/2.

49. Obv: Same.
Rev: Same, letter Λ
Copper. Dichalcon. 7.00 g, 21 mm, (?). (Bertier, 1913, plate, 3).

50. Obv: Same.
Rev: Same, letter M.
Copper. Dichalcon. 6.16 g, 21 mm, ↖. State Hermitage, No. 102.

51. Obv: Same.
Rev: Same, letter N.
Copper. Dichalcon (Bertier, 1912, p. 47).

52. Obv: Same.
Rev: Same, letter Ξ
Copper. Dichalcon. 6.22 g, 21 mm, ↖. State Chersonesus Museum, No. 9146.

53. Obv: Same.
Rev: Same, letter Ο
Copper. Dichalcon. 6.05 g, 22 mm, ↖. State Historical Museum, No. 3725.

54. Obv: Same.
Rev: Same, letter Π
Copper. Dichalcon. 6.20 g, 20 mm, ↖. State Hermitage, No. 108.

55. Obv: Same.
Rev: Same, letter P.
Copper. Dichalcon (Bertier, 1912, plate 5).

56. Obv: Same.
Rev: Same, letter Σ
Copper. Dichalcon. 5.44 g, 21 mm, ↓. State Hermitage, No. 110.

57. Obv: Janus-head (Hera and Zeus ?), letters HP.
Rev: XEP. Lion tearing bull, right.
Copper. Chalcon. 3.22 g, 16 mm, ↓. State Historical Museum, unnumbered.

58. Obv: Same, letters ΛY
Rev: Same.
Copper. Chalcon. 2.39 g, 14 mm, ↑. State Historical Museum, No. 1690.

59. Obv: Same, letters ΣA
Rev: Same,
Copper. Chalcon. 2.64 g, 14 mm, ↑. State Historical Museum, unnumbered.

Series about 330-320 B.C.

60. Obv: Griffon left.
Rev: XEP. Kneeling Maiden right, bow in left hand, arrow in right hand, at left letters APІ
Copper. Dichalcon. 8.92 g, 22 mm, ↑. State Chersonesus Museum, No. 7153.

61. Obv: Same.
Rev: Same, letters KPA.
Copper. Dichalcon. 10.19 g, 24 mm, ↗. D. I. Moshnyagin collection.

62. Obv: Same.
Rev: Same, letters ΠA
Copper. Dichalcon. 12.88 g, 23 mm, ↑. State Historical Museum, unnumbered.

63. Obv: Kneeling Maiden right, with bow and arrow, at left letters
Rev: XEP. Griffon left.
Copper. Dichalcon. 9.15 g, 24 mm, ↑. State Chersonesus Museum, No. 7148.

64. Obv: Same, letters KPA.
Rev: Same.
Copper. Dichalcon. 8.99 g, 23 mm, ↑. State Hermitage, No. 71.

65. Obv: Same, letters ΠA
Rev: Same.
Copper. Dichalcon. 11.73 g, 23 mm, →. State Hermitage, No. 73.

66. Obv: Biga right, Maiden in chariot with torch.
Rev: XEP. Lion with spear in jaws left, above letters ΠΑ
Copper. Chalcon. 3.78 g, 14 mm, ↑. State Hermitage, No. 74.

67. Obv: Same.
Rev: Same, inscription ΔΑΜΑΡΕ
Copper. Chalcon. 2.81 g, 16 mm, ↗. British Museum.

Issue about 320-310 B.C.

68. Obv: Kneeling Maiden right, with bow and arrow.
Rev: XEP. Griffon left, above it the name ΑΙΣΧΙ.
Copper. Dichalcon. 5.53 g, 20 mm, ↘. State Chersoneusus Museum. No. 7073.

69. Obv: Same.
Rev: Same, name ΘΕΟΠ
Copper. Dichalcon. 7.60 g, 22 mm, ↖. State Chersonesus Museum, unnumbered.

70. Obv: Same.
Rev: Same, name ΦΙΛΙΣΤΙΟ
Copper. Dichalcon. 7.97 g, 21 mm, ↗. State Chersonesus Museum, No. 7398.

71. Obv: Same.
Rev: Same, name ΦΙΛΙ
Copper. Dichalcon. 6.03 g, 23 mm, ↘. State Chersonesus Museum, No. 8295.

72. Obv: Same.
Rev: Same, name ΒΑΘΥΛΛΟ
Copper. Dichalcon. 6.51 g, 21 mm, ↘. State Hermitage, No. 516.

73. Obv: Same.
Rev: Same, name ΧΟΡΕΙΟ
Copper. Dichalcon. 7.56 g, 21 mm, →. State Chersonesus Museum, No. 32/2.

74. Obv: Same.
Rev: Same, name ΙΣΤΙΕΙΟ
Copper. Dichalcon. 7.01 g, 21 mm, ↘. D. I. Moshnyagin collection.

Issue about 310-300 B.C.

75. Obv: XEP. Griffon left.
Rev: Kneeling Maiden right, with bow and arrow, behind her the name ΕΥΔΡΟΜΟ.
Copper. Dichalcon. 6.31 g, 21 mm, ↓. State Chersonesus Museum, No. 7442.

76. Obv: Same. Countermark "dolphin".
Rev: Same, below exergue line the name ΕΥΔΡΟΜΟ
Copper. Dichalcon. 6.08 g, 20 mm, ↖ . State Chersonesus Museum, No. 7437.

Issue about 300-290 B.C.

77. Obv: XEP. Maiden striking down hind with spear left, in left hand a bow.
Rev: Butting bull on club left, beneath it the name ΕΥΔΡΟΜΟΥ, bow and quiver.
Copper. Dichalcon. 6.36 g, 21 mm, ↗. State Chersonesus Museum, No. 8218/10.

78. Obv: Same.
Rev: Same, name ΔΙΑΓΟΡΑ
Copper. Dichalcon. 4.66 g, 22 mm, ↘ . State Chersonesus Museum, No. 8218/3.

79. Obv: Same.
Rev: Same, name ΣΥΡΙΣΚΟΥ
Copper. Dichalcon. 5.89 g, 21 mm, ↑ . State Chersonesus Museum, No. 7226.

80. Obv: Same. Countermark "dolphin".
Rev: Same, name ΚΛΕΜΥΤΑΔΑ
Copper. Dichalcon. 5.63 g, 22 mm, ← . State Chersonesus Museum, No. 7563.

81. Obv: Same.
Rev: Same, name ΘΕΟΧΑΡΕ
Copper. Dichalcon (Bertier, 1912, plate 7).

Series about 290-280 B.C.

82. Obv: Head of Maiden right, behind it bow and quiver. Countermarks: monogram ΠΑΡ (a), "dolphin", "thunderbolt".
Rev: XEP. Butting bull, left, above it club left, beneath it name ΑΠΟΛΛΩΝΙΔΟΥ .
Silver. Tetradrachm. 13.94 g, 26 mm, ↑ . D. I. Moshnyagin collection.

83. Obv: Same. Same countermarks.
Rev: Same, name ΑΔΩΝΟΣ
Silver. Tetradrachm. 13.70 g, 28 mm, ↖ . State Chersonesus Museum, No. 7004.

84. Obv: Same. Same countermarks.
Rev: Same, name ΑΓΑΣΙΚΛΕΟΣ
Silver. Tetradrachm. 13.88 g, 28 mm, ↙ . State Chersonesus Museum, No. 6901.

85. Obv: Same. Same countermarks.
Rev: Same, name ΑΡΤΕΜΙΔΩΡΟΥ
Silver. Tetradrachm. 13.77 g, 27 mm, ↑. State Chersonesus Museum, No. 6902.

86. Obv: Same. Same countermarks.
Rev: Same, name ΙΣΤΡΩΝΟΣ
Silver. Tetradrachm. 12.72 g, 28 mm, ↑. State Chersonesus Museum, No 9150.

87. Obv: Same.
Rev: Same.
Silver. Didrachm. 6.56 g, (Bertier, 1913, p. 63, No. 33).

88. Obv: Same, same countermarks.
Rev: XEP. Maiden left, striking down hind with spear, to right the name ΑΡΤΕΜΙΔΩΡΟΥ
Silver. Didrachm. 6.88 g, 24 mm, ↑. State Chersonesus Museum, No. 6903.

89. Obv: Same.
Rev: Same. name ΙΣΤΡΩΝΟΣ
Silver. Didrachm. 6.71 g, 22 mm, ↑. D. I. Moshnyagin collection.

90. Obv: Same, same countermarks.
Rev: Same, name ΑΙΣΧΙΝΑ
Silver. Didrachm, 6.88 g, 21 mm, ↑. State Chersonesus Museum, No. 6904.

Issue about 280-270 B.C.

91. Obv: Head of Heracles right.
Rev: Maiden striking down hind left, to right the name ΒΑΘΥΛΛΟΥ
Silver. 9 obols. 5.23 g (Zograph, 1951, plate XXXV, 21).

92. Obv: Same.
Rev: Same, name ΗΡΑΚΛΕΙΤΟΥ
Silver. 9 obols. 5.07 g, 19 mm, ↓. State Hermitage, No. 148.

Issue about 270-260 B.C.

93. Obv: Head of Heracles left, a club below and to right.
Rev: XEP. Maiden seated on throne left, behind back a bow and quiver, in right hand arrow, at left the name ΝΑΝΩΝΟΣ
Silver. Tridrachm. 10.55 g, 22.5 mm, ↓. State Hermitage, No. 149.

Issue about 260-250 B.C.

94. Obv: Head of Heracles right, beneath it club.
Rev: Maiden seated on throne left, at right the name ΖΩΙΛΟΥ
Silver. 9 obols. 4.57 g, 19 mm, ↑. British Museum.

Series about 250-230 B.C.

95. Obv: Head of Herakles right, beneath it club. Countermark "thunderbolt".
Rev: XEP. Maiden seated on throne left, to left the name ΠΡΩΤΙ-ΠΠΟΥ, beneath exergue line a T. Countermark "dolphin".
Silver. Tridrachm. 9.35 g, 24 mm, ↑ . State Chersonesus Museum, No. 6917.

96. Obv: Same. Same countermark.
Rev: Same, name ΗΡΑΚΛΕΙΤΟΥ, on throne a T.
Silver. Tridrachm. 9.35 g, 24 mm, ↖ . State Chersonesus Museum, No. 7020.

97. Obv: Same. Same countermark.
Rev: Same, name ΔΙΩΝΟΣ. Same countermark.
Silver. Tridrachm, 9.41 g, 22 mm, ↑ . State Chersonesus Museum, No. 7010.

98. Obv: Same, Same countermark.
Rev: Same, name ΑΠΟΛΛΑ . Same countermark.
Silver. Tridrachm. 9.30 g, 23 mm, ↑ . State Chersonesus Museum, No. 7017.

99. Obv: Same. Same countermark.
Rev: Same, name ΑΠΟΛΛΩΝΙΔΟΥ. Same countermark.
Silver. Tridrachm. 9.30 g, 23 mm, ↑ . State Chersonesus Museum, No. 6916

100. Obv: Same. Same countermark.
Rev: Same, name ΠΡΥΤΑΝΙΟΣ. Same countermark.
Silver. Tridrachm. 9.03 g, 22 mm, ↑ . State Chersonesus Museum, No. 6920.

101. Obv: Same, same countermark.
Rev: Same, name ΝΕΥΠΟΛΙΟΣ.
Silver. Tridrachm. 9.37 g, 22 mm, ↑ . State Chersonesus Museum, No. 6921.

102. Obv: Same. Same countermark.
Rev: Same, name ΞΕΝΩΝΟΣ. Same countermark.
Silver. Tridrachm. 9.35 g, 21 mm, ↖ . State Chersonesus Museum, No. 7026.

103. Obv: Same. Same countermark.
Rev: Same, name ΑΓΑΘΟΚΛΕΟΣ
Silver. Tridrachm. 9.40 g, 22 mm, ↗. State Chersonesus Museum, No. 7023.

104. Obv: Same.
Rev: Same, name ΑΠΟΛΛΩΝΙΟΥ
Silver. Tridrachm. 9.05 g, 23 mm, ↖ . State Historical Museum, No. 9129.

105. Obv: Same. Same countermark.
Rev: Same, name ΗΡΑΚΛΕΟΥ.
Silver. Tridrachm. 9.13 g, 23 mm, ↖ . State Chersonesus Museum, No. 7019.

106. Obv: Same.
Rev: Same. name ΙΣΤΡΩΝ.
Silver. Tridrachm (Bertier, 1936a, p. 244, note 1).

107. Obv: Same. Countermark "thunderbolt".
Rev: ΧΕΡ. Butting bull left, beneath it the name ΠΡΩΤΙΠΠΟΥ . Countermark "dolphin".
Silver. 9 obols. 4.69 g, 21 mm, ↖ . State Chersonesus Museum, No. 10949.

108. Obv: Same.
Rev: Same, name ΗΡΑΚΛΕΙΤΟΥ.
Silver. 9 obols. 4.32 g, 17 mm, ↑ . Berlin Museum.

109. Obv: Same.
Rev: Same, name ΔΙΩΝΟΣ.
Silver. 9 obols. 4.48 g, 18 mm, ↑ . State Hermitage, No. 152.

110. Obv: Same.
Rev: Same, name ΑΡΤΕΜΙΔΩ
Silver. 9 obols. 4.51 g, 19 mm, ↑ . State Hermitage, No. 151.

111. Obv: Same.
Rev: Same, name ΑΠΟΛΛΑ
Silver. 9 obols. 3.72 g, 19 mm. British Musuem (↖).

112. Obv: Same. Same countermark.
Rev: Same, name ΑΠΟΛΛΩΝΙΔΟΥ. Same countermark.
Silver. 9 obols. 4.60 g, 19 mm, ↗. State Chersonesus Museum, No. 6925.

113. Obv: Same. Same countermark.
Rev: Same, name ΠΡΥΤΑΝΙΟΣ
Silver. 9 obols. 4.63 g, 18 mm, ↖ . State Chersonesus Museum, No. 6293.

114. Obv: Same. Same countermark.
Rev: Same, name ΝΕΥΠΟΛΙΟΣ. Same countermark.
Silver. 9 obols. 4.65 g, 18 mm, ↗. State Chersonesus Museum, No. 7037.

115. Obv: Same. Same countermark.
Rev: Same, name ΙΞΥΠΟΡΟΣ. Same countermark.
Silver. 9 obols. 3.57 g, 20 mm, ↗. State Chersonesus Museum, No. 9138.

116. Obv: Same. Same countermark.
Rev: Same, name ΞΕΝΩΝΟΣ. Same countermark.
Silver. 9 obols. 4.65 g, 19 mm, ↗. State Chersonesus Museum, No. 6934.

117\. Obv: Same. Same countermark.
Rev: Same, name ΑΠΟΛΛΩΝΙΟΥ. Same countermark.
Silver. 9 obols. 4.65 g, 18 mm, ↖ . State Chersonesus Museum, No. 7029.

118\. Obv: Same.
Rev: Same, name ΗΡΑΚΛΕΟΥ
Silver. 9 obols. 3.72 g, 17 mm, ↖ . State Hermitage, No. 153.

119\. Obv: Same. Same countermark.
Rev: Same, name ΠΥΡΡΙΝΟΥ
Silver. 9 obols. 4.63 g, 17 mm, ↑ . State Chersonesus Museum, No 7040.

120\. Obv: Same.
Rev: Same, name ΖΩΙΛΟΥ
Silver. 9 obols (Bertier, 1906, p. 243, note 2).

Series about 230-220 B.C.

121\. Obv: Head of Maiden right.
Rev: Butting bull left, beneath it the name ΞΑΝΘΟΥ.
Silver. $4\frac{1}{2}$ obols. 2.89 g, 14 mm, ?. Berlin Museum.

122\. Obv: Same.
Rev: Same, name MIKA (two first letters in ligature).
Silver. $4\frac{1}{2}$ obols. 2.57 g, 14 mm, ↑ . State Historical Museum, No. 9124.

123\. Obv: Same.
Rev: Same, name YMNOY.
Silver. $4\frac{1}{2}$ obols. 2.21 g, 14 mm, ?. (Oreshnikov, 1915, plate II, 31).

124\. Obv: Same.
Rev: Same, the name ΝΑΝΩ above.
Silver. $4\frac{1}{2}$ obols. 2.40 g, 14 mm, ↗ . State Hermitage, No. 154.

125\. Obv: Griffon right.
Rev: XEP. Bow in case, the name ΞΑΝΘΟΥ below.
Silver. 2 obol. 1.27 g, 12 mm, ↙ . British Museum.

126\. Obv: Same.
Rev: Same, a name NA above.
Silver. 2 obols. 0.83 g, 10 mm, ↑ . V.V. Pereplesnin collection.

Series about 220-210 B.C.

127\. Obv: Head of Herakles right, club beneath.
Rev: XEP. Butting bull left, beneath it a name ΝΕΟΠΟΛΙΟϹ.
Silver. Hemidrachm. 2.36 g, 15 mm, (?). (Naville, V, No. 1592).

128. Obv: Same.
Rev: Same, name ΗΡΩΙΔ
Silver. Hemidrachm. 2.09 g, 16 mm, ↑. British Museum.

129. Obv: Same.
Rev: Same, name ΖΩΙΛ
Silver. Hemidrachm. 1.93 g, 15 mm, (?). Pushkin State Museum for the Representative Arts, No. 28380.

130. Obv: Same.
Rev: Same, name MENE.
Silver. Hemidrachm (Bertier, 1906a, p. 243, note 1).

131. Obv: Same.
Rev: XEP. Prow of galley left, beneath it the name ΓΕΡΟΝΤΟΣ.
Copper. Dichalcon. 5.02 g, 22 mm, ↑. State Hermitage, No. 195a.

132. Obv: Same.
Rev: Same, name ΣΙΛΑΝΟΥ.
Copper. Dichalcon. 4.14 g, 20 mm, ↑. British Museum.

Series about 210-200 B.C.

133. Obv: Head of Maiden wearing wreath right, behind her a bow and quiver.
Rev: XEP. Maiden striking down hind with a spear left. beneath the name YMNOY.
Silver. Drachma. 4.48 g, 17 mm, ↖. V. N. Orekhov collection.

134. Obv: Same.
Rev: Same, name ΕΥΡΥΔΑΜΟΥ
Silver. Drachma. 3.90 g, 17 mm, ↖. British Museum.

135. Obv: Same.
Rev: Same, name ΕΥΡΥΔΑ
Silver. Drachma. 4.45 g, 19 mm, ↑. E. B. Shapiro collection.

136. Obv: Same.
Rev: Same, name ΜΕΝΕΣΤΡΑ
Silver. Drachma. 3.70 g, 17 mm, ↑. British Museum.

137. Obv: Same. Countermarks "star" and "club".
Rev: Same, name not preserved.
Silver. Drachma. 3.11 g, 17 mm, ↖. British Museum.

138. Obv: Same.
Rev: XEP. Bow with string upward, beneath it quiver; beneath this the name YMNOY.
Silver. Hemidrachm. 1.65 g, 14 mm, ↑. British Museum.

139. Obv: Same.
Rev: Same, quiver and beneath it bow with string downward.
Silver. Hemidrachm. 1.86 g, 14 mm (?) (Giel, 1891, plate IV, 7).

140. Obv: Same.
Rev: Same, quiver, beneath it the name ΞΥΡΥΔΑΜ
Silver. Hemidrachm. 1.92 g, 15 mm (?). Pushkin State Museum for the Representative Arts, No 28379.

141. Obv: Same.
Rev: Same, name ΜΕΝΕΣΤΡ
Silver. Hemidrachm. 1.53 g, 14 mm, ↑ . State Hermitage, No. 185.

142. Obv: Same.
Rev: Same, name above.
Silver. Hemidrachm. 2.02 g, 14 mm (?) (Giel, 1896, plate XVIII, 18).

143. Obv: Same.
Rev: XEP. Reclining hind left, beneath it the name
Copper. Dichalcon. 4.72 g, 18 mm, ↗. State Hermitage, No. 208.

144. Obv: Same.
Rev: Same. name ΧΟΡΕΙΟΥ
Copper. Dichalcon. 4.05 g, 17 mm, ↓ . State Chersonesus Museum, No. 9237.

145. Obv: Male head wearing fillet right.
Rev: XEP. Club left, beneath it the name ΞΕΝΟΚΛΕΟ
Copper. Chalcon. 2.63 g, 16 mm, ↑ . State Hermitage, No. 212.

146. Obv: Same.
Rev: Same, name ΧΟΡΕΙΟΥ
Copper. Chalcon. 2.28 g, 14 mm, ↑. State Chersonesus Museum, No. 216/2.

Series about 210-200 B.C.

147. Obv: Head of Heracles right.
Rev: XEP. Butting bull left, beneath it the name ΑΡΧΙΚΛΕΙΟ
Copper. Dichalcon. 2.43 g, 14 mm, ↑ . State Hermitage, No. 195.

148. Obv: Same.
Rev: Same, name ΒΟΛΛΙΩΝΟ
Copper. Dichalcon. 2.86 g, 15 mm, ↗ . V. V. Pereplesnin collection.

149. Obv: Same.
Rev: Same, name MATP.
Copper. Dichalcon. 2.12 g, 15 mm, ↙ . State Historical Museum, No. 1731.

150. Obv: Male head wearing fillet, right.
Rev: XEP. Club left, beneath it the name ΑΡΧΙΚΛΕ
Copper. Chalcon. 1.55 g, 15 mm, ↗. D. I. Moshnyagin collection.

151. Obv: Same.
Rev: Same, name ΒΟΛΛΙΩΝ
Copper. Chalcon. 1.42 g, 13 mm, ↖ . D. I. Moshnyagin collection.

152. Obv: Same.
Rev: Same, name ΜΑΤΡ.
Copper. Chalcon. 1.58 g, 13 mm, ↑ . State Hermitage, No. 211.

153. Obv: Same.
Rev: Same, name ΔΕΛΦΟΥ
Copper. Chalcon. 2.84 g, 14 mm (?) (Karyshkovski, plate I, 8).

Series of end of the IIIrd century B.C.

154. Obv: Head of Maiden wearing wreath, left.
Rev: ΧΕΡ. Kneeling Maiden shooting bow right, beneath her the name ΑΓΑΣ.
Copper. Chalcon. (?). 14 mm, Private collection.

155. Obv: ΧΕΡ. Protome of Pegasus left.
Rev: Standing warrior with spear and shield, to left the name ΑΓΑΣ
Copper. (Bertier, 1906a, plate I, 6).

Issue about 200-190 B.C.

156. Obv: Head of Maiden wearing wreath right, behind it bow and quiver.
Rev: ΧΕΡ. Butting bull left, beneath it the name ΑΓΑΣΙΚΛ
Copper. Dichalcon. 4.14 g, 17 mm, ↑ . State Historical Museum, No. 1717.

157. Obv: Same.
Rev: Same, name ΗΡΩΙΔΑ
Copper. Dichalcon. 2.85 g, 19 mm, ↑ . State Historical Museum, unnumbered.

Issue about 190-180 B.C.

158. Obv: Head of Maiden wearing mural crown, right. Countermarks "star" and "club".
Rev: ΧΕΡ. Bow with string upward, beneath it quiver, beneath these the name ΔΕΛΦΟϹ.
Silver. Hemidrachm. 1.57 g, 12 mm, → . State Hermitage, No. 238b.

Series about 180-170 B.C.

159. Obv: Head of Pallas Athena right. Countermark "star".
Rev: ΧΕΡ. Griffon right, beneath it the name ΑΠΟΛΛΟΔΩΡΟΥ
Copper. Dichalcon. 4.88 g, 17 mm, ↖ . State Historical Museum, No. 1746.

160. Obv: Same.
Rev: Same, name ΗΡΑΚΛΕΙΟΥ
Copper. Dichalcon. 4.31 g, 19 mm, ↑ . D. I. Moshnyagin collection.

161. Obv: Same.
Rev: XEP. Nike left, to right the name ΑΠΟΛΛ
Copper. Chalcon. (Giel, 1891, plate IV, 10).

162. Obv: Same.
Rev: Same, name ΣΙΜΑ (?).
Copper. Chalcon. 1.87 g, 15 mm, ↑ . State Hermitage, No. 220a.

163. Obv: Same.
Rev: Same, name .... ΑΡΩ....
Copper. Chalcon. 2.24 g, 14 mm, ↑ . State Historical Museum, No. 5.

Issue about 180-170 B.C.

164. Obv: Head of Maiden right, behind her bow and quiver.
Rev: XEP. Nike left.
Copper. Chalcon. 1.82 g, 14 mm, ↑ . State Historical Museum, No. 18.

Series about 170-160 B.C.

165. Obv: Head of a Dioscurus wearing pilos, right.
Rev: XEP. Prow left, beneath it the name ΑΛΚΙΝΟΥ
Copper. Dichalcon. 3.31 g, 18 mm, ↑ . State Hermitage, No. 218.

166. Obv: Same.
Rev: Same, name ΣΙΜΑΙΟΥ
Copper. Dichalcon. 1.98 g, 14 mm, ↗ . State Hermitage, No. 218b.

167. Obv: Male head left.
Rev: XEP. Prow left.
Copper. Chalcon. 1.70 g, 15 mm, → . State Hermitage, No. 241a.

Issue about 160-150 B.C.

168. Obv: Head of Maiden wearing wreath, right.
Rev: XEP. Bow and quiver left, beneath these the name ΣΙΜΑΙΟΥ
Copper. Chalcon. 1.16 g, 11 mm, ↗ . V. N. Orekhov collection.

169. Obv: Same.
Rev: Same, bow and quiver right.
Copper. Chalcon (Giel, 1891, plate IV, 8).

Issue about 150-140 B.C.

170. Obv: Head right.
Rev: XEP. Beak of galley, beneath it club and the name ΑΛΚΙΝΟΥ
Copper. Dichalcon. 2.42 g, 14 mm, ↓. State Historical Museum, No. 35.

171. Obv: Same.
Rev: Same. name [ΤΡ]ΥΘΩΝ
Copper. Dichalcon (Bertier, 1912, pp. 60-61).

Series about 140-130 B.C.

172. Obv: Head of Hermes wearing petasus, right. Border of dots.
Rev: XEP. Butting bull left, above it caduceus.
Copper. Dichalcon. 2.79 g, 14 mm (?). Private collection.

173. Obv: Head of Hermes wearing petasus right, at left caduceus.
Rev: XEP. Cornucopiae, at left the name ΠΥΘΙΩΝΟ
Copper. Dichalcon. 2.72 g, 18 mm, ↘. State Hermitage, No. 215.

174. Obv: Same.
Rev: Same, name ΠΡΟΜΑΘΙΩΝΟϹ
Copper. Dichalcon. 2.80 g, 16 mm, ↙. British Museum.

175. Obv: Head of Hermes wearing petasus, right.
Rev: Cornucopiae, to right a star.
Copper. Chalcon (?). 1.05 g, 13 mm, ↙. State Chersonesus Museum, No. 5987.

Issue about 130-120 B.C.

176. Obv: Head of Apollo wearing wreath, right.
Rev: XEP. Tripod, to right the name ΑΠΟΛΛΩ
Copper. Dichalcon. 1.88 g, 15 mm, ↗. State Chersonesus Museum, No. 8182.

Issue about the third quarter of the IInd century B.C.

177. Obv: Eagle standing with folding wings, left.
Rev: XEP. Standing goat left.
Copper. Dichalcon (?). 1.53 g, 12 mm, ↓. State Historical Museum, No. 3775.

178. Obv: Maiden standing right.
Rev: XEP. Standing goat right, before it obscure object.
Copper. Dichalcon (?). 1.58 g, 12 mm (?) (Bertier, 1912, plate, 8).

Series about 120-110 B.C.

179. Obv: Head of Maiden wearing mural crown right, behind it a bow and quiver.
Rev: XEP. Standing hind right, beneath it the name ΜΟΙΡΙΟΣ
Silver. Drachma. 3.63 g, 20 mm, ↑. State Historical Museum, No. 9132.

180. Obv: Same.
Rev: Same, name ΑΠΟΛΛΩΝΙΔΑ
Silver. Drachma. 4.15 g, 19 mm, ↑. State Historical Museum, No. 9141.

181. Obv: Same.
Rev: Same, name ΔΙΟΤΙΜΟΥ
Silver. Drachma. 3.17 g, 19 mm, ↑. British Museum.

182. Obv: Head of beardless Heracles wearing fillet.
Rev: XEP. Club left, beneath it the name ΜΟΙΡΙΟΣ
Silver. Hemidrachm, 1.35 g, 17 mm, (?) (Bertier, 1906a, plate I, 10).

183. Obv: Same.
Rev: Same, name ΔΙΟΤΙΜΟΥ
Silver. Hemidrachm. 1.83 g, 17 mm (?) (Bertier, 1906a, plate I, 9).

184. Obv: Head of Maiden wearing mural crown right, behind it a quiver.
Rev: XEP. Standing hind right, to right a trophy (?), beneath these the name ΑΠΟΛ
Copper. Dichalcon. 1.56 g, 17 mm, ↗. State Historical Museum, No. 12.

185. Obv: Same.
Rev: Same, name [H]ΡΟΞΕ
Copper. Dichalcon. 1.14 g, 13 mm, ↑. State Hermitage, No. 579.

186. Obv: Same.
Rev: Same, name ΣΩΤΗΡΙ
Copper. Dichalcon. 2.92 g, 17 mm, ↑. State Hermitage, No. 239.

Issue about 120-110 B.C.

187. Obv: Head of Maiden wearing wreath right, hair done up into a topknot, behind it a quiver.
Rev: XEP. Standing hind left, at left the name ΗΡΟΔΟΤ
Copper. Dichalcon (Oreshnikov, 1884, plate II, 17).

Issues about 110-100 B.C.

188. Obv: Bust of Maiden right, behind it a quiver.
Rev: XEP. Standing hind right.
Copper. Dichalcon. 3.77 g, 17 mm, ↗. V. N. Orekhov collection.

189. Obv: Head of Helios wearing radiate crown, right.
Rev: XEP. Cornucopiae, at its sides the caps of the Dioscuri, beneath this the name [H]ΡΑΚΛΕ
Copper. Dichalcon. 3.16 g, 16 mm, ↑. State Hermitage, No. 215B. (215c).

190. Obv: Jugate heads of Dioscuri, both wearing pilos, right, a star above each head.

Rev: XEP. Prow left.

Copper. Chalcon (?). 0.60 g, 12 mm, ↙ . D. I. Moshnyagin collection.

Issue about 100-90 B.C.

191. Obv: Head of Maiden wearing fillet, right.

Rev: Maiden striking down hind, left, at right the name ΔΗΜΗΤΡΙΟΥ

Silver. Drachma. 4.58 g, 16 mm, ↗. British Museum.

Issues about 90-80 B.C.

192. Obv: Bust of Maiden right, at back a bow and quiver.

Rev: Wreath, within it a hind with lowered head right, above it a monogram (b)

Copper. Tetrachalcon. 5.51 g, 23 mm, ↖ . State Historical Museum, No. 1774.

193. Obv: Same.

Rev: Same, monogram (c) beneath.

Copper. Dichalcon. 2.35 g, 17 mm, ↑ . D. I. Moshnyagin collection.

194. Obv: Same.

Rev: Same, beneath exergue line the monogram (d).

Copper (Giel, 1891, plate IV, 11).

195. Obv: Same.

Rev: Same, beneathe exergue line the monogram (h).

Copper (Zograph, 1951, plate XXXVI, 20).

Issue about 80-70 B.C.

196. Obv: Skull of hind facing.

Rev: XEP. Bow and case.

Copper. Dichalcon. 4.20 g, 16 mm, → . V. N. Orekhov collection.

Issue about 70-63 B.C.

197. Obv: Bust of Maiden right, at back bow and quiver.

Rev: XEP. Eagle with spread wings upon thunderbolt facing three-quarters left, at left monogram (c)

Copper. Tetrachalcon. 6.90 g, 22 mm, ↑ . State Historical Museum, No. 15.

198. Obv: Same, smaller size.

Rev: Same.

Copper. Tetrachalcon. 6.07 g, 19 mm, ↖ . State Hermitage, No. 242a.

Issue about 63-47 B.C.

199. Obv: Male head right. Countermark "star".
Rev: Maiden standing facing, in left hand bow, in right spear, at left monogram (c). Countermark "star".
Copper. Obol. 17.30 g, 31 mm, ↑. State Historical Museum, No. 21.

Issue about 47-44 B.C.

200. Obv: Butting bull left, above it the inscription ΕΛΕΥΘΕ, beneath exergue line [ΧΕΡCΟΝΗC]
Rev: Maiden striking hind with spear, at right monogram (ƒ).
Copper. Obol. 15.53 g, 25 mm, ↙. State Hermitage, No. 251.

201. Obv: ΧΕΡCΟ ΕΛΕΥ. Maiden striking hind with spear, left.
Rev: Butting bull left, around it the name ΑΠΟΛΛΩΝΙΔΟΥ
Copper. Obol. 11.11 g, 24 mm, ↓. State Chersonesus Museum, No. 4646/2.

Issues about 44-17 B.C.

202. Obv: Head of Maiden right. Countermark "star and crescent".
Rev: XEP. Caduceus, at right monogram (ƒ).
Copper. Tetrachalcon. 6.12 g, 20 mm, ↘. State Historical Museum, No. 1674.

203. Obv: Head of Zeus right.
Rev: ΧΕΡCΟΝΗCΟΥ. Thunderbolt. Countermark: monogram (ƒ).
Copper. Tetrachalcon. 3.53 g, 19 mm, ↓. State Historical Museum, No. 36.

204. Obv: XEP. Head of Zeus wearing fillet, right.
Rev: Maiden standing with bow and spear, at left monogram (ƒ).
Copper. Tetrachalcon. 8.32 g, 21 mm, ↑. State Hermitage, No. 247.

205. Obv: Same.
Rev: Same.
Copper. Tetrachalcon. 7.02 g, 21 mm, ↑. State Historical Museum, No. 1670.

Issues of End of Ist Century B.C.

206. Obv: XEP. Head of Zeus wearing fillet right, at right a star.
Rev: Maiden standing with bow and spear, at left monograms (ƒ) and (ȝ).
Copper. Tetrachalcon. 5.12 g, 19 mm, ↑. State Hermitage, No. 258.

207. Obv: Male bearded head left, with long hair at back (a Scythian?), at left undecipherable remains of inscription.
Rev: Maiden standing with bow and spear.
Copper. Tetrachalcon (?). 4.32 g, 19 mm, ↗. V. V. Pereplesnin collection.

Issue of End of Ist century B.C.—Beginning of Ist century A.D.

208. Obv: XEP. Head of divinity Chersonas wearing fillet right, at right a star.
Rev: Maiden standing with bow and spear, at left monogram (⨍).
Copper. Tetrachalcon. 4.69 g, 18 mm, ↘. State Historical Museum, No 1885.

209. Obv: Same.
Rev: Same.
Copper. Tetrachalcon. 2.88 g, 18 mm, ↘. State Historical Museum, No. 1770.

210. Obv: Same.
Rev: Same.
Copper. Tetrachalcon. 4.43 g, 17 mm, ↑. State Historical Museum, No. 4226.

Issue of First Quarter of Ist century A.D.

211. Obv: Head of divinity Chersonas laureate right, at right star and serpent.
Rev: Maiden standing with bow and spear, beneath an inscription XEP.
Copper. Tetrachalcon (3.30 g,). 18 mm, ↑. State Chersonesus Museum.

212. Obv: Same (same die).
Rev: Same, at sides an inscription X – E P.
Copper. Tetrachalcon. 3.86 g, 16 mm. ↙. State Chersonesus Museum, No 4632.

Issues of Second Quarter of Ist Century

213. Obv: Head of divinity Chersonas right, at right a serpent.
Rev: XEP. Wreath.
Copper. Tetrachalcon. 3.59 g, 13 mm, ↙. State Chersonesus Museum, No. 4630.

214. Obv: Head of divinity Chersonas laureate right.
Rev: XEP. Wreath.
Copper. Tetrachalcon. 6.16 g, 18 mm, ↘. State Chersonesus Museum, No. 218.

Issue of A.D. 47

215. Obv: XEP. Head of divinity Chersonas wearing fillet right.
Rev: Maiden standing with bow and spear, at right a hind; at left, monogram (h) and date—AO.
Gold. Stater. 7.75 g, 20 mm, ↗. State Historical Museum, No. 31539/A—372.

Series of A.D. 49

216. Obv: Head of divinity Chersonas wearing fillet right.
Rev: Maiden standing with bow and spear, at right a hind, at left monogram (ħ) and date—OΓ
Gold. Stater. 7.84 g, 20 mm, ↑ . Berlin Museum.

217. Obv: Head of divinity Chersonas right, at right a serpent.
Rev: Hind right, above a monogram (ħ), at right symbol Δ , beneath the date OΓ.
Copper. Tetrachalcon. 2.30 g, 17 mm, ↗ . State Hermitage, No. 266.

Issue of A.D. 50

218. Obv: Head of divinity Chersonas right, at right a serpent.
Rev: Hind right, above a monogram (ħ), at right a symbol (ι), beneath the date OΔ
Copper. Assarion (=tetrachalcon). 3.30 g, 18 mm, ↗ . State Chersonesus Museum, No. 995.

Issue of A.D. 51

219. Obv: XEP. Head of divinity Chersonas right, at right a serpent, beneath the date OЄ
Rev: Nike standing left, with wreath and palm branch, at left the symbol (i).
Copper. Assarion. 5.05 g, 17 mm, ↗. State Hermitage, No. 268.

Issue of A.D. 52

220. Obv: Same, beneath the date OϚ (76).
Rev: Same.
Copper. Assarion. 3.87 g, 16 mm, ↑ . State Chersonesus Museum, No. 6203.

Issue of A.D. 53

221. Obv: Same, beneath the date OZ.
Rev: Same.
Copper. Assarion. 4.02 g, 18 mm, ↑ . State Chersonesus Museum, No. 240.

Issue of A.D. 54

222. Obv: Same, beneath the date HO.
Rev: Same.
Copper. Assarion. 3.53 g, 19 mm, ↑ . State Chersonesus Museum, No. 11.

Issue about A.D. 63-68

223. Obv: ΧΕb. Head of divinity Chersonas right, at right a serpent and star.
Rev: Nike, at left the symbol (i).
Copper. Assarion. 7.83 g, 10 mm, ↘. State Chersonesus Museum, No 5824.

224. Obv: Same.
Rev: Same. at left the inscription XE.
Copper. Assarion. 2.49 g, 17 mm, ↓. State Historical Museum, No. 1751.

225. Obv: Same.
Rev: Same, no inscription.
Copper. Assarion. 3.95 g, 17 mm, ↘. Private collection.

Issue about A.D. 69-79

226. Obv: ΕΙΡΗΝΗC CΕΒΑCΤΗC. Bust of Maiden right, behind a quiver, at right monogram (h).
Rev: ΧΕΡΣΟΝΑΣΕΙΤΩΝ. Head of bearded male wearing fillet right, beneath it a symbol Δ.
Copper. Tetrassarion. 10.79 g, 23 mm, ↓. State Chersonesus Museum, unnumbered.

227. Obv: Same, monogram at left.
Rev: Same, no inscription.
Copper. Tetrassarion. 13.10 g, 26 mm, ↙. State Hermitage, No. 279.

Series of A.D. 80

228. Obv: ΧΕΡ. Bust of divinity Chersonas left, at left a serpent.
Rev: Maiden standing with bow and spear, at left monogram (f) and date ΔΡ.
Gold. Stater. 7.69 g, 19 mm, ↗. State Hermitage, No. 624.

229. Obv: ΕΙΡΗΝΗC CΕΒΑCΤΗC. Bust of divinity Chersonas right, at right a lyre, at left palm branch.
Rev: ΧΕΡΣΟΝΝΗΣΕΙΤ[ΩΝ] ΕΤ[ΟΥΣ] ϘΔ. Maiden standing with bow and spear.
Copper. Tetrassarion. 15.72 g, 29 mm, ↘. State Historical Museum, No. 1754.

230. Obv: Same (same die).
Rev: ΕΙΡΗΝΗC CΕΒΑCΤΗC. Bust of Maiden right, at right monogram (h).
Copper. Tetrassarion. 12.50 g, 28 mm, ↘. V. N. Orekhov collection.

Issue of A.D. 81

231. Obv: Same (same die).
Rev: Same, date ϘЄ
Copper. Tetrassarion. 8.76 g, 24 mm, ↘. State Chersonesus Museum, No. 2/1.

Issue of A.D. 82

232. Obv: Same (same die).
Rev: Same, date Ϙ[(106).
Copper. Tetrassarion. 19.00 g, 25 mm, ↘. Bakhchisarai Local History Museum, No. 5821.

Series of A.D. 85

233. Obv: XEP. Bust of divinity Chersonas left, at left a serpent.
Rev: ΒΑCΙΛΕΥΟΥCΗC ΕΤΟΥ[C] ΡΘ. Maiden standing, at right monogram (A).
Gold. Stater. 7.70 g, 20 mm, ↗. Bibliothèque Nationale, Paris.

234. Obv: ΕΙΡΗΝΗC CΕΒΑCΤΗC. Bust of divinity Chersonas right, at right lyre, at left palm branch.
Rev: Maiden standing with bow and spear, date Ε[ΤΟΥC] ΡΘ.
Countermark "Maiden".
Copper. Tetrassarion. 8.45 g, 26 mm, ↘. State Chersonesus Musuem, No. 3721 (Anokhin, 1963a, plate IV, 4).

Issue of A.D. 87

235. Obv: Same (same die as in Nos. 229-232).
Rev: XEP. Same, date ϘΙΑ
Copper. Tetrassarion. 12.00 g, 25 mm, ↘. State Historical Museum, No. 1759.

Issue of A.D. 96 and later (?)

236. Obv: Same.
Rev: Same, date ΕΤΟΥC ΡΚ
Copper. Tetrassarion (Giel, 1896, plate XIX, 37).

237. Obv: Same.
Rev: Same, at right a bucranium.
Copper. Tetrassarion. 11.81 g, 27 mm, ↘. State Chersonesus Museum, No. 4626.

238. Obv: Same.
Rev: Same.
Copper. Tetrassarion. 11.67 g, 25 mm, ↓. State Historical Museum, No. 1761.

239. Obv: Same.
Rev: Same, no bucranium.
Copper. Tetrassarion. 11.78 g, 27 mm, ↓. State Historical Museum, No. 1763.

240. Obv: Same.
Rev: Same.
Copper. Tetrassarion. 9.79 g, 27 mm, ↓. Bakhchisarai Local History Museum, No. 5821 (76/2).

241. Obv: Same.
Rev: Same, bucranium at right.
Copper. Tetrassarion. 11.91 g, 26 mm, ↓. State Chersonesus Museum, No. 4744/1.

242. Obv: Same. no inscription.
Rev: Same, no bucranium.
Copper. Tetrassarion. 10.37 g, 27 mm, ↓. Bakhchisarai Local History Museum, No. 5821 (76/3).

243. Obv: Same.
Rev: Same, bucranium.
Copper. Tetrassarion. 12.20 g, 26 mm, ↓. State Historical Museum, No. 1765.

244. Obv: Same.
Rev: Same, no bucranium. Countermark "Maiden".
Copper. Tetrassarion. 11.54 g, 27 mm, ↙. State Historical Museum, No. 1766.

245. Obv: Same, inscription ΕΙΡΗΝΗϹ ϹΕΒΑϹΤΗϹ
Rev: Same, countermark "Maiden".
Copper. Tetrassarion. 11.58 g, 28 mm, ↙. State Hermitage, No. 277.

246. Obv: Same.
Rev: Same, at right a bucranium.
Copper. Tetrassarion. 9.49 g, 26 mm, ↓. State Historical Museum, No. 1767.

Issue of A.D. 104

247. Obv: Head of divinity Chersonas left.
Rev: Maiden standing with bow and spear, at left monogram (ħ), at sides date ΡΚ-Η
Copper. Assarion (?).

Issue of A.D. 107

248. Obv: Bust of divinity Chersonas left, at left a serpent, traces of circular inscription.
Rev: Maiden standing with bow and spear, at left monogram (ħ), inscription ЄΤΟΥϹ ΡΛ-Α
Gold. Stater. 7.75 g, 19.5 mm, ↘. British Museum.

Issue of A.D. 134

249. Obv: Bust of divinity Chersonas left, at left a serpent.
Rev: Maiden standing with bow and spear, at left monogram (ħ), digits

of date Р-N-Н around her.
Gold. Stater. 6,95 g, 19 mm, (?). Odessa State Archeological Museum.

Issues about A.D. 138-161

250. Obv: ΧΕΡϹ. Bust of divinity Chersonas right, at right a lyre.
Rev: ΧΕΡ. Maiden standing with bow and spear, at left a hind, at right monogram (h).
Copper. Tetrassarion. 10.14 g, 24 mm, ↙. State Chersonesus Museum, No. 8315.

251. Obv: ΧΕΡ ΕΛΕ. Same.
Rev: ΧΕΡ. Same, hind at right, no monogram.
Copper. Tetrassarion. 11.22 g, 26 mm, ↓. D. I. Moshnyagin Collection.

252. Obv: ΧΕΡϹΟΝΗ ΕΛΕΥΘ. Bust of divinity Chersonas right.
Rev: ΠΑΡΘΕΝΟϹ. Maiden standing, hind at left.
Copper. Tetrassarion. 8.72 g, 24 mm, ↙. Stage Hermitage, No. 285.

253. Obv: ΕΛΕΥ. Bust of divinity Chersonas right.
Rev: ΧΕΡϹΟ ΕΛΕ. Maiden standing at right a hind, at left monogram (h).
Copper. Tetrassarion. 12.02 g, 24 mm, ↙. State Hermitage, No. 288.

254. Obv: Same (same die).
Rev: ΧΕΡ-ϹΟ (first two letters in ligature). Same, no monogram.
Copper. Tetrassarion (Oreshnikov, 1915, plate II, 38).

255. Obv: ΧΕΡ. Same (same die, inscription altered).
Rev: ΕΛΕΥΘΕΡΑϹ. Same.
Copper. Tetrassarion. 7.72 g, 26 mm, ↙. State Historical Museum, No. 1780.

256. Obv: ΘϵΡΑ-Ϲ. Same, at right lyre and branch.
Rev: ΧΕΡ ϵΛϵΥ. Same.
Copper. Tetrassarion. 11.48 g, 24 mm, ✓. State Historical Museum, No. 1784.

257. Obv: Same (same die, inscription altered).
Rev: ΕΛΕΥΘΕΡΑϹ. Same.
Copper. Tetrassarion. 10.51 g, 24 mm, ↙. State Chersonesus Museum, No. 20.

258. Obv: ΕΛΕΥΘΕΡΑϹ. Butting bull left.
Rev: ΧΕΡϹΟΝΗϹΟΥ (N and H in ligature). Maiden striking hind with spear, left.
Copper. Dupondius. 7.37 g, 20 mm, ←. State Chersonesus Museum, No. 14/2.

259. Obv: Same.
Rev: Same.
Copper. Dupondius. 6.67 g, 22 mm, ↙. State Hermitage, No. 290.

260. Obv: Same.
Rev: ΧΕΡϹΟ. Same.
Copper. Dupondius. 7.07 g, 21 mm, ↙. State Hermitage, No. 292.

261. Obv: Head of divinity Chersonas wearing wreath left, at left a palm branch.
Rev: ΧΕΡ–Ϲ. Maiden standing with bow and spear, crown upon head.
Copper. Assarion. 3.57 g, 18 mm, ↑. State Hermitage, No. 263.

262. Obv: ΧΕΡϹΟΝΗϹΟΥ. Bust of divinity Chersonas right, wreath upon head, at right, lyre.
Rev: ΕΛΕΥΘΕΡΑϹ. Same.
Copper. Tetrassarion. 7.33 g, 24 mm, ↙. State Hermitage, No. 307.

Issues about A.D. 161-180

263. Obv: ΧΕΡ. Head of divinity Chersonas left, lyre at left.
Rev: ЄΛЄ-Υ. Maiden standing with bow and spear, hind at left.
Copper. Tetrassarion. 9.20 g, 23 mm, ↘. State Historical Museum, No. 1813.

264. Obv: ΧЄΡϹΟΝΗϹΟΥ. Same, crown on head.
Rev: ΕΛΕΥΘΕΡΑϹ. Same.
Copper. Tetrassarion. 9.44 g, 24 mm, ↙. State Historical Museum, No. 1816.

265. Obv: ΧΕΡ. Same, right.
Rev: Ε-Λ-Ε-Υ. Same.
Copper. Tetrassarion. 6.57 g, 25 mm, ↓. State Hermitage, No. 336.

266. Obv: ΧΕΡ. Asclepius standing, head turned left, serpent staff at right hand, symbol Γ at right.
Rev: ΕΛ-Ε-Υ. Hygieia standing right, serpent in right hand, patera in left.
Copper. Tressis. 4.47 g, 19 mm, ↓. State Hermitage, No. 338 (reverse).

267. Obv: ΧΕΡ. Bust of divinity Chersonas right, lyre at right, wreath on head.
Rev: ΕΛΕΥΘΕΡ. Maiden standing facing, hind at left.
Copper. tetrassarion. 6.13 g, 25 mm, ↓. Simferopol Local History Museum, No. 280.

268. Obv: Same.
Rev: Same.

Copper. Tetrassarion. 6.32 g, 23 mm, ↓ . State Historical Museum, No. 1934 (obverse). 8.29 g, 23 mm, ↘ . State Historical Museum, No. 6202 (reverse).

269. Obv: Same.
Rev: Same.
Copper. Tetrassarion. 6.63 g, 23 mm, ↙ . State Hermitage, No. 326.

270. Obv: Maiden striking hind, left.
Rev: ΧΕΡ. Butting bull left.
Copper. Dupondius. 7.15 g, 23 mm, ↙. State Hermitage, No. 333.

271. Obv: Same.
Rev: Same.
Copper. Dupondius. 5.30 g, 19 mm, ↓ . State Chersonesus Museum, No 5822.

272. Obv: Same.
Rev: Same.
Copper. Dupondius. 4.80 g, 17 mm, → . State Historical Museum, No. 1881.

Issues about A.D. 180-192

273. Obv: ΧΕΡ. Bust of divinity Chersonas right, wreath on head, lyre at right.
Rev: ΕΛΕΥΘΕΡΑC . Maiden standing with bow and spear, hind at left.
Copper. Tetrassarion. 8.26 g, 24 mm, ↙ . State Hermitage, No. 311.

274. Obv: Same.
Rev: Same, symbol Δ and hind at left.
Copper. Tetrassarion. 7,10 g, 22 mm, ↙ . State Hermitage, No. 311.

275. Obv: Same, lyre and palm branch at left.
Rev: Same.
Copper. Tetrassarion. 5.45 g, 22 mm, ↙. State Hermitage, No. 318.

276. Obv: Same, no lyre or palm branch.
Rev: ΕΛΕΥΘΕ . Same.
Copper. Tetrassarion. 6.43 g, 23 mm, ↘ . State Historical Museum, No. 1805.

277. Obv: ΧΕΡ . Asclepius standing, symbol Γ at right.
Rev: ΕΛΕΥΘΕΡΑC . Hygieia standing right.
Copper. Tressis. 3.40 g, 22 mm, ↙ . State Historical Museum, No. 1894.

278. Obv: Same.
Rev: Same.

Copper. Tressis. 5.69 g, 22 mm, ↓. State Historical Museum, No. 1900.

279. Obv: ЄΛΕΥΘЄΡΑϹ. Hygieia.
Rev: ΧЄΡ. Asclepius.
Copper. Tressis. 4.46 g, 21 mm, ↓. State Chersonesus Museum, No. 4/2.

280. Obv: ΧΕΡ. Maiden striking hind with spear, right.
Rev: ЄΛΕΥΘΕΡΑϹ. Bull right.
Copper. Dupondius. 5.77 g, 20 mm, ↓. State Hermitage, No. 321.

281. Obv: ЄΛЄΥΘЄΡΑϹ. Bull right.
Rev: ΧЄΡ. Maiden striking hind with spear, right.
Copper. Dupondius. 4.53 g, 18 mm, ↑. State Hermitage, No. 315.

282. Obv: Same.
Rev: Same.
Copper. Dupondius. 3.45 g, 21 mm, →. State Chersonesus Museum, No. 80.

283. Obv: ΧΕΡ. Bust of divinity Chersonas right, wreath on head, lyre to right.
Rev: Nike standing left, monogram (j) at left.
Copper. Assarion. 2.05 g, 17 mm, ↓. State Hermitage, No. 1289.

Series about A.D. 192-211

284. Obv: ЄΛЄΥΘЄΡΑϹ. Asclepius.
Rev: ΧЄΡϹΟΝΗϹϹΟΥ. Hygieia, symbol 7 at left.
Copper. Tressis. 4.65 g, 20 mm, ↓. State Hermitage, No. 308.

285. Obv: ЄΛЄΥΘЄΡΑΑϹ. Butting bull left.
Rev: ΧЄΡϹΟΝΗϹϹΟΥ. Maiden striking hind with spear, left.
Copper. Dupondius. 4.27 g, 20 mm, ↙. State Chersonesus Museum, No. 19/1.

Issues about A.D. 212-217

286. Obv: ΕΛΕΥΘΕΡΑϹ. Bust of Caracalla right, wreath on head, lyre at right.
Rev: ΧΕΡϹΟΝΗϹΟΥ. Maiden standing right, hind at left.
Copper. Tetrassarion. 6.23 g, 24 mm, ↗. State Hermitage, No. 298.

287. Obv: Same, bust of Julia Domna right, lyre at left.
Rev: Same, hind at right.
Copper. Tetrassarion. 5.62 g, 23 mm, ↙. State Hermitage, No. 301.

288. Obv: Same.
Rev: Same.
Copper. Tetrassarion. 6.07 g, 22 mm, ↙. State Chersonesus Museum, No. 82.

Issues about A.D. 218-222

289. Obv: ΕΛΕΥΘΕΡΑC. Bust of Elagabalus right, wreath on head, lyre at right.
Rev: ΧΕΡCΟΝΗCΟΥ. Maiden standing left, hind at left.
Copper. Tetrassarion. 6.16 g, 24 mm, ↑. State Chersonesus Museum, No. 99.

290. Obv: Same, bust of Severus Alexander right, lyre at right.
Rev: Same.
Copper. Tetrassarion. 5.77 g, 24 mm, ↙. State Hermitage. No. 300.

Issues about A.D. 212-222

291. Obv: ΧΕΡCΟΝΗCΟΥ. Hygieia.
Rev: ΕΛΕΥΘΕΡΑC. Asclepius.
Copper. Tressis. 5.05 g, 20 mm, ↓. State Chersonesus Museum, No 3129.

292. Obv: ΕΛΕΥΘΕΡΑC. Butting bull left.
Rev: ΧΕΡCΟΝΗCΟΥ. Maiden striking hind with spear, left.
Copper. Dupondius. 4.16 g, 19 mm, ↘. State Chersonesus Museum, No. 81.

293. Obv: Same, bull right.
Rev: Same.
Copper. Dupondius. 3.55 g, 18 mm, ↗. V. N. Orekhov collection.

294. Obv: Same.
Rev: Same.
Copper. Dupondius. 2.85 g, 20 mm, ↙. State Hermitage, No. 306.

295. Obv: Χ-Ε.... Head wearing fillet right.
Rev: Nike left, letters ΠΑ (?) at left.
Copper. Assarion. (1.69 g,). 18 mm, ↓. State Hermitage, No. 311b.

Issues about A. D. 222-235

296. Obv: ΕΛΕΥΘΕΡΑC. Bust of divinity Chersonas right, lyre at right.
Rev: ΧΕΡCΟΝΗC. Maiden standing, hind at right.
Copper. Tetrassarion. 5.13 g, 21 mm, ↓. State Chersonesus Museum, No. 5/1.

297. Obv: Same.
Rev: Same.

Copper. Tetrassarion. 7.44 g, 24 mm, ↗. State Chersonesus Museum, No. 5/2.

298. Obv: Same.
Rev: Same.
Copper. Tetrassarion. 5.74 g, 23 mm, ↗. State Historical Museum, No. 2031.

299. Obv: Same.
Rev: Same.
Copper. Tetrassarion. 7.45 g, 21 mm, ↘. State Chersonesus Museum, No. 2046.

300. Obv: Same.
Rev: Same, countermark Γ
Copper. Tetrassarion. 4.64 g, 22 mm, ↑. Berlin Museum.

301. Obv: Same,
Rev: Same.
Copper. Tetrassarion. 5.98 g, 21 mm, ↑. State Hermitage. No. 328.

302. Obv: Same.
Rev: Same.
Copper. Tetrassarion. 6.10 g, 20 mm, ↗. State Hermitage, No. 590.

303. Obv: Same.
Rev: Same.
Copper. Tetrassarion. 5.64 g, 23 mm, ↙. State Chersonesus Museum, No. 4741.

Issues about A.D. 253-268

304. Obv: ЄΛЄΥΘЄΡΑϹ. Bust of divinity Chersonas right, lyre at right.
Rev: ΧЄΡϹΟΝΗϹΟΥ. Maiden standing, lyre at left. symbol B at right.
Copper. Dupondius (?). 5.17 g, 20 mm, ↗. State Historical Museum, No. 2044.

305. Obv: Same.
Rev: Same.
Copper. Dupondius (?). 5.80 g, 21 mm, ↗. State Hermitage. No. 349.

306. Obv: Same.
Rev: Same.
Copper. Dupondius (?). 3.62 g, 23 mm, ↗. State Hermitage, No. 352.

307. Obv: Same.
Rev: Same.
Copper. Dupondius (?). 4.70 g, 18 mm, ↗. State Hermitage, No. 334e.

308. Obv: Same.
Rev: Same.
Copper. Dupondius (?). 3.34 g, 19 mm, ↓ . State Chersonesus Museum, No. 4883.

Issue of period of Zeno (474-491)

309. Obv: DN ZENO PF AVG. Bust of emperor right.
Rev: CONCODIAR. Emperor standing right, spear in right hand, orb in left, foot placed upon captive.
Copper. 4.50 g, 18 mm, ↙ . State Chersonesus Museum, No. 4792.

Issues of period of Justinian I (527-565)

310. Obv: DN IVSTINIANVS. Bust of emperor right.
Rev: VICTORIA AVGGGЄ. Emperor standing, long cross in right hand, orb in left.
Copper. Pentanummion. 2.40 g, 18 mm, ↓ . State Chersonesus Museum, No. 6416.

311. Obv: Same.
Rev: VICTOR. Same.
Copper. Pentanummion. 3.49 g, 16 mm, ↓ . Private collection.

312. Obv: Same.
Rev: Same, left hand resting on shield.
Copper. Pentanummion. 2.65 g, 16 mm, ↙ . State Chersonesus Museum, unnumbered.

313. Obv: Same.
Rev: Same, standard (labarum) in right hand.
Copper. Pentanummion. 2.91 g, 12 mm, ↘ . Private collection.

314. Obv: DN I VSTIN I ANVSPP. Bust of emperor right.
Rev: Monogram (K)
Copper. Pentanummion. 2.55 g, 15 mm, ↓ . State Chersonesus Museum, No. 4757/6.

Issues of period of Justin II (565-578)

315. Obv: XЄPCWNOC . Emperor and consort standing.
Rev: Standing figure with chrism, symbol M at right, cross above symbol.
Copper. 40 nummia. 13.69 g, 30 mm, ↙ . State Historical Museum, No. 1923.

316. Obv: Same.
Rev: Same, symbol K at left.
Copper. 20 nummia. 6.95 g, 24 mm, ↓ . D. P. Vashkov. collection.

317. Obv: XЄPCONOC. Emperor and consort standing.
Rev: Standing figure with chrism, symbol at right.
Copper. 8 pentanummia. 13.96 g, 31 mm, ↙ . State Historical Museum, No. 1928.

318. Obv: Same.
Rev: Same, symbol Δ at right.
Copper. 4 pentanummia. 5.85 g, 25 mm, ↙ . State Chersonesus Museum, No. 4778.

319. Obv: Same
Rev: Same.
Copper. 4 pentanummia. 6.90 g, 21 mm, ↘ . State Historical Museum, No. 1935.

Series of period of Mauricius Tiberius (582-602)

320. Obv: DN MAVRIC PP AVG. . Emperor and consort standing.
Rev: Standing figure with chrism, symbol H at right.
Copper. 8 pentanummia. 13.36 g, 31 mm, ↗ State Hermitage No. 1995.

321. Obv: Same.
Rev: Same, symbol Δ
Copper. 4 pentanummia. 6.90 g, 23 mm, ↗ . State Chersonesus Museum, No. 9018.

Issue of period of Heraclius (610-641)

322. Obv: DD NN HЄR ЄT HЄRACON. Emperor and his son Heraclius Constantine standing.
Rev: Standing figure with chrism, symbol H at left.
Copper. 8 pentanummia. 7.90 g, 25 mm, ↗ . State Hermitage, No. 2700.

Issues of second half of VIIIth century.

323. Obv: Two standing figures.
Rev: Standing figure, Δ at right.
Copper. 4 pentanummia. Cast. 5.71 g, 19 mm, ↓ . State Chersonesus Museum, No 4190.

324. Obv: Same.
Rev: Same.
Copper. 4 pentanummia. Cast. 3.57 g, 16 mm, ↓ . State Hermitage, No. 5895.

325. Obv: Same, symbol B at right.
Rev: Same.
Copper. 4 pentanummia. Cast. 4.61 g, 18 mm, ↙ . State Hermitage, No. 5937.

326. Obv: Bust of emperor right.
Rev: Emperor standing with cross and orb.
Copper. Pentanummion. Cast. 2.56 g, 12 mm, ↘ . State Chersonesus Museum, unnumbered.

Issues of end of VIIth century to first third of IXth

327. Obv: Letter П
Rev: Letter X (?).
Copper. Cast. (Sokolova, 1971a plate II).

328. Obv: Letter П
Rev: Letter П
Copper. Cast. 1.93 g, 13 mm, ↑ . D. P. Vashkov collection.

329. Obv: Same.
Rev: Same.
Copper. Cast. 2.56 g, 16 mm, ← . State Chersonesus Museum, No. 9623.

Issue of the period of Theophilus (829-842), about 834-842

330. Obv: Inscription in two lines: DN - TH
Rev: Letters П°Λ
Copper. Cast. 1.25 g, 13 mm, ↖ . State Chersonesus Museum, No. 5344.

Issues of the period of Michael III (842-867)

Series I

a) of the emperor

331. Obv: Letter M
Rev: Cross.
Copper. Cast. 1.55 g, 13 mm. V. N. Orekhov collection.

332. Obv: Same, at right a small letter B (?).
Rev: Same.
Copper. Struck (?). 0.38 g, 13 mm, V. N. Orekhov collection.

b) of the proteuon

333. Obv: Letter П
Rev: Cross.
Copper. 1.21 g, 13 mm. State Chersonesus Museum, No. 4924.

334. Obv: Letter П
Rev: Cross.
Copper (Oreshnikov, 1911, plate B, 4).

335. Obv: Same.
Rev: Same.
Copper (Oreshnikov, 1911, plate B, 3).

336. Obv: Same.
Rev: Same.
Copper. 0.48 g, 15 mm. V. N. Orekhov collection.

c) <u>of the archon</u>

337. Obv: Letter A
Rev: Cross.
Copper. 0.75 g, 12 mm. V. N. Orekhov collection.

<u>Series II</u>

a) <u>of the emperor</u>

338. Obv: Letters MB
Rev: Letters Π°X
Copper. Cast. 1.92 g, 14 mm, ↑ . V. V. Pereplesnin collection.

339. Obv: Same.
Rev: Same.
Copper. Cast. 1.74 g, 14 mm, ↑ . State Chersonesus Museum, No. 8538.

340. Obv: Letters MB (in ligature).
Rev: Same.
Copper. Cast. 1.42 g, 13 mm, ↑ . Private collection.

341. Obv: Letters BM
Rev: Same.
Copper. Cast. 2.25 g, 13 mm, ↑ . V. N. Orekhov collection.

342. Obv: Letters MB
Rev: Same.
Copper. Cast. 0.88 g, 14 mm, ↑ . Private collection.

343. Obv: Same, but from right to left.
Rev: Same, but from right to left.
Copper. Cast. 1.05 g, 11 mm, ↑ . V. V. Pereplesnin collection.

344. Obv: Letters MB
Rev: Letters ΠX
Copper. Cast. 1.74 g, 13 mm, ↓ . State Hermitage, No. 3529.

b) <u>of the proteuon</u>

345. Obv: Letter Π
Rev: Letter X
Copper. 0.86 g, 15 mm, State Chersonesus Museum, No. 4710.

346. Obv: Same, to right a cross.
Rev: Same.
Copper. 0.94 g, 13 mm, V. N. Orekhov collection.

347. Obv: Same, no cross.
Rev: Same.
Copper. Cast. 2.02 g, 14 mm. State Chersonesus Museum, No. 252.

348. Obv: Same.
Rev: Same.
Copper. Cast. 3.01 g, 15 mm, State Chersonesus Museum, No. 9769.

c) <u>of the archon</u>

349. Obv: Letters ΠοΧ
Rev: Letter Α
Copper. 1.75 g, 15 mm, ↙ . State Chersonesus Museum, No. 8842.

Issue of first half of IXth century

350. Obv: Letter Μ (?).
Rev: Letters Πο , at right a cross.
Copper. Cast. 1.79 g, 14 mm. V. V. Pereplesnin collection.

Issues of period of Basil I (867-886)

Issue I

351. Obv: Letter Β
Rev: Cross, traces of inscription (?) around it.
Copper (Oreshnikov, 1911, plate B, 12).

352. Obv: Letter Β , cross at right.
Rev: Letters Πο
Copper (Oreshnikov, 1911, plate B, 5).

353. Obv: Same.
Rev: Same, cross at right and at left.
Copper. 0.86 g, 15 mm, ↓ . V. V. Pereplesnin collection.

354. Obv: Same.
Rev: Same.
Copper. Cast. 1.19 g, 15 mm, ↖ . Private collection.

355. Obv: Same.
Rev: Same, cross at right.
Copper. Cast. 1.30 g, 14 mm, ↓ . Private collection.

356. Obv: Same.
Rev: Same.
Copper. Cast. 1.80 g, 14 mm, ↘ . Private collection.

357. Obv: Same.
Rev: Letter Π
Copper. Cast. 1.92 g, 13 mm, ↑ . D. P. Vashkov collection.

358. Obv: Letter Β
Rev: Letters Πο
Copper. Cast. 1.48 g, 14 mm, ↘ . D. I. Moshnyagin collection.

359. Obv: Letter Β (reversed).
Rev: Letters Πο
Copper. Cast. 1.17 g, 13 mm, ↙ . State Hermitage, No. 3570.

Issue II

360. Obv: Letter
Rev: Cross.
Copper. Cast. 4.91 g, 20 mm, ↑ . V. N. Orekhov collection.

361. Obv: Same.
Rev: Same.
Copper. Cast. 2.10 g, 15 mm, ↑ . State Chersonesus Museum, No. 2042/2.

362. Obv: Same.
Rev: Same.
Copper. Cast. 3.38 g, 18 mm, ↑ . V. N. Orekhov collection.

363. Obv: Same.
Rev: Same.
Copper. Cast. 5.59 g, 18 mm, ↑ . Private collection.

364. Obv: Same.
Rev: Same.
Copper. Cast. 3.28 g, 17 mm, ↑ . Private collection.

365. Obv: Same.
Rev: Same.
Copper. Cast. 3.12 g, 17 mm, ↑ . Private collection.

366. Obv: Same.
Rev: Same.
Copper. Cast. 4.14 g, 16 mm, ↑ . Private collection.

367. Obv: Same.
Rev: Same.
Copper. Cast. 3.52 g, 16 mm, ↑ . State Chersonesus Museum, unnumbered.

368. Obv: Same.
Rev: Same.
Copper. Cast. 3.40 g, 18 mm, ↑ . E. B. Shapiro collection.

369. Obv: Same.
Rev: Same.
Copper. Cast. 5.21 g, 18 mm, ↑ . State Hermitage, No. 3576.

370. Obv: Same.
Rev: Same, no points.
Copper. Cast. 3.43 g, 17 mm, ↑ . State Hermitage, No. 3603.

371. Obv: Same. left.
Rev: Cross, point to either side.
Copper. Cast. 3.83 g, 17 mm, ↖ . Private collection.

372. Obv: Same.
Rev: Same.
Copper. Cast. 3.27 g, 18 mm, ↖ . Private collection.

373. Obv: Same.
Rev: Same.
Copper. Cast. 4.30 g, 18 mm, ↖ . Private collection.

374. Obv: Same.
Rev: Same.
Copper. Cast. 2.57 g, 16 mm, ↖ . Private collection.

375. Obv: Same, reversed.
Rev: Same.
Copper. Cast. 2.40 g, 16 mm, ↑ . E. B. Shapiro collection.

Series III

376. Obv: Letter B , point in lower loop.
Rev: Cross.
Copper. Cast. 2.68 g, 17 mm, ↖ . State Chersonesus Museum, No. 10221.

377. Obv: Letter B , two points to sides.
Rev: Same.
Copper. Cast. 2.79 g, 17 mm, ↑ . State Chersonesus Museum, No. 5287.

378. Obv: Same, left.
Rev: Same.
Copper. Cast (Oreshnikov, 1911, plate B, 11).

379. Obv: Same, right.
Rev: Same.
Copper. Cast. 2.69 g, 17 mm, ↑ . State Historical Museum, No. 1952.

380. Obv: Same.
Rev: Same.
Copper. Cast. 3.20 g, 17 mm, ↑ . Private collection.

381. Obv: Same.
Rev: Same.
Copper. Cast. 2.44 g, 16 mm, ↑ . Private collection.

382. Obv: Same.
Rev: Same.
Copper. Cast. 2.34 g, 14 mm, ↑ . Private collection.

383. Obv: Same.
Rev: Same.
Copper. Cast. 2.38 g, 16 mm, ↑ . Private collection.

Issue of last third of IXth century

384. Obv: Cross on globe-like base.
Rev: Cross on three-stepped base, two points at sides.
Copper. Cast. 3.33 g, 19 mm, ↓ . State Chersonesus Museum, No. 4786/2.

Issues of period of emperor Leo VI and Alexander (886-912)

385. Obv: Letters ΛЄ
Rev: Cross.
Copper. Cast. (3.89 g,). 21 mm, ↑. State Chersonesus Museum, No 8055.

386. Obv: Same (mould impressed with coin No. 385).
Rev: Same (mould impressed with coin No. 385).
Copper. Cast. 3.31 g, 19 mm, ↑. State Hermitage, No. 3704.

387. Obv: Same.
Rev: Same.
Copper. Cast. 3.64 g, 17 mm, →. State Chersonesus Museum, No. 1914.

388. Obv: Same.
Rev: Same (same stamp as in No. 387).
Copper. Cast. 2.25 g, 17 mm, →. V. N. Orekhov collection.

389. Obv: Letters ΛA
Rev: Same (same stamp as in No. 387).
Copper. Cast. 2.97 g, 18 mm, ↑. State Chersonesus Museum. No. 1570.

390. Obv: Letters Λ and A, cross between them.
Rev: Same (same stamp as in No. 387).
Copper. Cast. 3.15 g, 18 mm, ↑. Private collection.

391. Obv: Letters ΛЄ
Rev: Same.
Copper. Cast. 2.06 g, 17 mm, ↑. State Chersonesus Museum, No. 355.

392. Obv: Letters Λ and Є, between them cross.
Rev: Portrait of Leo.
Copper. Cast. 2.50 g, 16 mm, ↑. V. N. Orekhov collection.

393. Obv: Letters ΛЄ (mould impressed with coin No. 391).
Rev: Cross (mould impressed with coin No. 391).
Copper. Cast 1.86 g, 16 mm, ↑. State Chersonesus Museum, No. 10405.

394. Obv: Letters Λ and Є, between them cross (mould impressed with coin No. 392).
Rev: Portrait of Leo (mould impressed with coin No. 392).
Copper. Cast. 3.42 g, 16 mm, ↑. State Chersonesus Museum, No. 61.

395. Obv: Letters Kω, two points at sides.
Rev: Portrait of Constantine.
Copper. Cast. 3.12 g, 17 mm, ↑. State Chersonesus Museum, No. 4702.

396. Obv: Letters ΛЄ (mould impressed with coin No. 393).
Rev: Cross (mould impressed with coin No. 393).
Copper. Cast. 2.25 g, 14 mm, ↑. State Chersonesus Museum, No. 1552.

Issues of period of Constantine Porphyrogenitus (913-959)

Issue I, 913-919

397. Obv: Letters Kω
Rev: Portrait of Constantine.
Copper. Cast. 2.94 g, 17 mm, ↓. State Chersonesus Museum, No. 5509.

398. Obv: Same.
Rev: Same.
Copper. Cast. 2.87 g, 17 mm, ↗. Private collection.

399. Obv: Same (mould impressed with coin No. 397?).
Rev: Same.
Copper. Cast (Oreshnikov, 1905, plate X, 45).

400. Obv: Same (mould impressed with coin No. 398).
Rev: Same (mould impressed with coin No. 398).
Copper. Cast. 1.49 g, 16 mm, ↑. Private collection.

Issue II, A.D. 920

401. Obv: Portrait of Constantine.
Rev: Portrait of Helen.
Copper. Cast. 2.52 g, 16 mm, ↙. State Chersonesus Museum, No, 4664.

402. Obv: Same.
Rev: Same.
Copper. Cast. 2.98 g, 15 mm, ↓. State Chersonesus Museum, No. 4664

Issue III, A.D. 921

403. Obv: Portrait of Constantine, letters P - O at sides.
Rev: Portrait of Helen, letters X - P at sides.
Copper. Cast. 3.37 g, 15 mm, ↓. State Chersonesus Museum, No. 111.

Issue IV, 920-944

404. Obv: Monogram for name of Romanus (I)
Rev: Portrait of Romanus.
Copper. Cast. 2.52 g, 17 mm, ↑. State Chersonesus Museum, No. 4793.

405. Obv: Same.
Rev: Same.
Copper. Cast. 2.80 g, 15 mm, ↑. V. N. Orekhov collection.

406. Obv: Same.
Rev: Same.
Copper. Cast. 2.82 g, 16 mm, ↑ . State Chersonesus Museum, No. 10360.

407. Obv: Same.
Rev: Same.
Copper. Cast. 1.95 g, 14 mm, ↑ . V. N. Orekhov collection.

408. Obv: Monogram for the name Romanus (m)
Rev: Cross, two points at sides.
Copper. Cast. 2.92 g, 17 mm, ↑ . State Chersonesus Museum, No. 4668.

409. Obv: Monogram for the name Romanus (n)
Rev: Cross (same stamp as No. 408).
Copper. Cast. 3.25 g, 18 mm, ↓ . State Chersonesus Museum, No. 1780.

410. Obv: Same, two points at sides.
Rev: Cross (same stamp as No. 408).
Copper. Cast. 3.05 g, 17 mm, ↓ . State Chersonesus Museum, No. 110/2.

411. Obv: Same, different design (o)
Rev: Cross (same stamp as No. 408).
Copper. Cast. 2.70 g, 18 mm, ↓ . V. N. Orekhov collection.

412. Obv: Same.
Rev: Cross (same stamp as No. 408).
Copper. Cast. 2.41 g, 18 mm, ↓ . Private Collection.

413. Obv: Same.
Rev: Cross (mould impressed with coin of type of Nos. 408-412).
Copper. Cast. 2.29 g, 18 mm, ↓ . Private Collection.

414. Obv: Letters Kω
Rev: Same.
Copper . Cast. 3.30 g, 18 mm, ↖ . State Chersonesus Museum, No. 2867/3.

415. Obv: Same.
Rev: Same.
Copper. Cast. 3.60 g, 18 mm, ↘ . Private collection.

416. Obv: Same.
Rev: Same.
Copper. Cast. 2.11 g, 18 mm, ↑ . State Historical Museum, No. 2030.

417. Obv: Same.
Rev: Same.
Copper. Cast. 3.13 g, 17 mm, ↘ . Private collection.

418. Obv: Same.
Rev: Same.
Copper. Cast. 3.65 g, 18 mm, ↘ . State Hermitage, No. 3923.

419. Obv: Monogram for the name Romanus (o)
Rev: Cross.
Copper. Cast. 3.50 g, 19 mm, ↓. State Historical Museum, unnumbered.

420. Obv: Same (mould impressed with coin No. 419).
Rev: Same.
Copper. Cast. 4.06 g, 19 mm, ↓. V. N. Orekhov collection.

421. Obv: Same.
Rev: Same.
Copper. Cast. 2.98 g, 18 mm, ↓. ↙. V. N. Orekhov collection.

422. Obv: Letters Kω
Rev: Cross.
Copper. Cast. 2.22 g, 17 mm, ↑. State Chersonesus Museum, No. 8101/2.

423. Obv: Monogram for the name Romanus (p)
Rev: Cross.
Copper. Cast. 2.45 g, 15 mm, ↗. State Chersonesus Museum, No. 1190.

424. Obv: Same.
Rev: Same.
Copper. Cast. 1.42 g, 15 mm, ↑. State Chersonesus Museum, No. 5505.

425. Obv: Letters Kω
Rev: Cross (mould impressed with coin of type of Nos. 414-418).
Copper. Cast. 1.95 g, 16 mm, ↗. Private collection.

426. Obv: Monogram for the name Romanus (p)
Rev: Cross.
Copper. Cast. 1.42 g, 14 mm, ↑. V. N. Orekhov collection.

427. Obv: Letters Kω
Rev: Cross.
Copper. Cast. 1.63 g, 15 mm, ↑. Private collection.

Issue V. 948-959

428. Obv: Monogram for the name Constantine (i)
Rev: Monogram for the name Romanus (o)
Copper. Cast. 3.50 g, 18 mm, ↓. State Chersonesus Museum, No. 1973/2.

429. Obv: Same.
Rev: Same.
Copper. Cast. 2.30 g, 18 mm, ↓. State Chersonesus Museum, No. 8102/12.

430. Obv: Same.
Rev: Same.
Copper. Cast. 3.18 g, 17 mm, ↓. V. N. Orekhov collection.

Issues of period of the emperor Romanus II (959-963)

Issue No. I 960-960

431. Obv: Monogram for the name Romanus (s)
Rev: Monogram for the name Basil (t)
Copper. Cast. 2.92 g, 18 mm, ↑ . State Chersonesus Museum, No. 145.

432. Obv: Same (mould impressed with coin No. 431).
Rev: Same.
Copper. Cast. 2.76 g, 16 mm, ↑ . State Chersonesus Museum, No. 6520.

Issue No. II, 961-963

433. Obv: Letters BA
Rev: Letters KωT
Copper. Cast. 4.82 g, 19 mm, ↖ . State Chersonesus Museum, No. 696.

434. Obv: Same.
Rev: Same.
Copper. Cast. 2.41 g, 18 mm, ↑ . V. N. Orekhov collection.

Issues of period of the emperor Nicephorus (963-969).

435. Obv: Monogram for the name Nicephorus (u)
Rev: Monogram for the title δεστότης (v)
Copper. Cast. 4.14 g, 19 mm, ↓ . State Chersonesus Museum, No. 10615.

436. Obv: Same.
Rev: Same.
Copper. Cast. 3.12 g, 18 mm, ↓ . State Chersonesus Museum, No. 6524.

437. Obv: Same (mould impressed with coin No. 436).
Rev: Same (mould impressed with coin No. 436).
Copper. Cast. 3.20 g, 17 mm, ↓ . State Hermitage, No. 4039.

Issues of the period of John Zimisces (969-976)

438. Obv: Monogram for the name John (v)
Rev: Monogram for the title δεσπότης (w)
Copper. Cast. 3.68 g, 18 mm, ↓ . State Chersonesus Museum, unnumbered.

439. Obv: Same (mould impressed with coin No. 438).
Rev: Same (mould impressed with coin No. 438).
Copper. Cast. 2.65 g, 17 mm, ↓ . State Chersonesus Museum, No. 96.

440. Obv: Same (mould impressed with coin No. 439).
Rev: Same (mould impressed with coin No. 439).
Copper. Cast. 2.36 g, 16 mm, ↓ . V. N. Orekhov collection.

Issues of the period of Basil II and Constantine (976-1025)

Issue No. I, 976-988

441. Obv: Monogram for the name Basil (x)
Rev: Monogram for the title δεσπότης (w)
Copper. Cast. 2.67 g, 17 mm, ↖ . State Chersonesus Museum, No. 109.

442. Obv: Same.
Rev: Same.
Copper. Cast. 2.24 g, 16 mm, ↑ . State Chersonesus Museum, No. 6874.

443. Obv: Same, but from right to left (y)
Rev: Same.
Copper. Cast. 2.94 g, 18 mm, ↓ . State Historical Museum, No. 2067.

444. Obv: Same (mould impressed with coin No. 441).
Rev: Same (mould impressed with coin No. 441).
Copper. Cast. 3.22 g, 16 mm, ↗ . State Hermitage, No. 4101.

Issue No. II, about 1016-1025

445. Obv: Letters KBω
Rev: Cross, two points at sides.
Copper. Cast. 10.62 g, 24 mm, ↑ . State Chersonesus Museum, No. 11773.

446. Obv: Same.
Rev: Same.
Copper. Cast. 4.71 g, 23 mm, ↑ . State Chersonesus Museum, No. 11370.

447. Obv: Same (mould impressed with coin No. 445).
Rev: Same (mould impressed with coin No. 445).
Copper. Cast. 7.91 g, 22 mm, ↑ . Private collection.

448. Obv: Same (mould impressed with coin No. 447).
Rev: Same (mould impressed with coin No. 447).
Copper. Cast. 5.96 g, 21 mm, ↑ . State Chersonesus Museum, No. 10499.

Issues of period of Romanus III (1028-1034)

449. Obv: Monogram for the name Romanus (z)
Rev: Monogram for the title δεσπότης
Copper. Cast. 7.98 g, 24 mm, ↘ . State Chersonesus Museum, No. 2469.

450. Obv: Same (mould impressed with coin No. 449).
Rev: Same (mould impressed with coin No. 449).
Copper. Cast. 6.53 g, 23 mm, ↘. State Hermitage, No. 3870.

451. Obv: Same.
Rev: Same, different design.
Copper. Cast. 7.65 g, 25 mm, ↘. (Bellinger, III, plate XL, 34, 2).

452. Obv: Same,
Rev: Same, different design.
Copper. Cast. 5.60 g, 24 mm, ↓. State Historical Museum, No. 1998.

453. Obv: Same.
Rev: Cross (same stamp as on coin No. 445).
Copper. Cast. 7.63 g, 25 mm, ↓. Private collection.

454. Obv: Same (same stamp as on coin No. 449).
Rev: Monogram for the name Romanus (same stamp as on coin No. 454).
Copper. Cast. (Oreshnikov, 1915, plate I, 21).

<u>Issues of period of Romanus IV (1067-1071</u>)

455. Obv: Monogram for the name Romanus (ьь)
Rev: Monogram for the title δεσπότης (same stamp as on coin No. 449).
Copper. Cast (Oreshnikov, 1915, p. 45, drawing).

456. Obv: Same.
Rev: Cross.
Copper. Cast (Oreshnikov, 1905, plate IX, 34).

457. Obv: Same.
Rev: Same.
Copper. Cast. 8.34 g, 25 mm, ↑. State Chersonesus Museum, No. 102.

458. Obv: Same.
Rev: Same.
Copper. Cast. 8.41 g, 26 mm, ↑. State Chersonesus Museum, No. 583/3.

459. Obv: Same.
Rev: Same.
Copper. Cast. 6.12 g, 26 mm, ↑. State Chersonesus Museum, No. 6833.

460. Obv: Same.
Rev: Same.
Copper. Cast. 6.73 g, 25 mm, ↑. Private collection.

461. Obv: Same.
Rev: Same.
Copper. Cast. 6.76 g, 25 mm, ↑. Private collection

462. Obv: Same.
Rev: Same.
Copper. Cast. 6.58 g, 25 mm, ↑ . Private collection.

463. Obv: Same (same stamp as on coin No. 458).
Rev: Monogram for the name Romanus (same stamp as on No. 458).
Copper. Cast. 6.58 g, 24 mm, ↖ . State Chersonesus Museum, No. 10677.

464. Obv: Same.
Rev: Same.
Copper. Cast. 9.47 g, 25 mm, ↑ . V. N. Orekhov collection.

Issues of end of XIth century and beginning of XIIth

465. Obv: Monogram for the name Romanus (bb)
Rev: Cross.
Copper. Cast. 5.57 g, 24 mm, ↑ . State Chersonesus Museum, unnumbered.

466. Obv: Same.
Rev: Same.
Copper. Cast. 3.12 g, 24 mm, ↑ . Private collection.

467. Obv: Same.
Rev: Lily or cross (?)
Copper. Cast. 4.30 g, 23 mm, ↑. State Chersonesus Museum, No. 4655.

468. Obv: Same.
Rev: Blank.
Copper. Cast (Oreshnikov, 1911, plate B, 14).

469. Obv: Same.
Rev: Blank.
Copper. Cast. 3.80 g, 23 mm. Private collection.

470. Obv: Same.
Rev: Blank.
Copper. Cast. 3.96 g, 22 mm, State Chersonesus Museum, No. 4718.

471. Obv: Same.
Rev: Blank.
Copper. Cast. 3.02 g, 21 mm, Private collection.

472. Obv: Same.
Rev: Blank.
Copper. Cast. 3.52 g, 21 mm, Private collection.

473. Obv: Same (mould impressed with coin No. 466).
Rev: Blank.
Copper. Cast. 3.26 g, 22 mm. State Chersonesus Museum, No. 6841.

474. Obv: Same (mould impressed with coin No. 467).
Rev: Blank.
Copper. Cast. 4.40 g, 23 mm. State Chersonesus Museum, No. 3418/2.

475. Obv: Same.
Rev: Letter
Copper. Cast. 2.24 g, 20 mm. State Hermitage. No. 3274.

476. Obv: Same (mould impressed with coin No. 474).
Rev: Blank.
Copper. Cast. 2.60 g, 21 mm, State Chersonesus Museum. No. 6126/2.

477. Obv: Same (mould impressed with coin No. 475).
Rev: Blank.
Copper. Cast. 3.43 g, 22 mm. State Chersonesus Museum, No. 6844.

478. Obv: Same (mould impressed with coin No. 477).
Rev: Blank.
Copper. Cast. 3.52 g, 20 mm. State Chersonesus Museum, No. 6853.

479. Obv: Same (mould impressed with coin No. 479?).
Rev: Blank.
Copper. Cast. 2.38 g, 19 mm. State Chersonesus Museum, unnumbered.

480. Obv: Same (mould impressed with coin No. 480).
Rev: Blank.
Copper. Cast. 2.22 g, 18 mm. Private collection.

BIBLIOGRAPHY

Anokhin, V. A., Khronolohiya Tetrasariiv Khersonesa, Arheolohiya, vol. XIV, Kiev, 1962.

Anokhin, V. A., O Nachale Éry Khersonesa Tavricheskogo, Numismatika i Sfragistika, No. 1, Kiev, 1963.

Anokhin, V. A., Monetnoye Delo Khersonesa I-III vv. n.é., Numismatika i Epigrafika, vol. IV, Moscow, 1963a.

Anokhin, V. A., K Voprosu ob Olviiskoi Ery, Numismatika i Sfragistika, No. 3, Kiev, 1958.

Anokhin, V. A., Yeshcho o Monetakh Ateya, Numismatika i Sfragistika, No. 4, Kiev, 1971.

Anokhin, V. A., Sitsiliiskaya Tekhnika Litya Monetnykh Zagotovok v Khersonese, Numismatika i Sfragistika, No. 5, Kiev, 1975.

Artamonov, M. I., Istoriya Khazar, Leningrad, 1962.

Belova, L. N., Khronologicheskoye Opisaniye Monet, Naidyonnykh v Khersonese pri Raskopkakh 1926 g., Khersonesski Sbornik, vol. II, Sebastopol, 1927.

Belova, L. N., Opisaniye Monet, Naidyonnykh pri Raskopkakh Severo-Vostochnoi Chasti Khersonesa v 1908-1912 gg., Khersonesski Sbornik, vol. III, Sebastopol, 1931.

Belova, L. N., Monety iz Raskopok Khersonesa v 1934 g. In Belov, G. D., Raskopki Khersonesa v 1934 g., Simferopol, 1936.

Belova, L. N., Opisaniye Monet iz Raskopok Khersonesa 1935-1936 gg. In Belov, G. D., Otchot o Raskopkakh v Khersonese za 1935-1936 gg., Simferopol, 1938.

Belova, L. N., Monety iz Raskopok Khersonesa 1931-1932 gg., MIA, No. 4, 1941.

Belova, L. N., Neizdannyye Monety Khersonesa, Sovietskaya Arkheologiya, VII, 1941a.

Belova, L. N., Opisaniye Monet iz Raskopok Nekropolya Khersonesa v 1937 g., Khersonesski Sbornik, vol. IV, Simperopol, 1948.

Belova, L. N., Monety iz Raskopok Kvartalov XV-XVIII, MIA, No. 34, 1953.

Belova, L. N., Opredeleniye Monet, Naidyonnykh pri Raskopkakh Khersonesa v 1955 g., Khersonesski Sbornik, vol. V, Simferopol, 1959.

Belov, G. D., Khersones Tavricheski, Leningrad, 1948.

Bertier de la Garde, A. L., Nadpis Vremeni Imperatora Zenona v Svyazi s Otryvkami iz Istorii Khersonesa, ZOOID, vol. XVI, Odessa, 1893.

Bertier de la Garde, A. L., Znacheniye Monogramm na Monetakh Khersonesa Tavricheskago, ZNORAO, vol. I, No. 1, St. Petersburg, 1906.

Bertier de la Garde, A. L., Neskolko Novykh ili Maloizvestnykh Monet Khersonesa, ZOOID, vol. XXVI, 1906a.

Bertier de la Garde, A. L., O Khersonese, IAK, No. 21, 1907.

Bertier de la Garde, A. L., Popravki Obshchego Kataloga Monet P. O. Burachkova, Moscow, 1907a.

Bertier de la Garde, A. L., O Monetakh Vlastitelei Bospora Kimmeriiskago, Opredelyayemykh Monogrammami, ZOOID, vol. XXIV, 1911.

Bertier de la Garde, A. L., Monetnye Novosti Drevnikh Gorodov Tavridy, ZOOID, vol. XXX, 1912.

Bertier de la Garde, A. L., Materialy dlya vesovykh Issledovanii Monetnykh System Drevnegrecheskikh Gorodov i Tsarei Sarmatii i Tavridy, Numizmaticheski Sbornik, vol. II, Moscow, 1913.

Burachkov, P. O., Obshchii Katalog Monet, Prinadlezhashchikh Ellinskim Koloniyam, Sushchestvovavshim v Drevnosti na Severnom Beregu Chornago Morya, Part I, Odessa, 1884.

Gilevich, A. M., Novy Klad Monet iz Okrestnostei Khersonesa, Sovietskaya Arkheologiya, XXVIII, 1958.

Gilevich, A. M., Monety iz Raskopok v Khersonese v 1950, Khersonesski Sbornik, vol. V., Simferopol, 1959.

Gilevich, A. M., Klad Monet iz Okrugi Strabonova Khersonesa, Sovietskaya Arkheologiya, 1960, No. 4.

Gilevich, A. M., Opisaniye Monet iz raskopok v Zapadnoi Chasti Khersonesa v 1958-1960 gg., in Surov, E., Khersones Tavricheski, Sverdlovski, 1961.

Gilevich, A. M., Novy Klad Khersono-Vizantiiskikh Monet, Vizantiiski Vremmenik, vol. XXIV, 1964.

Gilevich, A. M., Antichnye Inogorodnye Monety iz Raskopok Khersonesa, Numizmatika i Sfragistika, No. 3, Kiev, 1968.

Gilevich, A. M., Kuchuk-Moinakski Klad Khersoneskikh Monet Iv-III vv, do n. é, Numizmatika i Epigrafika, vol. VIII, 1970.

Gilevich, A. M., Klad Khersono-Vizantiiskikh Monet iz Okrugi Khersonesa, Numizmatika i Sfragistika, No. 5, Kiev, 1974.

Giel, Ch. Ch., Novyye Priobreteniya Moyego Zobraniya, ZRAO, vol. V, St. Petersburg, 1891.

Giel, Ch. Ch., Opisaniye Monet, Pristupivshikh v Moyo Sobraniye v 1892 i 1893 gg., ZRAO, vol. VI, St. Petersburg, 1896.

Golenko, K. V., Iz Istorii Monetnogo Dela na Bospore v I v. do n. é., Numizmatika i Epigrafika, vol. II, 1960.

Golenko, K. V., K Datirovke Nekotorykh Monet Khersonesa, Numismatika i Epigrafika, vol. III, 1962.

Golenko, K. V., Khersonesskiye Drakhmy s Imenem Magistrata Demetriya, SGMII, No. II, Moscow, 1964.

Golenko, K. V., Sostav Denezhnogo Obrashcheniya Khersonesa v I v. do n.é, VDI, 1964a, No. 4.

Golenko, K. V., Monety iz Raskopok Gosudarstvennogo Istoricheskogo Muzeya v Khersonese (1958-1969), Sovietskaya Arkheologiya, 1972, No. 4.

Grakov, B. N., Materialy po Istorii Skifii v Grecheskikh Nadpisyakh Balkanskogo Poluostrova i Maloi Azii, VDI, 1939, No. 3.

Dombrovski, O. I., Rozkopki Antichnoho Teatru v Khersonesi, Arkheolohiya, vol. X, Kiev, 1957.

Dyakov, V. N., Okkupatsiya Tavriki Rimom v I v. n.é., VDI, 1941, No. 1.

Zhebelyov, S. A., Severnoye Prichernomorye, Moscow-Leningrad, 1953.

Zograf, A. N., Statuarnye Izobrazheniya Devy v Khersonese po Dannym Numizmatiki, IRAIMK, vol. II, 1922.

Zograf, A. N., Dve Gruppy Khersonskikh Monet z Zaimstvovannym Tipami, IRAIMK, vol. V, 1927.

Zograf, A. N., Antichnye Monety, MIA, No. 16, 1951. (Published in English as Ancient Coinage, BAR-S33, Oxford, 1977).

Zograf, A. N., Denezhnoye Obrashcheniye i Monetnoye Delo Severnogo Prichernomorya, vol. I, 1955.

Zograf, A. N., Monety Tiry, Moscow, 1957.

Kadeyev, V. I., Solntsev, A. A. and Fomin, A. D., Nekotorye Resultaty Spektralnogo Issledovaniya Tsvetnykh Metallov, Sovietskaya Arkheologiya, 1963, No. 1.

Kallistov, D. P., Svidetelstvo Strabona o Skifskom Tsare Ateya, VDI, 1969, No. 1.

Karyshkovski, P. O., Neskolko Neizdannykh Monet Antichnogo Prichernomorya, Studies of the State Historical Museum, No. XXVI, Moscow, 1957.

Koehne, B. V., Issledovaniya ob Istorii i Drevnostyakh Goroda Khersonesa Tavricheskago, St. Petersburg, 1848.

Koehne, B. V., Opisaniye Muzeuma Knyazya V. V. Kochubeya, vol. I, St. Petersburg, 1857.

Kósciuszko-Walużynycz, D. N., Zametki o Tekhnike Monetnago Dela v Khersonese Tavricheskom, Numizmaticheski Sbornik, vol. III, Moscow, 1915.

Krushkol, Iulia S., Monety iz Raskopok v Khersonese v 1946 g., Studies of the State Historical Museum, No. XXVI, Moscow, 1957.

Kulakovski, Yu., Sonni, A., Ammian Martsellin, No. I, Kiev, 1906.

Latyshev, V. V., Grecheskiye i Latinskiye Nadpisi, Naidyonnyie v Yuzhnoi Rossii v 1889-1891 gg., MAR, No. 9, St. Petersburg, 1892.

Latyshev, V. V., Sbornik Grecheskikh Nadpisei Khristianskikh Vremyon iz Yuzhnoi Rossii, St. Petersburg, 1896.

Latyshev, V. V., Zhitiya Sv. Episkopov Khersonskikh, Zap. IAN, vol. VIII, No. 3, St. Petersburg, 1906.

Latyshev, V. V., ΠΟΝΤΙΚΑ, St. Petersburg, 1909.

Makhov, I. I., Amfornyie Ruchki Khersonesa Tavricheskogo, ITUAK, No. 48, Simferopol, 1912.

Murzakievich, N., Khersonesskaya Moneta Imperatora Irakliya I, ZOOID, vol. XI, 1879.

Nadel, B. I., Iz Politicheskoi Istorii Bosporskogo Gosudarstvo v Krymu v Nachale IV v. n.é., "Acta antiqua," IX, parts 1-2, Budapest, 1961.

Novikova, R. A., Simmnamony i Nomofilaki Khersonesa Tavricheskogo, VDI, 1961, No. 2.

Oreshnikov, A. V., Materialy po Drevnei Numismatike Chornomorskago Poberezhya, Moscow, 1884.

Oreshnikov, A. V., Katalog Sobraniya Drevnostei Gr. A. S. Uvarova, No. VII, Moscow, 1887.

Oreshnikov, A. V., Opisaniye Monet, Naidyonnykh v Khersonese v 1888-1889 gg, MAR, No. VII, 1890.

Oreshnikov, A. V., Khersono-Visantiiskiye Monety, TMNO, vol. III, No. 2, Moscow, 1905.

Oreshnikov, A. V., Khersono-Visantiiskiye Monety, Supplement, Numizmaticheski Sbornik, vol. I, Moscow, 1911.

Oreshnikov, A. V., Khersono-Vizantiiskaya Moneta Romana I, Numizmaticheski Sbornik, vol. I, Moscow, 1911a.

Oreshnikov, A. V., Monety Khersonesa Tavricheskago, Tsarei Bospora Kimmeriiskago, i Polemona II Pontiiskago, Numizmaticheski Sbornik, vol. II, Moscow, 1913.

Oreshnikov, A. V., Ekskursy v Oblasti Drevnei Numizmatiki Chornomorskago Poberezhya, Numizmaticheski Sbornik, vol. III, Moscow, 1915.

Oreshnikov, A. V., Khersonas, Bozhestvo Khersonesa Tavricheskogo, IAK, No. 65, 1918.

Oreshnikov, A. V., Olitsetvoreniye Obshchiny Khersonesa Tavricheskogo, IRAIMK, vol. II, 1922.

Oreshnikov, A. V., Etyudy po Numizmatike Chornomorskogo Poberezhya, IRAIMK, vol. II, 1922a.

Pyatysheva, N. V., Material Sklepa No. 1012 i yego znacheniye dlya Istorii Khersonesa Ellinisticheskogo Vremeni, In Istoriya i Kultura Vostochnoi Yevropy po Arkheologicheskim Dannym, Moscow, 1971.

Rostovtsev, M. I., Novyie Latinskiye Nadpisi s Yuga Rossii, IAK, No. 27, 1908.

Rostovtsev, M. I., Delo o Vzimanii Prostitutsionnoi Podati v Khersonese, IAK, No. 60, 1916.

Rostovtsev, M. I., K Istorii Khersonesa v Epokhu Rannei Rimskoi Imperii, In., Sbornik Statyei v Chesti Gr. P. S. Uvarovoi, Moscow, 1916a.

Rostovtsev, M. I., Tsesar i Khersones, IAK, No. 63, 1917.

Skrzynskaya, E. Ch., Review of the book: A. L. Yakobson, Srednevekovyi Khersones, Vizantiiski Vremennik, Vol. VI, 1953.

Sokolova, I. V., Khersonesskiye Monety X v. s Portretami, Numizmatika i Epigrafika, vol. V, 1965.

Sokolova, I. V., Datirovka Nekotorykh Monet Khersonesa, Numizmatika i Sfragistika, No. 3, Kiev, 1968.

Sokolova, I. V., Pechati Georgiya Tsuly i Sobytiya 1016 g. v Khersone, Palestinski Sbornik, No. 23, 1971,

Sokolova, I. V., Mednyie Monety Yustina I i Yustiniana I, Chekanennyie v Vizantiiskom Khersone, Communications of the State Hermitage, No. XXXII, 1971a.

Sokolova, I. V., Klad Khersonesskikh Monet Serediny IX v., Studies of the State Hermitage, vol. XII, 1971b.

Sokolova, I. V., Administratsiya Khersona v IX-XI VV, po Dannym Sfragistiki, In: Antichnaya Drevnost i Sredniye Veka, No. 10, Sverdlovsk, 1973.

Sokolova, I. V., Monety i Pechati Vizantiiskogo Khersona (Datirovka i Atributsiya. Author's abstract of Candidate Dissertation, Leningrad, 1975.

Solomonik, E. I., Novyie Epigraficheskiye Panyatniki Khersonesa, Kiev, 1964.

Solomonik, I. I., Novyie Epigraficheskiye Panyatniki Khersonesa, Kiev, 1973.

Strzeletski, S. F., Klery Khersonesa Tavricheskogo, Khersonesski Sbornik, vol. VI, Simferopol, 1961.

Tatishchev, B., Istoriya Rossiiskaya, vol. 2, Moscow-Leningrad, 1963.

Takhtai, A. K., Dva Klada Khersonesskikh Antichnykh Monet, Khersonesski Sbornik, vol. IV, Simferopol, 1948.

Tolstoi, I. I., Vizantiiskiye Monety, Nos. L-IX, St. Petersburg, 1908-1916.

Tolstoi, I. I., O Vizantiiskikh Pechatyakh Khersonskoi Femy, ZRAO, vol. II, 1887.

Tyumenev, A. I., Khersonesskiye Etyudy, VDI, 1938, No. 2.

Uspenski, F. I., Vizantiiski Tabel o Rangakh, IRAIK, vol. III, Sofiya, 1898.

Frolova, N. A., Neizdannaya Zolotaya Moneta Antichnogo Khersonesa, KS OGU and OGAM for 1960, Odessa, 1961.

Shangin, M., Nekotoryie Nadpisi Khersonesskogo Muzeya. VDI, 1938, No. 3.

Shelov, D. B., Monetnoye Delo Bospora VI-II vv. do n.é. Moscow, 1956.

Shestakov, S. P., Ocherki po Istorii Khersonesa v VI-X vv. po R. Kh., Pamyatniki Khristianskogo Khersonesa, No. III, Moscow, 1908.

Shcheglov, A. N., Osnovnyie étapy Istorii Zapadnogo Kryma v Antichnuyu Epokhu, In: Antichnaya Istoriya i Kultura Sredizemnomorya i Prichornomorya, Leningrad, 1968.

Yakobson, A. L., Srednevekovy Khersones (XII-XIV vv.), MIA, No. 17, 1950.

Yakobson, A. L., Rannesrednevekovy Khersones, MIA, No. 63, 1959.

Babelon, E., and Reinach, Th., Receuil générale des monnaies grecques d'Asie Mineure, Vol. I, fasc. 1, Paris 1925.

Barron, J. P., The Silver Coins of Samos, London 1966.

Bellinger, A. R. and Grierson, Ph., Catalogue of the Byzantine Coins in the Dumbarton Oaks Collection and in the Whittemore Collection, Vols. I-III, Washington, 1966-1973.

BMC. The Tauric Chersonese, Sarmatia, Dacia, Moesia, Thrace, etc., London 1877.

BMC. Pontus, Paphlagonia, Bithynia, and the Kingdom of Bosporus, London, 1889.

Coin Hoards, vol. I, London, 1975.

Franke, P. R., Zur Tyrannie des Klearchos und Satyros in Herakleia am Pontos, AA, 1966, H. 2, Berlin.

Garnett, R., The Story of Gycia, The English Historical Review, vol. XII, 1897.

Golenko, K., Gegenstempel auf Chersoner Münzen, HBN, H. 18/19, 1964-1965.

Grierson, Ph, and Jenkins, R. I. H., The Date of Constantine VII's Coronation, Byzantion, Vol. 32, fasc. 1 (1962).

Grierson, Ph., The Crimean Countermark of Heraclius, NC, 1966.

Head, B. V., Historia Numorum, Oxford, 1911.

Hill, G. F., Becker the Counterfeiter, Part I, London, 1924.

Hirsch, J., Sammlung Consul E. F. Weber, I Abteilung-Griechische Münzen, München, 1908.

Imhoof-Blumer, F., Monnaies grecques, Amsterdam, 1883.

Imhoof-Blumer, F., Kleinasiatische Münzen, Band II, Wien, 1902.

Koehler, H. K. E., Description des médailles de Chersonesus, ville de la Chersonèse Taurique, Serapis, t. II, St. Petersburg, 1850.

MacDonald, G., Catalogue of the Greek Coins of the Hunterian Collection, Vol. III, Glasgow, 1905.

Mattingly, H., Roman Coins, London, 1960.

Minns, E. H., Scythians and Greeks, Cambridge, 1913.

Muralt, M. E., Essai de Chronographie Byzantine, 1057-1453, T. I, St. Petersburg, 1871.

Naster, P., La collection Lucien de Hirsch, Bruxelles, 1959.

Sabatier, J., Description générale des monnaies byzantines, T. I-II, Paris, 1862.

Sallet, A. von, Die Münzen von Chersonesus in der Krim, ZfN, Band IV, 1877.

Sallet, A, von, Jahreszahlen auf Münzen der taurischen Chersonesus, ZfN, Band X, 1883.

Schönert-Geiss, E., Die Münzprägung von Byzantion, Teil I, Autonome Zeit, Berlin, 1970.

Seltman, Ch., Greek Coins, London, 1960.

Seyrig, H., Monnaies hellénistiques de Byzance et de Chalcédoine, in: Essays in Greek Coinage Presented to Stanley Robinson, ed. by C. M. Kraay and G. K. Jenkins, Oxford, 1968.

Seyrig, H., Un Pseudo-Lysimaque de Crimée, RN, 1971.

Six, J. P., Sinope, NC, 1885.

SNG, Sammlung H. von Aulock, H. 1-15, Berlin, 1957-1967.

Trésor de Numismatique et de Glyptique. Mythologie, Paris, 1960.

West, L. C., The Relation of Subsidiary Coinage to Gold under Valerianus and Gallienus, MN, vol. VII, New York, 1957.

Wroth, W., Catalogue of the Imperial Byzantine Coins in the British Museum, vols. I-II, London, 1908.

LIST OF ABBREVIATIONS

BIAM	Bakhchisaraiski Istoriko-Kraevedcheski Muzei
VV	Vizantiiski Vremennik
VDI	Vestnik Drevnei Istorii
GIM	State Historical Museum
GMII	Pushkin State Museum for the Representational Arts
GKhM	Chersonesus State Historical and Archaeological Museum
GE	State Hermitage
ZAP. IAN	Zapiski Imperatorskoi Akademii Nauk
ZNORAO	Zapiski Numizmaticheskago Otdeleniya Russkago Arkheologicheskago Obshchestva
ZOOID	Zapiski Odesskago Obshchestva Istorii i Drevnostei
ZRAO	Zapiski Russkago Arkheologicheskago Obshchestva
IAK	Izvestiya Arkheologicheskoi Komissii
IRAIK	Izvestiya Russkago Arkheologicheskago Instituta v Konstantinopole
IRAIMK	Izvestiya Rossiiskoi Akademii Istorii Materialnoi Kultury
KS OGU i OGAM	Kratkie Soobshcheniya Odesskogo Gosudarstvennogo Universiteta im. I. I. Mechnikova i Odesskogo Gosudarstvennogo Arkheologicheskogo Muzeya
MAR	Materialy po Arkheologii Rossii
MIA	Materialy i Issledovaniya po Arkheologii SSSR
NiS	Numizmatika i Sfragistika
NS	Numizmaticheski Sbornik
NE	Numizmatika i Epigrafika
OGAM	Odessa State Archeological Museum
PS	Palestinski Sbornik
PKhKh	Pamyatniki Khristianskago Khersonesa
SA	Sovietskaya Arkheologiya
SGMII	Soobshcheniya Gosudarstvennogo Muzeya Isobrazitelnykh Isskustv im. A. S. Pushkina
SGE	Soobschsheniya Gosudarstvennogo Ermitazha
SKM	Simferopolski Kraevedcheski Muzei
TGE	Trudy Gosudarstvennogo Ermitazha
TMNO	Trudy Moskovskago Numizmaticheskago Obshchestva
KhSb	Khersonesski Sbornik
AA	Archäologischer Anzeiger
BMC	British Museum Catalogue, A Catalogue of the Greek Coins in the British Museum
HBN	Hamburger Beiträge für Numismatik
MN	Museum Notes
RN	Revue Numismatique
SNG	Sylloge Nummorum Graecorum
ZfN	Zeitschrift für Numismatik

PLATE I

PLATE II

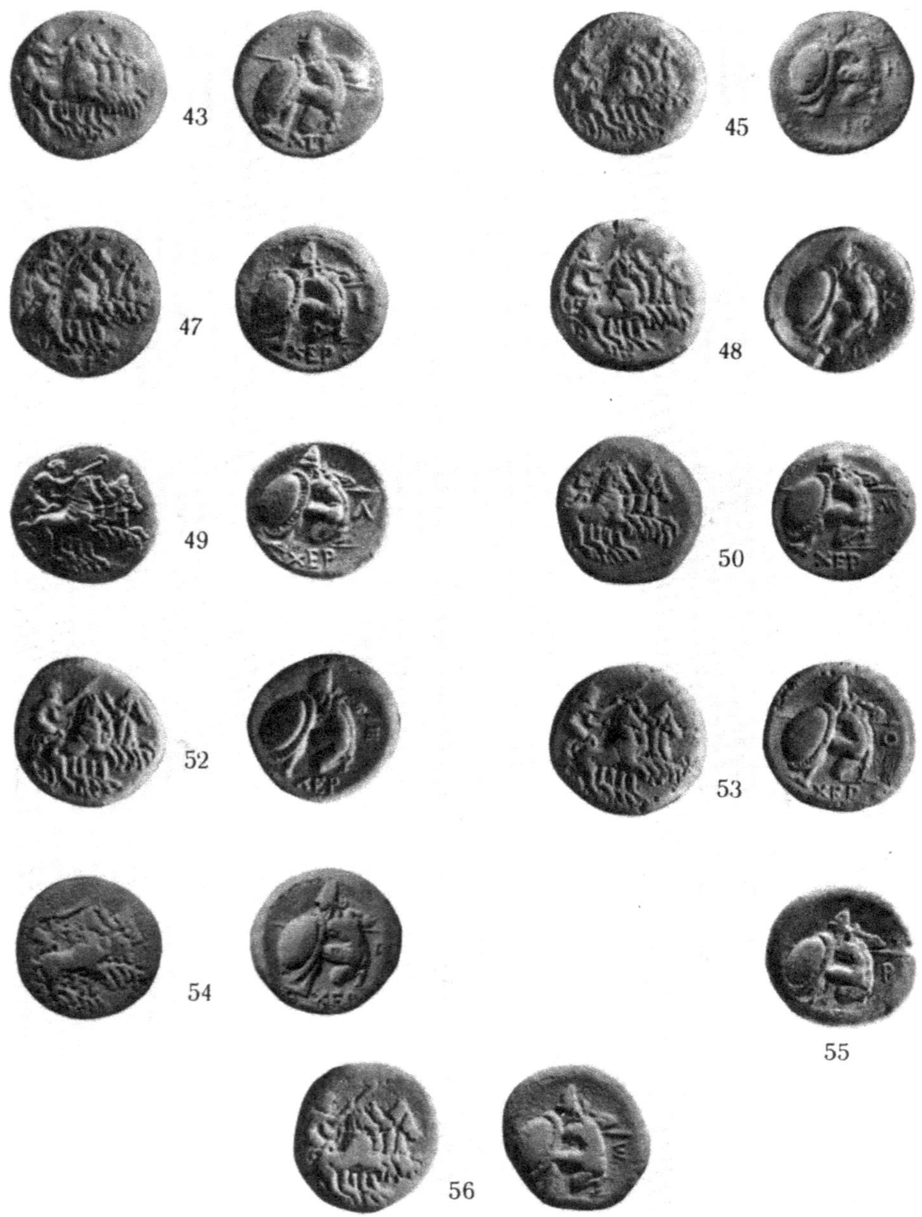

PLATE III

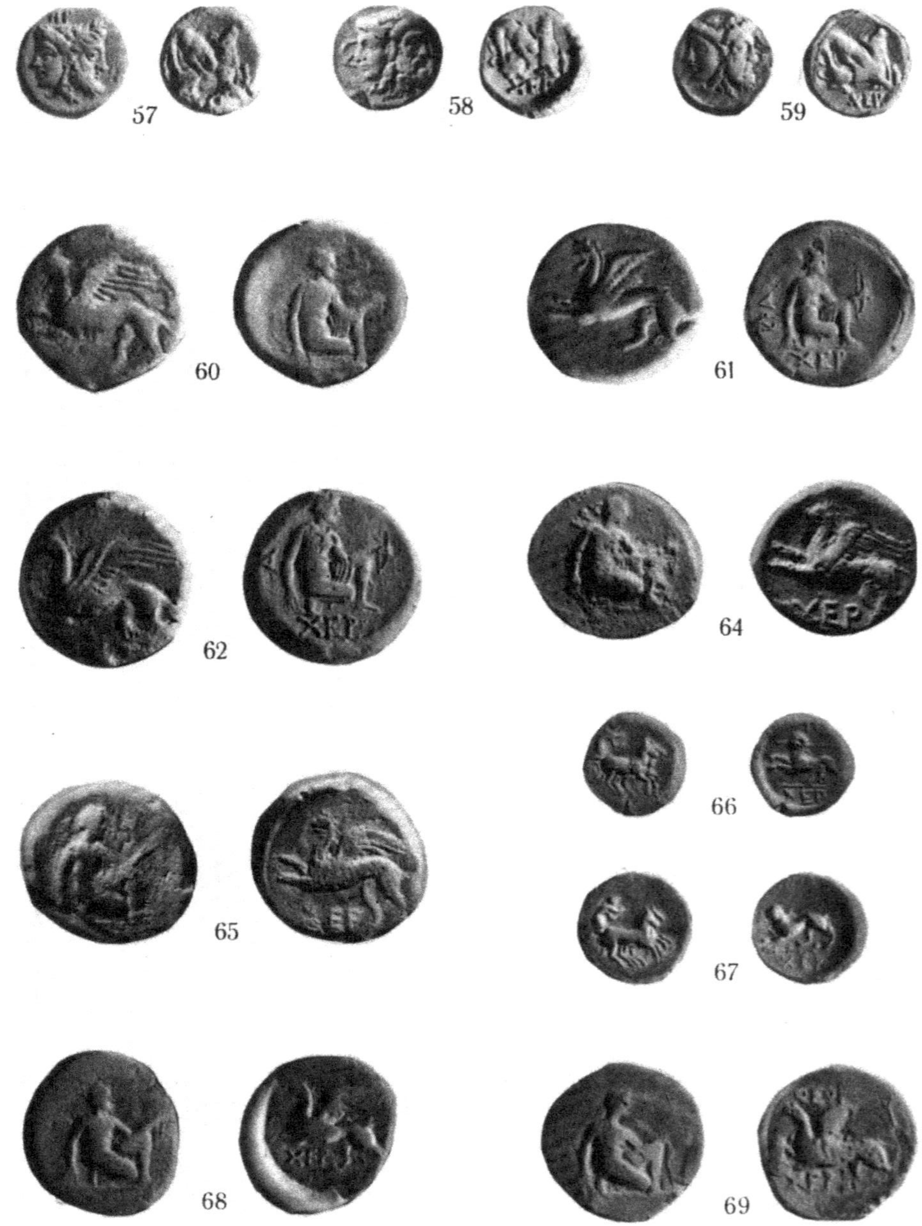

PLATE IV

PLATE V

PLATE VI

PLATE VII

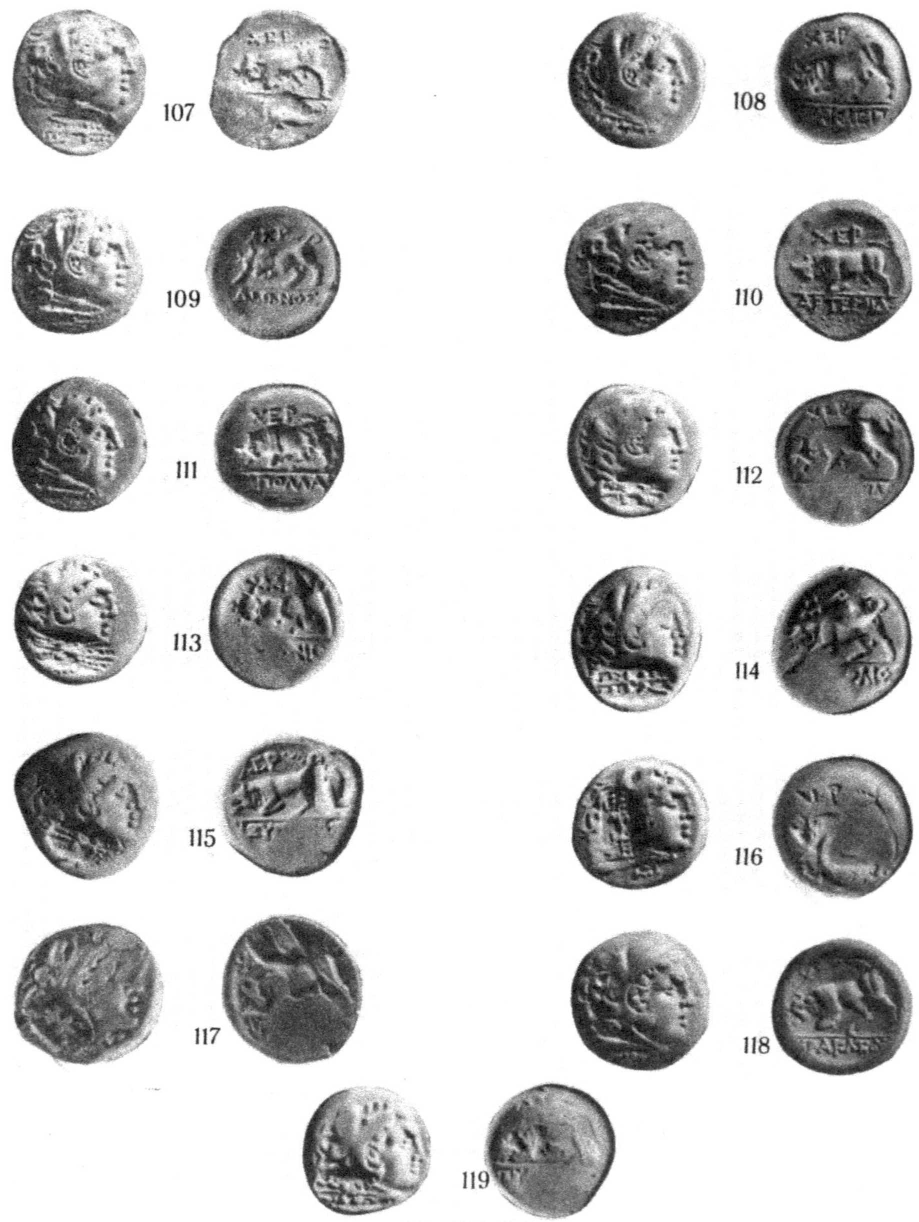

PLATE VIII

PLATE IX

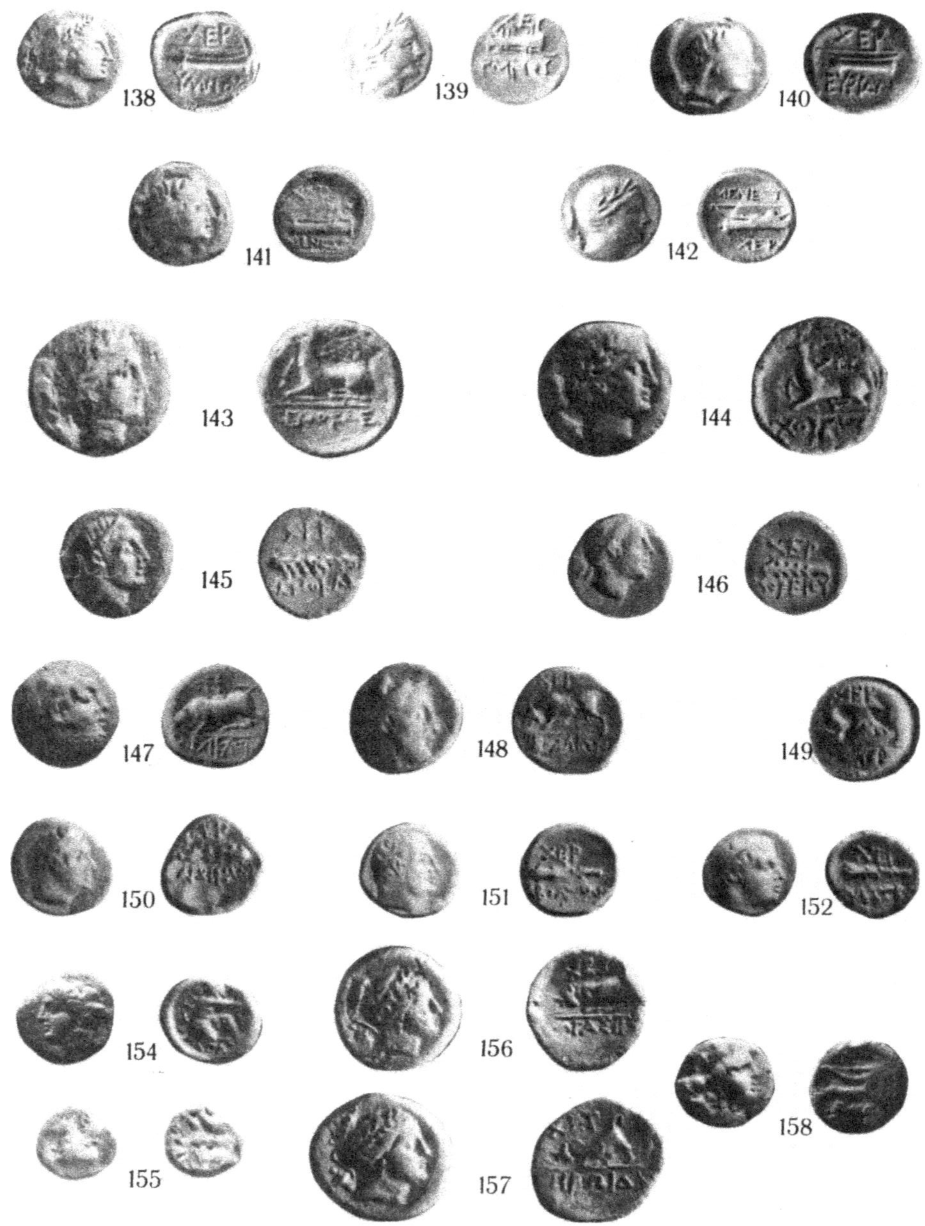

PLATE X

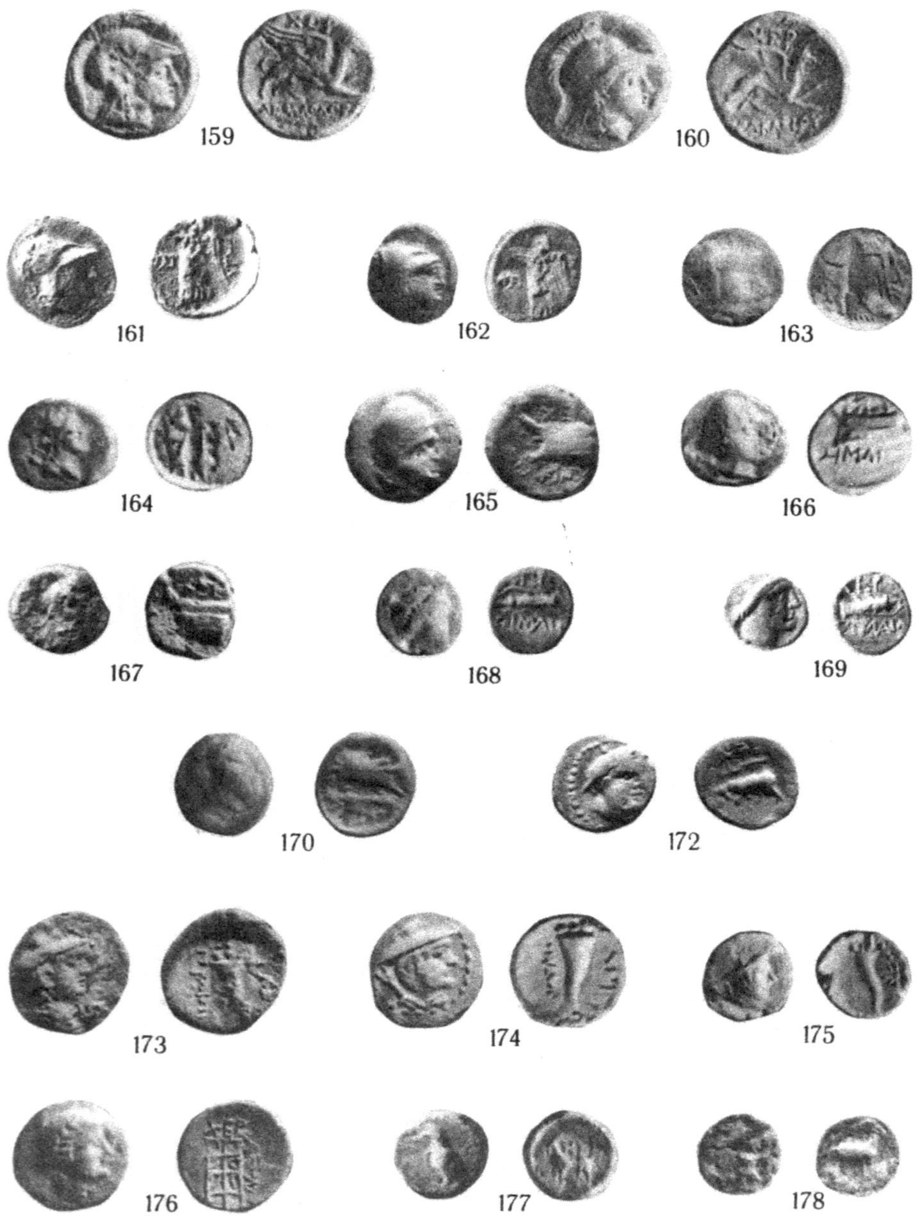

PLATE XI

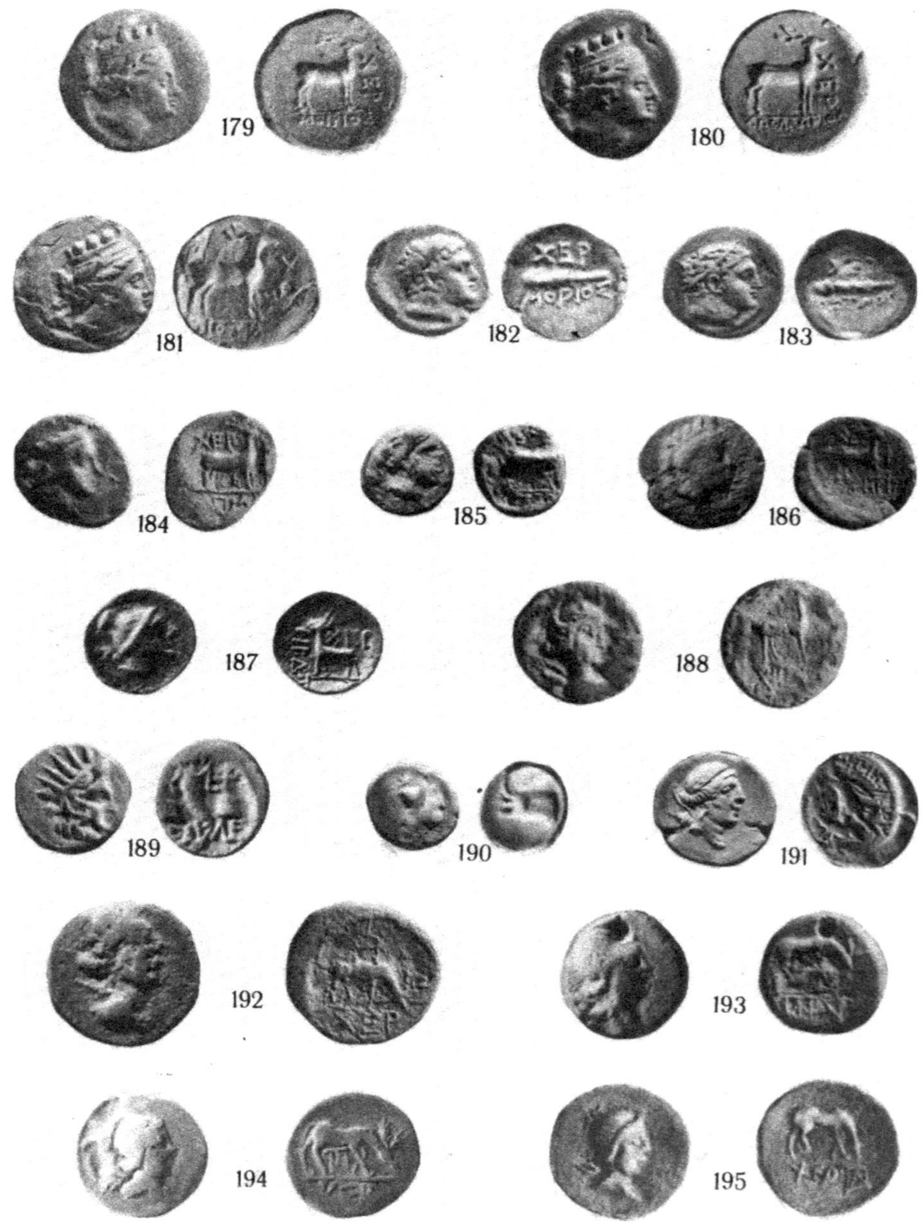

PLATE XII

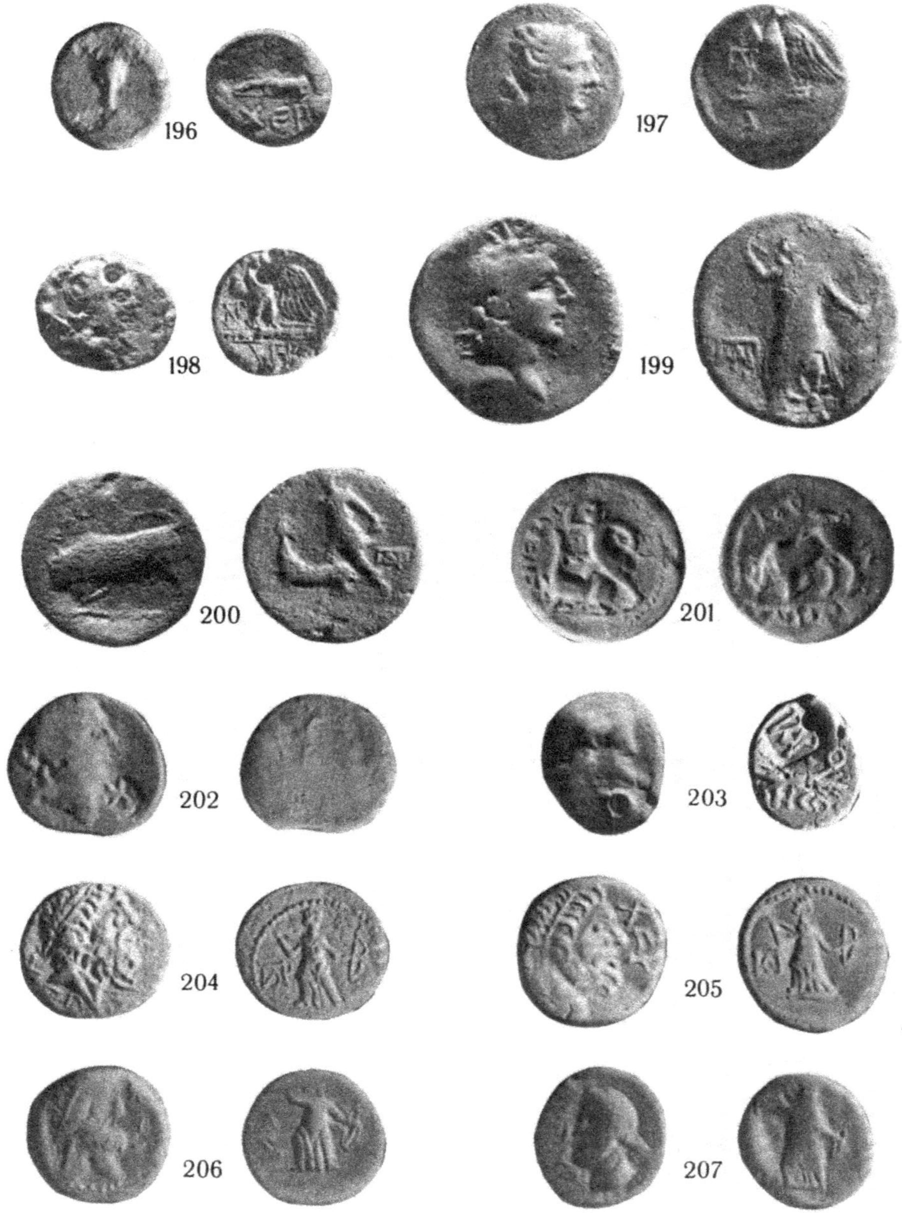

PLATE XIII

PLATE XIV

PLATE XV

PLATE XVI

PLATE XVII

PLATE XVIII

273 274 275 276 277 278 279 280 281 282 283

PLATE XIX

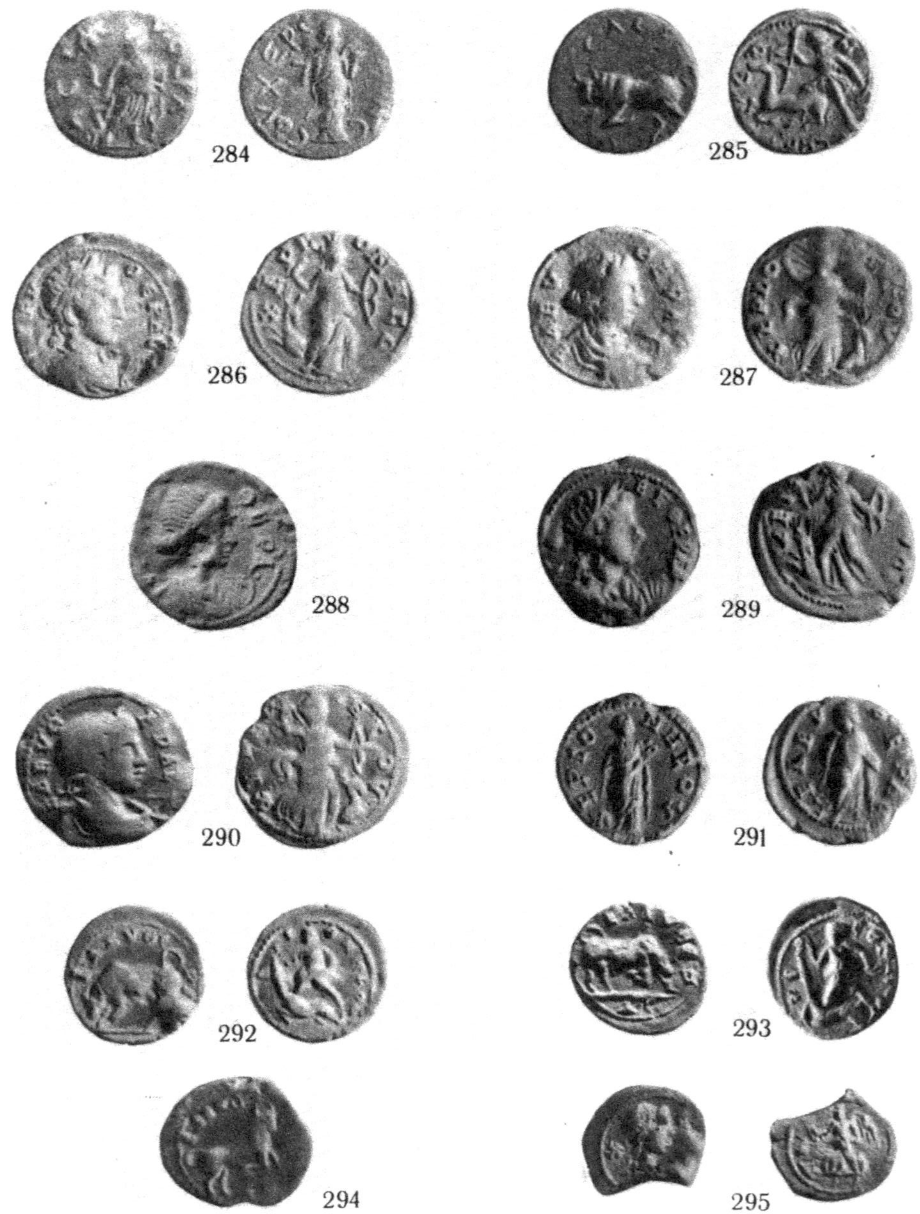

284 285 286 287 288 289 290 291 292 293 294 295

PLATE XX

PLATE XXI

PLATE XXII

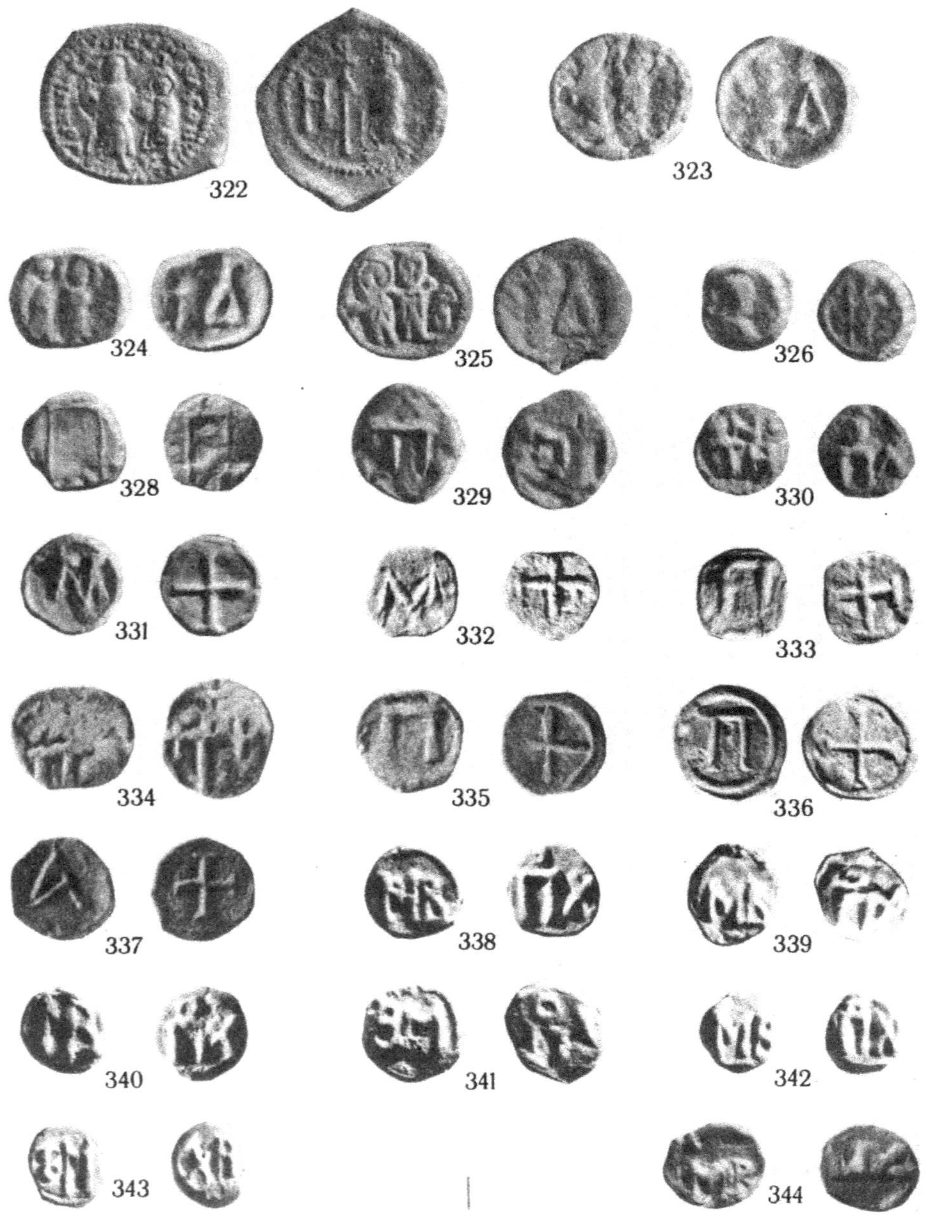

PLATE XXIII

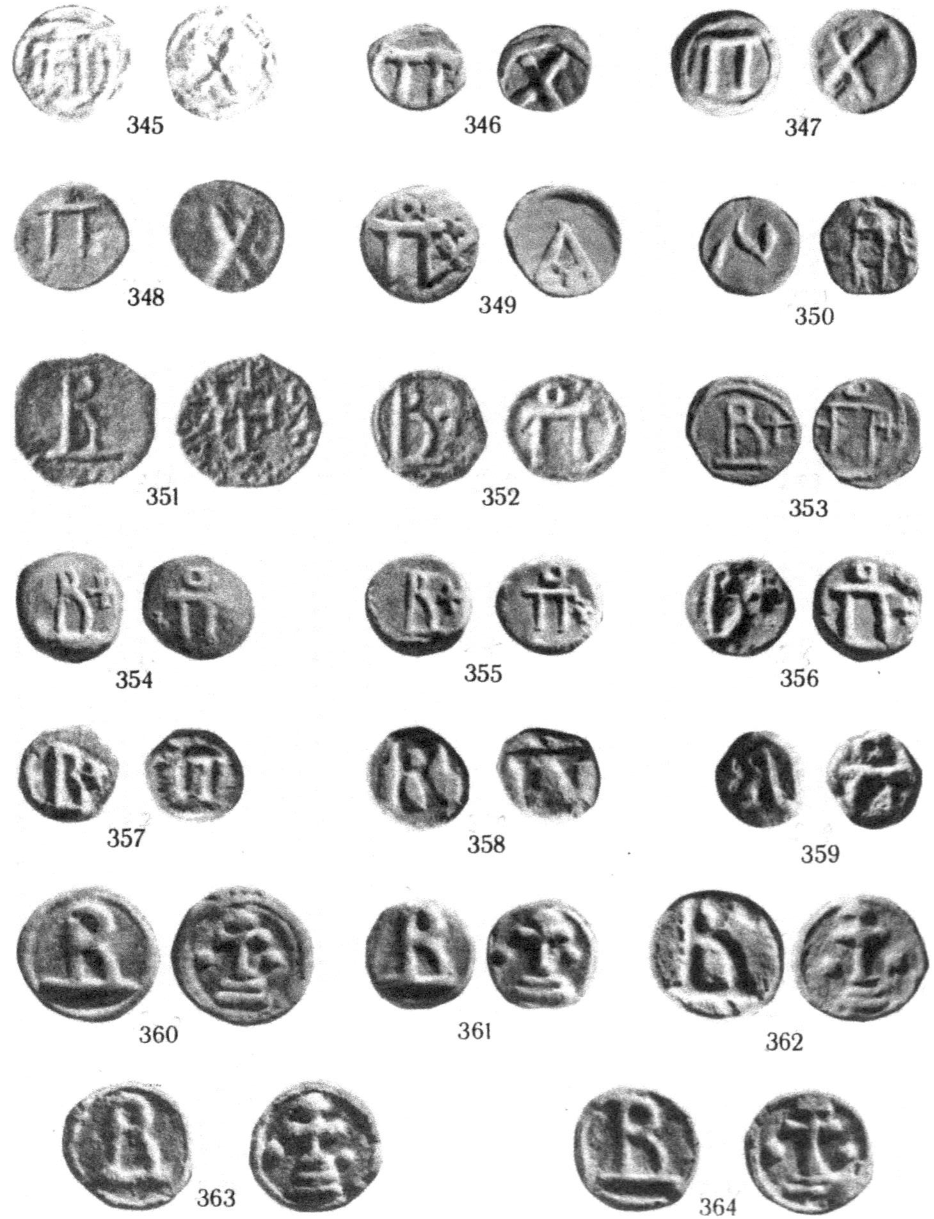

PLATE XXIV

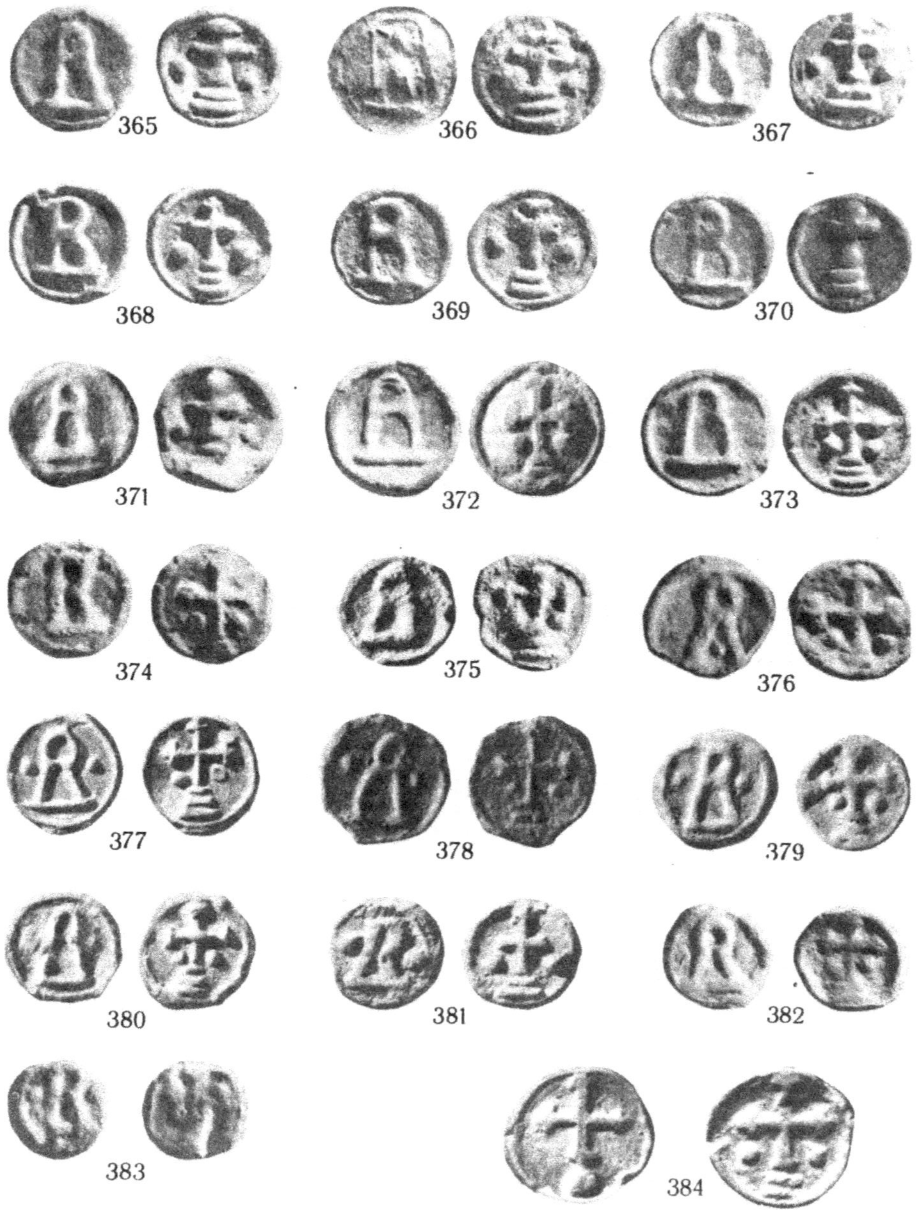

PLATE XXV

PLATE XXVI

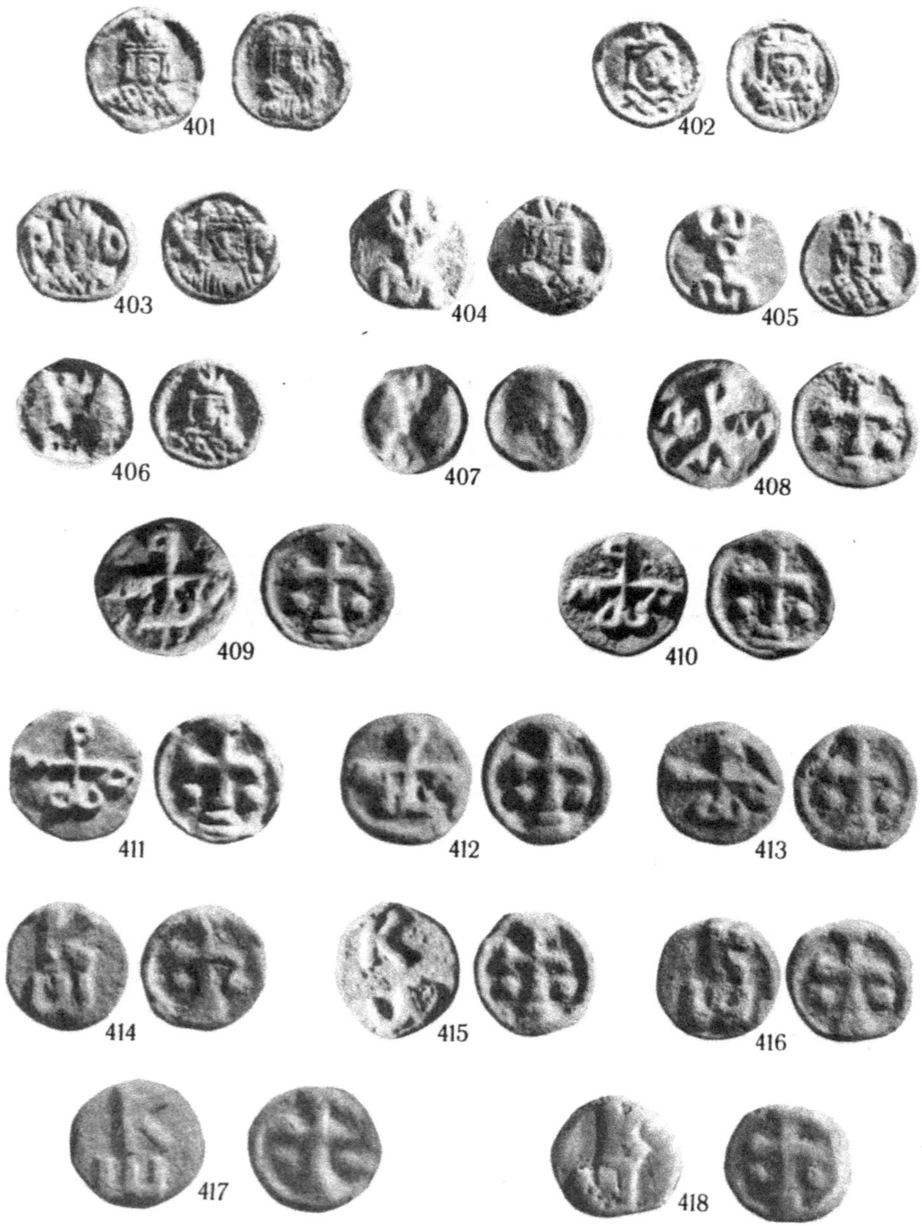

PLATE XXVII

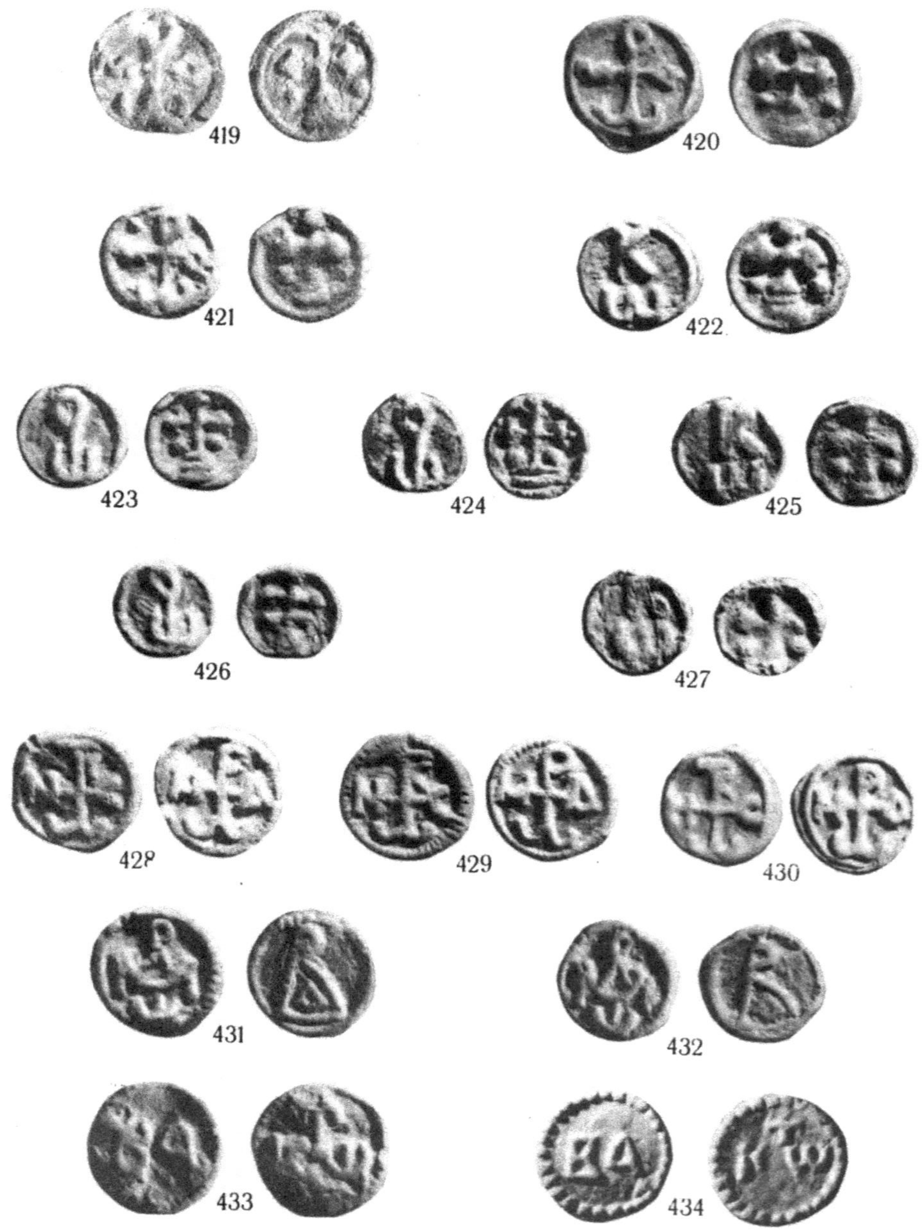

PLATE XXVIII

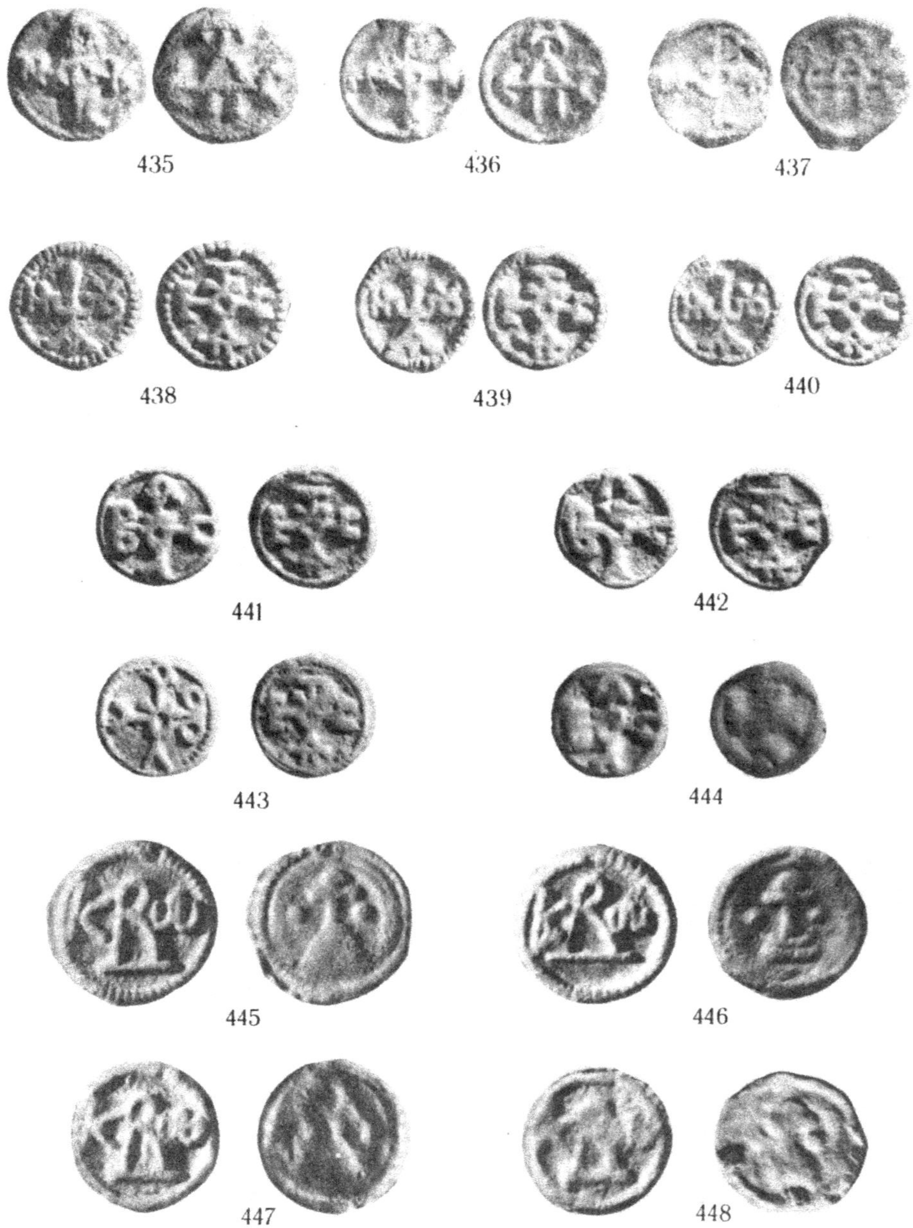

435 436 437 438 439 440 441 442 443 444 445 446 447 448

PLATE XXIX

449 450 451 452 453 454 455 456 457

PLATE XXX

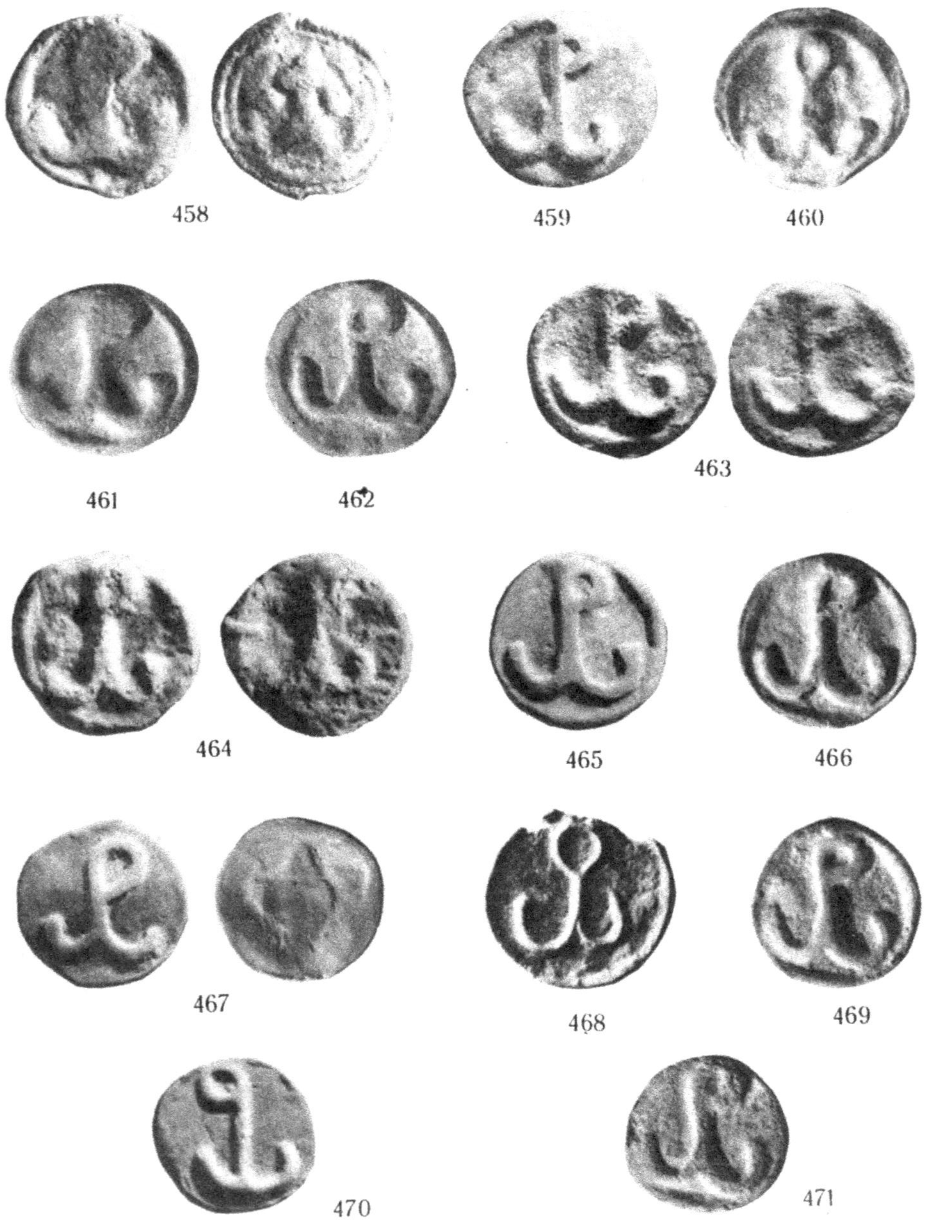

PLATE XXXI

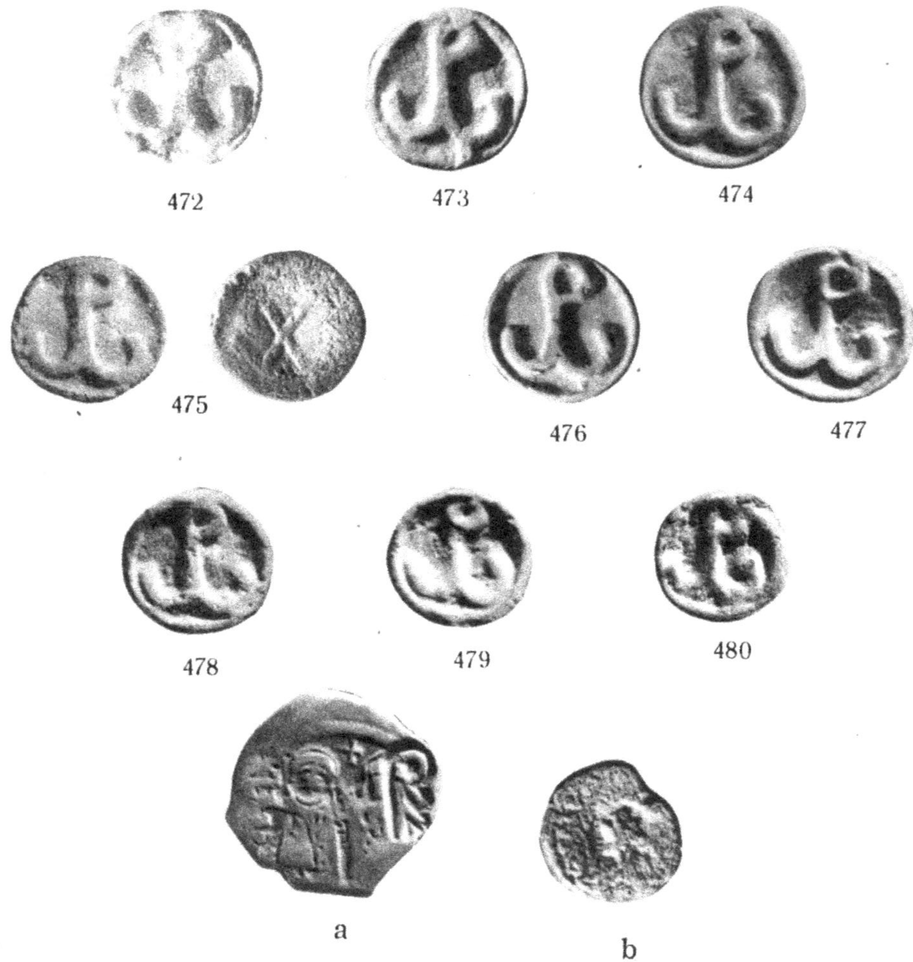

PLATE XXXII

www.ingramcontent.com/pod-product-compliance
Lightning Source LLC
La Vergne TN
LVHW071209210926
848482LV00015B/761